Land
Of The
Long Wild
Road

Land
Of The
Long Wild
Road

Braiswick

Braiswick
61 Gainsborough Road, Felixstowe,
Suffolk IP11 7HS

ISBN 1 898030 37 5 softback, 1 898030 13 8 casebound

copyright © 2003 **Bob Goddard**
www.author.co.uk/goddard

British Library Cataloguing in Publication Data
available.

Printed
by Cromwell Press
Braiswick is an imprint of Author Publishing Ltd

For Nicholas

who lived for adventure

Contents

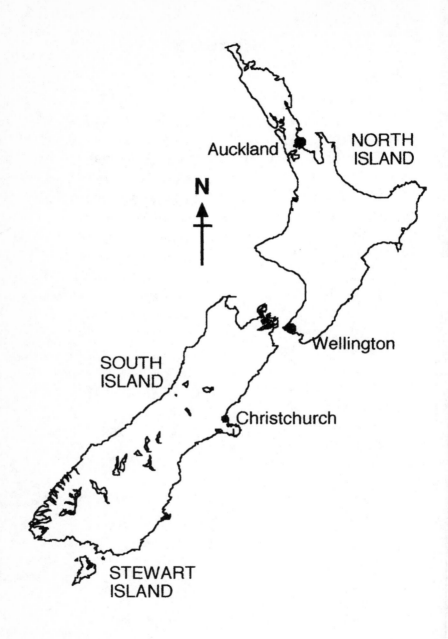

Introduction

'*Ketchi-boy-nuzu!*' Sabatin exclaimed with a broad smile, as he held aloft what appeared to be a long dried dog turd. This weird looking object - black, lumpy and curved - was one of many we had seen scattered beneath the parched tree behind Sabatin's café. Too many for even a pack of dogs. We were intrigued to the point of jabbing at them with a curious toe.

Our curiosity had already taken us a long way off the beaten track on this sunny April day in south west Turkey. Far from the Germans hogging the poolside sunloungers. Far from the excursion buses packed with sweating and cursing British tourists. Far from anywhere in fact, since we'd headed off that morning into the unknown distance on a whim and a prayer and a little red motorcycle. And now, with the sun rapidly slipping down the sky, we were lost.

We knew we shouldn't be there. We'd wobbled off what passed for a road into a neat little cluster of houses, looking for a coffee and a toilet, not necessarily in that order. From the surprised looks on the faces of the well-dressed Turks we passed as we weaved around the end of a checkpoint-type barrier and down the neatly-paved road of this orderly village, it was evident they didn't see middle-aged British couples squeezed on to a tiny 125cc Honda every day.

Then I saw tables and chairs beside one of the houses, shouted over my shoulder to Viv that I'd found what we were looking for and pulled up with a flourish, trying to show more confidence than I felt. Despite Viv's protests that it was obviously a private development for the Turkish well-to-do and that tourists wouldn't be welcome, we were greeted with a grin by a very small, nut-brown man who wiped his hands on his apron before shaking ours and announcing he was Sabatin.

It quickly became apparent that this was the only word we were going to understand, but Sabatin picked up on the word coffee and disappeared to produce two cups of bitter

1

brown sludge with a strange, sand-like texture. We would later learn to ask for Nescafé, to distinguish what we found palatable from the traditional Turkish brew, but this was all a part of the learning process.

We wandered off clutching our cups, looking for somewhere to tip their contents without causing offence, when we came across these doggy-doos which Sabatin, hot on our heels, now told us were ketchi-boy-nuzu. Frankly, it didn't help a lot.

So he broke one in half and motioned for us to eat it. Viv, still chewing on her first mouthful of gritty coffee, had gone quite far enough with sampling the local flavour. I put aside my fears and took a bite. It was sort of chewy, crunchy and sticky, full of hard seeds and a vaguely nutty flavour, but we were still none the wiser.

Sabatin, delighted that someone had taken a shine to the dog-turd seed pods under his tree, insisted we take some away with us. Which is how we identified it and why, to this day, whenever we see a carob tree we gleefully call it by its Turkish name - keçiboynuzu.

All of which has precious little to do with our travels in New Zealand, except to explain how we came to rediscover our misspent youth on two wheels and a delight in making unexpected discoveries, which ultimately led, via many gravelly paths, to the land of the long white cloud.

It was April 1998, in Marmaris, Turkey, that we suddenly had the urge to take to two wheels again after years of playing the role of middle aged, responsible parents. Well, why not? We were on our own, holidaying *sans enfants* for the first time. And the tour operator's brochures and holiday reps had all issued the same grave warnings - *'Don't hire motorcycles or scooters - you may not live to regret it'* ... or words to that effect. We've always had a rebellious streak, so we promptly hired a shiny red Honda 125 and wobbled off into the Terrifying Turkish Traffic.

As we escaped from the Marmaris madness and emerged on to clear open roads, we realised we were FREE! Free from the heaving crowds of sweaty tourists, Free from the accursed excursion buses, Free to venture where we wished, Free to rearrange our vertebrae into random patterns as we crashed into the biggest pot-holes we'd ever seen...

Chapter 1

You Must Be Joking!

Fast forward to November 2001 and we are in Christchurch, New Zealand, admiring the impressive range of bikes offered by New Zealand Motorcycle Rentals who have promised to provide us with two machines suitable for the rugged roads of the outback. All the arrangements have been made via email, with just a phone call to confirm we were on our way.

'Ah, Bob and Viv. Pleased to meetcha guys!' smiled Gordon Lidgard, one of the partners of the booming bike business. *'We've got your bikes all ready for you out the back, come on through and take a look.'*

There in the workshop area, among the towering GS1150 BMWs, the hulking Honda Gold Wings and everything in between, were two tiny red 50cc scooters with panniers and fuel cans strapped beside their fat little seats and 'Bob' and 'Viv' labels fixed to their front mudguards. After a silent second or two filled with shock, wonder, horror and finally realisation, we both burst out laughing. What a great joke! To have the nerve to pull such a stunt on two unknown Pommy customers spoke volumes for the bike shop's sense of humour and their relaxed and happy lifestyle.

We tried the scoots out for size and took photographs to remind us of this comic moment, then Gordon led us to two more suitable mounts: A pair of Yamaha XT225 Serows, dual-purpose trailie bikes with single cylinder four-stroke motors and brand new semi-knobbly tyres, ready to take us into the bush and beyond and hopefully, bring us back again in one piece. Perfect.

If the bikes were ideal, the gear the bike rental shop provided to go with them was excellent. Full face helmets (we'd brought our own jackets, trousers, gloves and boots with us, or we could have had these too) and strap-on soft panniers to carry all our luggage. Also included was an aerosol can of chain-lube and a spare bottle of engine oil to keep the motors' tiny sumps topped up, plus free servicing whenever we were near either of the company's Christchurch or Auckland depots. Cushty. This was five-star treatment compared to our first bike hire experience in Turkey...

Back in Marmaris, Abdul had scribbled a few hieroglyphics on a scrap of paper which he assured us was insurance, handed us the key and took our money with a beaming, gold-toothed smile. He was still smiling when we asked if he had crash helmets. *'Specially for nice Inglis peeples, we have helmets,'* he laughed, and pointed to two battered, black objects sitting on the shelf of his little hut.

He thought it was funny, because no self-respecting Turk would be seen dead wearing a crash helmet. They'd rather go to meet Allah without one. It just isn't the done thing in Mediterranean countries to show off your virility with high-speed, death-defying swoops through the honking traffic, then ruin the whole macho effect by wearing a sissy skid lid. And anyway, it would spoil your hairstyle.

We had no such qualms, but these helmets were less than ideal. Apart from being unpleasantly grimy and smelly with the residue from a thousand previous heads, both were extra large. Mine was loose, Viv's rattled around on her head like an upturned coal-scuttle. But being British, we had gone to Turkey in April prepared for all eventualities, and Viv had packed a cosy woolly winter hat. It fitted snugly underneath her helmet and helped protect her from the greasy interior.

This Mediterranean motorcycling had been completely unplanned. For riding jackets we had cagoules, which kept the dust off while we were riding and created an instant boil-in-the-bag experience whenever we were stopped in traffic. Sunglasses stood in for goggles and only the backs of my hands really suffered. They turned bright red and swollen from being held out in the fierce sun while gripping the handlebars. For the following days, in the absence of gloves, I slapped on extra-thick layers of suncream, which stopped my hands burning to a crisp, but made holding on to the grips and operating the controls somewhat tricky.

5

By the time we arrived in New Zealand, three and a half years later, we were better prepared. We had brought our chunky walking boots to serve the dual purposes of riding and tramping. This latter activity does not involve sifting through dustbins, sleeping in bus shelters or swigging a bottle of meths. Tramping is the New Zealander's term for walking in the bush, and with vast areas of unspoiled and gorgeous wilderness to choose from, it's a very popular activity.

We had also brought our riding gloves, which on hot summer days in the UK prove too warm, but in NZ's very generous weather were to reveal another amusing side to their nature, but more on that later. Plus waterproof overtrousers and our big, waterproof, padded and armoured riding jackets, which took up an inordinate amount of suitcase space and which I was convinced would be far too hot for the scorching southern summer to come. Stay with us and you'll find out how wrong I can be.

On this bright November morning in downtown Christchurch we felt more than adequately equipped as we wheeled the two Serows out of NZ Motorcycle Rentals workshop into the spring sunshine, jabbed the electric start buttons to fire up their little single cylinder four-stroke engines and rode away between the smart rows of colonial buildings. We didn't have far to go on this first trip through the orderly, drive-on-the-left, Kiwi traffic. We were staying with my brother John and his wife Jill in the suburbs of the city, on the first slope of the Port Hills which lead to the stunningly scenic Banks Peninsula.

John had taken the afternoon off work in order to take us on a shakedown ride into the rugged country which lies just minutes from his door. Astride his big red BMW R80RT, he led us up to the Summit Road which weaves along the rim of the first of two extinct volcanoes that created this extraordinary landscape of steep ridges, vertical clefts and shimmering expanses of blue water. It was all a bit too much to take in. We had left behind the flat fields of our Norfolk home as damp autumn was being overtaken by dark and dreary winter. After two flights and a brief stopover in Singapore, we were suddenly riding on top of the world,

6

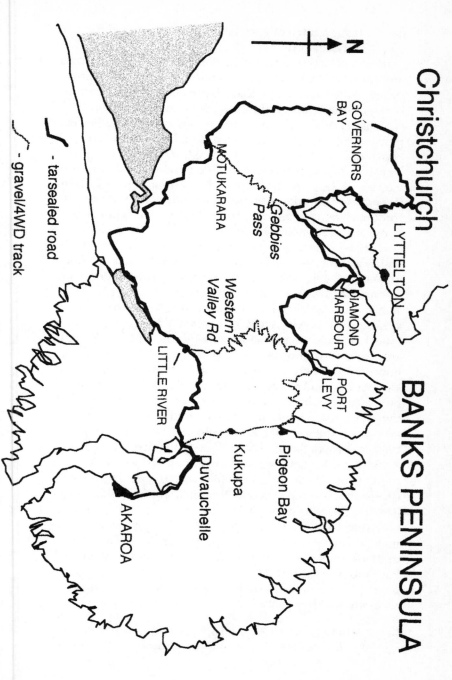

our senses assaulted by spectacular scenery bathed in bright spring sunshine.

Residual jetlag and unfamiliarity with the bikes did nothing to help us overcome our nervousness of the narrow, twisty, switchback tarmac that we were soon careering along. I tried to keep the rear of John's bike in sight while hanging back to see Viv's headlight in my mirrors as we rose and plunged, twisted and turned past Governor's Bay, Diamond Harbour and Port Levy on the shoreline of Lyttelton Harbour. It was almost impossible to take in the stunning views as well as ride and my head was spinning. When John pulled over to take a photo of an impossibly cute little wooden church with a red corrugated tin roof, I slumped on to the grass and fell instantly asleep.

The ten minute power-nap recharged a few brain cells, which was just as well as big brother then led us up a steep gravel track overlooking a precipitous drop into a gorgeous green valley - the Western Valley Road. While Viv and I were skidding and slithering on the unfamiliar loose surface, John was fast disappearing on his stately BMW as if his big touring bike had been expressly made for it. This was most disconcerting and as the slippery track dropped ear-poppingly quickly down to the settlement of Little River, Viv and I slowed to a crawl as we fought to stay in control of our skittish mounts. Catching our breath at the bottom, we agreed there was nothing wrong with the bikes, it was our lack of experience that was making us over-cautious and this was preventing the Yamahas from giving their best.

Back on flat and smooth tarmac again, we were soon flying around the long sweeping bends heading back to Christchurch at top speed - although in the case of our little Serows, this was only 100kph (60mph). We were pleased with our machines but the biggest impression my bike had made on me was in the region of my posterior. The narrow and stiff seat felt like a plank after an hour and my bum had been numb and painful for most of the day. If we were going to spend three months on these bikes, we needed to get to the bottom of this problem.

Our introduction to the delights of the New Zealand countryside, and the traffic-free trails that we could ride into the very heart of it, was excellent if a little overwhelming. We decided we needed more practice at off-road riding and resolved to revisit the craggy tracks of Banks Peninsula, where we could weave our way across to the former French colony of Akaroa at the centre of the second volcano crater, the following day.

Unfortunately, the weather had other ideas. We woke to rain rattling against the windows of John and Jill's lovely traditional wooden house. We're not complete wimps, but it seemed silly to set out in a downpour, so we wrote letters, studied maps, read guides and started to plan our antipodean mega-enduro instead.

New Zealand was called Aotearoa - Land of The Long White Cloud - by the Maori after the lenticular (lens shaped) clouds formed by moist sea air rising over the hills and mountains. But it wasn't just New Zealand's skies that were different. Every photo we'd seen and every book we'd read told us we were in for a scenic feast.

With so much spectacular country to see, spread across two main islands and with climate ranging from sub-tropical in the north to the chilly end of temperate in the south, from monsoonally wet in the west to arid in parts of the east, we decided weather should play a part in our planning. John assured us it had been 30^{0}C in Christchurch just a week before we arrived, but right now - November 20th 2001 - it was colder here than London! It would make sense, we thought, to head for the sunnier climes in the north to start with, then explore the cooler and wetter south after Christmas by which time the southern summer should have finally decided to play ball.

Meanwhile, we figured it would be wise to test out the luggage on our bikes and if there were a few drops of rain the next day, well... hey, it would be a good chance to try out our wet weather gear too. Whatever the weather, we would set off for Akaroa in the morning.

Don't you just hate yourself for making those 'come hell or highwater' type proclamations? We woke to a steady drizzle and a positively polar 9^{0}C! Fortunately, neither of us asked the obvious question - why had we travelled half way round the world to weather worse than at home? We pulled on our gear with the encouraging thought that it could only get better. And anyway, it would be an ideal extreme-weather evaluation of our clothing and equipment.

First we had to persuade the equipment to fit on to the bikes. Both Serows had been modified with substantial metal carrier-cum-pannier frames fixed behind their seats. We had two entirely different panniers to fit to them. The one we had brought with us from England was an ancient throw-over type saddlebag with rusted buckles, loose fitting lids and a major hole in the bottom where it had melted on the exhaust pipe of a Kawasaki 500 on the way back from Milan in the winter of 1977. We had kept it all these years partly out of sentimentality - a reminder of our mad dash to Italy to cover a motorcycle show for the magazine I worked for at the time - and partly because I was too stingy to throw it away. It had sat, quietly rusting, mouldering and stiffening in the garage all these years, waiting for an opportunity to be put to good use again.

We patched up the hole with Duct Tape*, filled the bags with a few oddments of clothing to pack them out, and lobbed them over the seat of my bike. Just as in 1977, one bag lay against the exhaust pipe where it promised to acquire another gaping hole amid dripping, burning, smelly plastic.

(* Don't let anyone tell you that this aluminium-coloured, cloth-reinforced sticky tape should be called Duck Tape. I once had lunch with Mr Roe, the man who invented it specifically for joining together sections of aluminium air ducting in factories and restaurants. He would be amused with the suggestion it be used for sticking two ducks together)

Sister-in-law Jill came to the rescue. Among her enviable list of talents which include being a violinist, long-distance tramper, apiarist, yachtswoman and former aerobatic display pilot, she is also an accomplished artist. Jill produced an offcut of artboard which we taped on to the rack to hold the pannier away from the exhaust and the problem was solved.

I was so impressed with this spot of DIY bodging that I stuffed the string we'd not needed into my jacket pocket, thinking: *'I'll hang on to that, you never know when it might come in handy.'* Unlike the thousands of other odd pieces of

10

wire, screws, bent nails, rubber bands and suchlike that I've hoarded for just such an eventuality, that little piece of string was later to perform a minor miracle.

By the time we'd filled the Serows' small petrol tanks and headed south, below the Port Hills towards Motukarara, it was late morning and the drizzle was definitely getting heavier. We turned off the main road to cut up through Gebbies Pass and eventually arrived, cold and wet, at Diamond Harbour which looks across the water towards Lyttelton. Or it would do, if the rain wasn't hammering down into the sea. The café looked welcoming and the owner didn't flinch at the sight of two dripping bikers seeking warmth, shelter and coffee.

It was at this little café that I discovered one of the greatest delights of Kiwi culture - Cookie Time! Intrigued by a garish sign on the café's roof, which depicted a manic monster raiding a cookie jar, I spotted the same cardboard figure standing by a glass jar on the counter. The jar contained the biggest, fattest, most choclatey biscuits I'd ever clapped eyes on - Cookie Time cookies. It was love at first bite, and the start of a serious addiction that was soon to reduce me to hunting for trousers with an elastic waistband.

But that was to come later. Right now we had to pull our cold, damp helmets back on and ride off into the persistent downpour to prove to ourselves we could handle the worst that New Zealand could throw at us.

After the winding, narrow road to Port Levy we took the steep gravel track high into the clouds to reach Pigeon Bay. The map says this road is not suitable for towing or caravans and it's not kidding. On a good day it would be challenging. Today it was a torment of gravel, mud and energetic rivulets carrying water down from the high peaks on our right to the plunging valley that disappeared into cloud on our left.

My visor, chilled by the colder air at this altitude, was now covered with rain droplets on the outside and fully misted on the inside. I had no choice but to flip it up. Within 100 metres my glasses were covered with rain droplets on the outside and fully misted on the inside. I had no choice but to stop and take them off. The track was now visible, if out of focus, and with eyes squinted against the stinging rain, we pressed on, up and over the summit and down to Pigeon Bay.

Then it was south through the valley to Kukupa and Barrys Bay where we picked up the main road, Highway 75, past Duvauchelle and into civilisation once more in Akaroa. By now it was raining stair rods, water was pouring across the road in great sheets and we could barely see a few metres ahead as we put-putted into town like a pair of drowned rats on wheels.

Through the thick curtain of water, salvation appeared in the form of The Dolphin, a nautical-themed restaurant with a roaring log fire, bowls of hot soup and a delightful attitude. In response to the sight of two squelching figures clutching dripping helmets and muddy baggage, not even a raised eyebrow. I thought the proprietor might not have noticed the state we were in, and would any minute eject us from his premises.

'Er... is it okay to come into your nice restaurant... we're a bit wet you see...?'

He looked genuinely surprised that I'd bothered to ask: 'Yeah, no worries mate! Helluva day for biking. Just dry yourselves out by the fire, you'll be right.'

So we did. One of the disadvantages of motorcycling in heavy rain is that all the water funnels unerringly down to your crotch. As we peeled off the layers and left huge puddles on the Dolphin's carpet, it became apparent that we were both soaked right through to our underpants and looked for all the world as if we'd been stricken with simultaneous incontinence. Viv elected to keep her waterproof (hah!) overtrousers on to cover her embarrassment, while I held my nether regions as near to the flames as I dared and delighted in the warmth and steam that issued forth.

But you can only make soup and coffee last so long and mid-afternoon we pulled our sodden, clammy outer layers back on and trudged outside to find it was still raining cats and dogs. Now we had two new problems: Firstly, our bikes were almost out of fuel, Christchurch was 82km away, and there was no certainty that we would find petrol anywhere. Secondly, my bike wouldn't start. In fact, it had no lights, no spark of life at all when I turned the key. Great - the rain had shorted out the electrics...

These little Yamahas have push-button starters which are excellent when there is electricity to spin the motor, but no kick-starter for when there isn't. I cast my mind back to 30 years before when I push-started Triumph Tiger Cubs at Cadwell Park and Snetterton in a brief but painful flirtation with club road racing. Into first gear, pull the bike back against the engine's compression then pull in the clutch. Now push the bike forward in a ragged run, jump side-saddle on the seat and let out the clutch at the same instant.

Of course, when I'd last done this I was young, fit and dressed in one-piece racing leathers. Today I was old, fat and swathed in copious layers of slippery nylon. The bike fired and roared off towards Akaroa Harbour no more than 15 metres away, while I slid off the seat and was suddenly doing a Superman impression, but without the smug grin. With boot-toes dragging along the ground and only my chest and right hip perched on the seat, I somehow managed to bring the machine to a halt just inches before it launched us into the sea, without dropping the bike or stalling the engine. I was thrilled, bruised, breathless and shaking in equal measure.

The Gods were either impressed with my efforts or felt sorry for these two soggy and frozen Poms, because we suffered no further mishaps that day. Down the road in Duvauchelle we found fuel and I managed to bump-start the bike on the slippery garage forecourt without any more drama. After the long, cold, wet ride back to Christchurch John and Jill resuscitated us with hot baths followed by spare ribs, kumara (native sweet potatoes), roast potatoes and pumpkin accompanied by a fine New Zealand Shiraz. Wonderful.

However, their magnificent hospitality couldn't hide the fact that their undoubtedly splendid country was, for now at least, bloody cold and outrageously wet. We had some serious rethinking to do. We'd done only 200 kilometres that day but had been soaked to the skin, chilled to the bone and one of our bikes had suffered complete electrical failure. The thin nylon overtrousers we'd brought from England were neither use nor ornament and our gloves had soaked up the rain like sponges, turning our hands bright red with leather dye.

Not only that, our old patched up panniers, relics of our trip to Milan 24 years previously, had let in such copious quantities of water through their loose-fitting lids, that even double-wrapping our clothing in plastic bags had not prevented everything from getting soaked. All in all, our first real test of ourselves, our bikes and our equipment had been an unmitigated disaster.

We were back at NZ Motorcycle Rentals next morning (still raining, 13⁰C) getting my sick Serow fixed and borrowing some better gear. The lads at the shop were brilliant. While the mechanics stripped the bike to find and insulate a faulty electrical connector, Gordon let us have free choice of overtrousers, gloves and panniers from their extensive selection. By lunchtime we had two fully-functioning machines, two sets of decent panniers, warmer and almost waterproof overtrousers plus spare gloves.

We also treated ourselves to spare trousers, found for a few pounds in one of Christchurch's many secondhand clothing shops, just in case we got soaked through again. Browsing through the racks and chatting to the friendly locals, we started to tune in to the twangy Kiwi accent. A big step forward came when we asked where to find something to eat.

'Have you tried our fashion shops?'

'Er... why fashion shops?'

'No, no, not fashion shops - fush 'n' chups!'

Being a country with a devotedly British culture, fish and chips are *de rigueur* in New Zealand. And jolly good they are too. The South Pacific's Blue Cod is altogether more succulent and delicious than the near-extinct North Sea or Atlantic cod we are used to back home. To add insult to injury, this top-class tucker together with a bagful of 'chups' costs around a pound. So 'fush 'n' chups' were added to Cookie Time cookies on our list of tasty Kiwi treats. Fortunately the trousers we'd bought had room for expansion.

Our last day as John and Jill's pampered guests was spent lubricating chains, checking oil, adjusting tyre pressures and finding ways to bungy-strap our newly acquired fuel cans on to the bikes, together with two sets of bulky panniers and a rucksack. Finally it all fitted. Everything we would need before returning in a month's time for Christmas was double-wrapped, packed, stashed and stuffed into pockets. We were now ready for anything.

Or nearly ready. I just needed a brainwave to solve the serious problem of my bum-numbing motorbike seat. Much to everyone's amusement, I adapted my inflatable in-flight neck pillow so it could be tied on to the seat to provide some extra squishy support for my posterior. Half expecting it to exhale like a whoopee cushion, I lowered myself gently on to the bloated horseshoe and... it worked! My reputation as master of improbable bodge-ups remained intact.

Saturday November 24th 2001, we headed north on Highway 71 through Kaiapoi to Amberley where we topped up the tanks and fuel cans. We went on to Waipara before turning off the coast road and heading inland through the wonderfully bendy Weka Pass to Culverden and finally Hanmer Springs.

The way in to this picturesque spa town is over the Waiau Ferry Bridge, a heart-stopping, single file suspension bridge. This provides an unsettling view, between the timbers rattling under your wheels, of the boiling waters of the Waiau River far below. It is also the site of 'Thrillseekers Canyon Adventure Centre' which offers those less fond of life than ourselves the opportunity to sample the delights of bungy-jumping, jetboating and white-water rafting. We didn't linger.

Hanmer Springs itself, nestling ten kilometres further up into the hills, is a tourist town with a touch of Swiss kitsch, wrapped around thermal sulphur springs. We weren't too sure of the welcome at first, when three B&Bs claimed to be full, despite vacancy signs hanging outside. Perhaps they didn't want Hell's Grannies biting off chickens' heads and lowering the tone of the neighbourhood?

No such worries for Merna and Robin, the cheery proprietors of the Glenalvon B&B, who welcomed us into their smart and modern establishment and provided a first class motel-like apartment for just NZ$89 (about £25) for the pair of us. For that modest sum we got a large room with double and single bed, dining area with table and four chairs, kitchenette with fridge, kettle, toaster and tea, coffee and milk provided, en-suite shower, loo and handbasin, plus a sofa and Sky TV! Even a brolly was thoughtfully provided, and was to come in handy later on when we strolled into town for supper.

But first, we had a mission to accomplish. I had seen on the map that north of town there was a 4WD track leading up and through Jollies Pass. This connected, via a short piece of the Molesworth track, to Jacks Pass, which would take us around Mt Isobel (1319 metres) and back down into town. We'd only done 140km so far, all on tarseal (tarmacadam) roads and I was itching to get down and dirty on the southern end of one of the most famous off-road tracks in the South Island. If Viv was less keen, she kept it to herself.

The top end of Jollies Pass became very steep and rocky. Keeping the bike moving and weaving between the biggest outcrops of rock called for first gear and a deft touch on the twistgrip. Each touch of throttle threatened to lift the front wheel and flip me over backwards, so I stood up on the footpegs and leant over the handlebars to keep my weight well forward. It was quite a challenge for me, with 32 years of biking experience. How would Viv handle it, having learned to ride only three years previously?

Fortunately, Viv's short motorcycling career had been inspired by our experience of two-wheeled freedom in Turkey and later that same year in Cyprus, where a little DT125 Yamaha trailbike had carried us all over the western end of the island. Exploring the dirt roads and gravel tracks into the Akamas peninsula and up into the Troodos Mountains had convinced Viv of two things: Getting off the beaten track on a motorbike was excellent; bouncing about on the back of a tiny bike was not. This little Yamaha had nowhere near enough seat for two people of our age and dimensions. Either I was sitting on the petrol tank and out of control, or Viv was sitting on the steel rack behind the

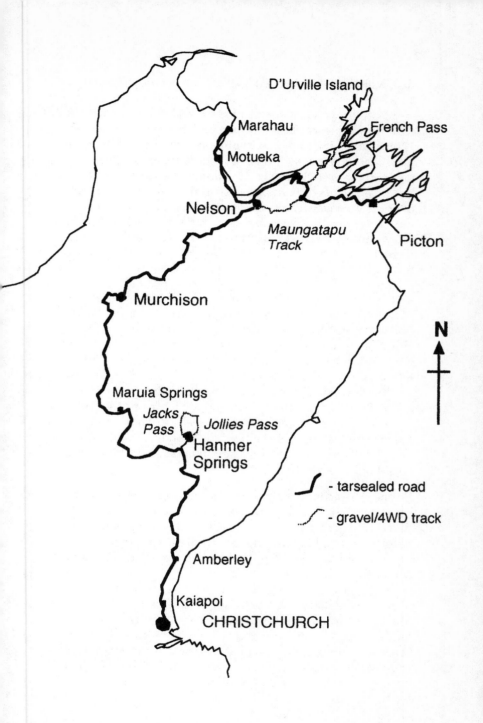

D'Urville Island

French Pass

Marahau

Motueka

Nelson

Maungatapu Track

Picton

Murchison

N

Maruia Springs

Jacks Pass

Jollies Pass

Hanmer Springs

— - tarsealed road

⌢ - gravel/4WD track

Amberley

Kaiapoi

CHRISTCHURCH

seat, which proved excruciating. It was obvious - we needed a bike each.

So a plan was hatched: Viv would take her motorcycle CBT (Compulsory Basic Training) to enable her to ride a 125cc bike on the road and to hire one of her own when we went abroad. It was a daunting task for a middle-aged mother of three to learn to ride a motorcycle from scratch on the greasy roads of rain-soaked Norwich alongside a bunch of fearless teenage tearaways. But she stuck at it, fought back the tears when the bike clipped the kerb and pitched her off during the low-speed U-turn in the morning training, and passed first time. By the next spring we were riding along the gravel tracks of Cyprus on a pair of trail bikes.

Since then we'd clocked up a few thousand miles on several trips to this Mediterranean island, during which we'd had numerous thrills and spills and gained some modest off-road experience. Back home, on the much more crowded roads of the UK, Viv had survived her first year on a 125, then took more training and a further gruelling test to allow her to ride a more powerful machine. She had graduated first to a 500cc KLE Kawasaki and then a brand new Honda 650cc Transalp. As the months slipped by and the miles disappeared under her spinning wheels, Viv had grown to love motorcycling and the big blue Honda was her pride and joy, a magic carpet to whisk her away from the humdrum world of housework.

But here, nearing the summit of Jollies Pass, the steep and rocky track was testing that experience to the limit. I only dared to snatch a glance behind to check she was still there before we reached the top. We pulled up alongside an equally middle-aged couple who had pedalled their way up on mountain bikes.

If we felt wobbly-legged and breathless, this intrepid pair of Brits were scarlet and steaming and quite unable to talk at first. It turned out they'd arrived ten minutes before us and had been gulping air and praying to be spared cardiac arrest ever since. If they ever got their breath back, they said, they would turn around and freewheel down to Hanmer Springs for a long reviving soak in the town's hot thermal baths.

Convinced we had already overcome the most difficult part of the track, I said airily that we were off to circumnavigate the mountain before supper, *'See you back in town!'* Viv was very quiet.

The rocky road we'd encountered on the way up was now transformed into a deeply rutted mud track at the summit of the pass, and now plummeted out of view before us. Rain had gouged miniature canyons and crevasses and the chunky tyres of 4WD vehicles had churned up the rest into deep puddles of sticky goo. If coming up Jollies Pass was tricky, getting down the other side was a real challenge.

Descending a steep hill on a motorcycle presents a different set of problems. Instead of wanting to slow to a stop and tip you over backwards, now the bike wants to race away madly downhill to certain destruction.

Applying the front brake risks a front wheel skid, followed a micro-second later by a hefty crash. Using the rear brake simply locks the rear wheel which then skids and slithers, neither slowing you down nor improving control. Applying both brakes in short, desperate dabs checks the speed, but threatens to pitch you over the handlebars instead. The way to stop that happening is to stand up on the footrests and stretch your body as far back as possible, so that your backside is hovering somewhere near the rearlight.

Doing all this while trying to steer around deep muddy gullies, wheel-swallowing ruts, treacherous puddles and chunks of rock is extremely difficult. If you've ever seen professional trials riders inching smoothly down a vertical cliff face and bouncing untroubled over the odd car-sized rock on the way, don't be fooled. They are super-human and what they can do on their wasp-like machines is clearly impossible. For ordinary mortals, a modest one-in-three downgrade full of obstacles calls for a steely resolve, a delicate touch and a tight control of all sphincters.

I couldn't stop to see if Viv was coping, but a quick glance in the mirror revealed she was still upright and edging her way down in my tyre-tracks, with an occasional flailing leg showing she was finding it tricky too.

Near the bottom of the descent there was a fast-flowing, axle-deep stream to cross. The trouble with mountain streams

19

is that the bubbling, raging waters conceal both their depth and the hazards that lurk beneath. Invariably there are large, spherical boulders like gigantic marbles lying in wait for motorcycle wheels. After millions of years of rounding, smoothing and polishing they are the perfect trap, able to hop and jump from beneath a bike's slender tyres and cause the machine to lurch uncontrollably to a watery fate.

As ever, there is a technique to overcome these aquatic challenges, but, like so much in life, it feels all wrong at first. The natural instinct is to cross the stream as slowly as possible sitting down with feet ready to paddle the bike upright if it threatens to fall, as it appears it must. This guarantees two things: Firstly the bike will stop midstream when the front wheel hits the biggest rock; secondly the bike will fall sideways and you'll get a wet leg if you're lucky, and a thorough dunking if you're not.

The trick is to accelerate smartly through the stream to lighten the front wheel so it skims over the boulders, while standing up on the footpegs to keep feet dry and balance maintained. Knowing it and doing it are two different things. I went too fast and got splashed from head to toe. Viv went too slow and got a bootfull.

Otherwise unscathed, we joined the wide gravel Molesworth Station Road before turning left again for the easier Jacks Pass track back to Hanmer. Back at our digs, the owners helpfully provided a bucket of water to wash the mud off our bikes and our riding gear, then we changed clothes and headed into the dusk and a light drizzle to find a bite to eat.

Keith's Café was cheerful and inexpensive, but with the same track playing repeatedly on their tinny sound system. After the sixth repeat we pointed it out to our schoolgirl waitress who hadn't noticed. She nudged the machine to play the rest of the CD - some sort of country rap with every track worse than the last - so we beat a hasty retreat and had our dessert in the street. This consisted of a wonderful ice cream confection called 'Hokey Pokey' (yes, really!). We were to discover that NZ ice creams are universally scrummy, old fashioned and irresistible.

Chapter 2

Bathed In Hot Oil

Sunday November 25th dawned cold but bright, with wispy white clouds wrapped like a cotton-wool scarf around the neck of Mt Miromiro (1875m) shining in the early morning sun. It was to the west, where we were headed, over the Lewis Pass. This follows the course of the original bridle track opened in 1866 after surveyors Christopher Maling and Henry Lewis discovered a route to join the east and west coasts.

First stop was scheduled for Maruia Springs, just 80km further on and perfectly positioned for a coffee break and bottom resuscitation. I had given up on my home-made whoopee cushion. For all the ingenuity and improvisation this great bodge represented, it proved to be more hassle than it was worth. It slipped backwards and forwards and side to side with every bump in the road or wriggle of my posterior. It was rather like sitting on a jelly.

And if I ever raised myself off the seat (as us chaps must from time to time to rearrange delicate parts of our anatomy) the cushion wasn't there when I sat down again. There followed several hundred metres of loony swerving while I groped around with one hand to locate it as it flapped around at the end of its tether, then stuffed it back under my bottom.

These lapses of concentration posed a greater risk than my petrified posterior, so the cushion was deflated and filed with a thousand other brilliant ideas under 'heroic failures'. Which left me with the unresolved problem of my agonised bottom. I said I would have to just grin and bear it, but Viv thought I would get arrested for high-speed mooning.

As it turned out, the coffee break at Maruia Springs provided more than ample time to massage life back into my aching buttocks. When we rolled to a stop outside the thermal-springs mini-resort's restaurant, Viv discovered her right boot was covered in oil. A quick inspection showed it was leaking from an oil-pressure switch that the rental company had added to the engine's right-hand crankcase.

Because these bikes carry so little oil in their tiny sumps and some hirers forget to keep a close eye on the oil level, there's a real danger the oil pressure could drop and wreck the motor. Hence the switch to illuminate a warning light near the speedo and alert the rider to stop and top up.

Ironically, the leak from the seal where the switch passed through the casing had nearly caused disaster, both for the bike and for Viv. Besides her boot, the hot lubricant had sprayed over the entire right side of the bike and had started to spread across the rear tyre. A few more kilometres and the wheel would have slid from under her in mid-bend. We had to fix it, or we could go no further.

We phoned the rental company but, being a Sunday, they had no mechanics at their disposal. If we could get a garage to fix it, they said, they would pay the bill. Great - but where would we find a garage? We were precisely in the middle of nowhere, halfway between the east and west coasts of The South Island. The nearest help would be hours away on a weekday, and the first one of those - 9am Monday - was a yawning 22 hours from now. Not for the last time did we get a real sense of how large and empty this country is.

If ever I needed the inspiration for a roadside bodge, this was the moment. As I rummaged in my jacket pocket for a tissue to wipe the oil off my fingers, I felt the piece of thin hemp twine I'd saved when fixing the pannier protector board a few days earlier. By winding multiple turns of this string around the switch and pulling it tight like a tourniquet, I was able to force the little rubber gasket into the joint and, hopefully, staunch the flow of the bike's lifeblood.

Thanks to the spare half-litre of oil we carried we were able to top up the sump. After wiping as much of the mess as we could off the bike and Viv's boot, and wrapping the latter in a plastic bag to protect it from further anointment, we set off gingerly for our destination, Murchison, 100km to the north. Repeated stops along the way showed that not one further drop of oil had seeped out past my garden twine instant fix. At last - a bodge to be proud of!

By the time we reached Maruia Falls, just half an hour from Murchison, our concern had been replaced by confidence and we stopped for a picnic lunch and to take in the splendid view. Up until 1929 the Maruia River sluiced north to join the mighty Buller untroubled. Then a huge earthquake shook the region, causing a rift in the river bed so that the water had to make a spectacular ten metre leap. The waterfall is now much used for TV commercials cashing in on the Kiwis' predilection for hurling themselves off any available precipice.

Despite our worries over the oil leak and occasional light drizzle, we couldn't escape the beauty of this region, from the Alpine quality of Hanmer's skyline to the lush and unspoiled native forests of the Victoria Forest Park on our way north.

Murchison, when we arrived mid-afternoon, was burning under the fierce antipodean sun and looking for all the world like a frontier town from a Western movie. Opposite the Commercial Hotel on Main Road (SH6), Fairfax Street heads south between single-storey wooden stores supporting wide porches casting deep shadows on the pavement. All it needed was a few hitching rails and Wyatt Earp could ride through town without raising an eyebrow. The picturesque little clapboard church with its red tin roof (yes, another one) and bell over the door tempted us back for a photo, but we pressed on to find the Kiwi Park Motel we had booked that morning.

After the frustration of being turned away from three motels in Hanmer Springs and the suspicion that they weren't really full, we'd consulted the accommodation guidebooks (we were to find these provided free in every motel in NZ) and phoned the cheapest. At NZ$60 (£17) our detached cabin was stunning value for money. In a more time-worn structure that fitted this Wild West town, we got everything our Hanmer accommodation had provided, plus a fully equipped kitchen and a cheery, joking proprietor, Maurice Horner, to welcome us and make us feel 'right at home'.

We'd only covered 178km but, with the drama and delay of the oil leak, it felt like a full day and I was pooped. While Viv took a stroll back into town to visit the shops, the big double bed swallowed me in dreams, where I was pushing a huge, luggage-laden motorcycle through deep sand in a vast desert. My feet and the bike's wheels kept sinking in, but I had to keep pushing if I was ever to see civilisation again.

It was a relief when Viv woke me, eager to show me a fabulous bird she'd seen on her walk. Still rubbing the sleep from my eyes and trying to shake the dream from my brain, I was suddenly wide awake when faced with this spectacular big black bird with white ruff and greeny-blue tail with two distinctive white wattles hanging below his chin. He was hopping about, sipping nectar from the flowers of a yukka plant at the pavement's edge, and seemed unconcerned that we had stopped two metres away to examine his every move.

The most extraordinary feature of our feathered friend, however, was his amazing song: Between hearty slurps of nectar he regaled us with a symphony of tinkles, whistles, clicks and bell-like chimes, plus a perfect rendition of a creaking rusty gate-hinge. He was a tui, a clown and mimic who was to delight and entertain us throughout our travels in NZ.

With his song still ringing in our ears we strolled the covered sidewalks in the dying sunshine to soak up the atmosphere of this charming old gold-rush town. When gold was discovered in the district in 1862, Murchison flourished. Here the Matakitaki and Matiri Rivers flow into the Buller and the Maruia, Mangles and Owen Rivers join nearby. Prospectors paddled their way upstream to Murchison, or led their mules down from the headwaters to cash in their gold dust and nuggets for a hot meal, whisky and a bed with sheets before setting out next day with fresh supplies for a more spartan existence back in the hills working their claim once more.

The colonial Hampden and Commercial Hotels bear witness to the glory days and there is a museum full of quaint relics. These tell the story of the town's history and some of the colourful locals who achieved fame for their pioneering spirit. One such was Charlie Collins and the eatery named after him on the opposite side of the street provided us with a massive if unpretentious meal.

Once the gold ran out, Murchison survived as a supply centre for the local farming community. Population was just 750 by the time of our visit, but looked set to grow with tourism as Murchison provides an ideal base for white-water rafting, kayaking, fishing, hunting and gold panning - there's still enough left to quicken the pulse. We hope Murchison survives. We loved its open-hearted frontier town nature.

Bright sunshine woke us early, so by 8.30am we were ready for a walk to start the day with a little light exercise. Having packed already, we left our bags at the office with Maurice, telling him we were just going for a walk down the lane.

'The 'lane'? Hell, yeah!' guffawed Maurice. 'You go for a walk down the 'lane' why dontcha! And while you're at it, you can go up all the hills and down the dales and all those other funny English things. Don't let me stop ya, ha ha ha!'

His uninhibited mirth at our eccentric Pommy ways kept us chuckling as we strolled through farmland beside the Matakitaki River, and reminded us that however Anglophilic the Kiwis are, we were in a foreign country on the far side of the globe. And New Zealanders have some odd little quirks of their own...

On our first afternoon in Christchurch we had noticed children playing barefoot in the street. The way in which they ran unflinching across the sharp chippings on the road surface made it clear they were used to going without shoes.

I was just puzzling over how this apparent poverty could exist in an apparently affluent city, when a smart Subaru pulled up and a businessman in a dark suit stepped out and crossed the road, barefoot! We soon came to realise this was another expression of Kiwi's love of the great outdoors and their oneness with nature - they like to feel it between their toes.

By 10.30 we were back on the road again for a modest 130km hop, skirting Kahurangi National Park, to Nelson, capital of the north coast. This thriving, lively city prides itself on having more sunshine than the rest of The South Island and was living up to its claim when we arrived, the hot southern sun blazing down unimpeded through a clear navy blue sky.

We had people to see here, but none knew we were coming. It was no big surprise they were not at home. So we escaped the searing brightness by checking in early to our accommodation (another Kiwi Park motel) at Appleby, ten kilometres to the west. We still hadn't got over the surprise and delight we felt at how much these motels provided for so little money. A new cabin at the Greenwood Park at Appleby provided everything you'd need to live there permanently for just NZ$75 (£21) a night. After a siesta we headed back into Nelson to find Chalkie White.

Twenty years earlier Chalkie had been a regular contributor to a UK motorcycling magazine I edited. His tales of trail bike riding in this wild and beautiful country, adrift in the southern Pacific Ocean, had delighted our readers and inspired me. The seeds he'd sown back in 1980 had slowly germinated and ultimately blossomed into the great adventure Viv and I were now undertaking. The least we could do was call and say thank you.

When we had corresponded in those distant days, I'd told Chalkie I had a plan to visit his country. He responded by sending me a superb pictorial book revealing some of the scenic magnificence of New Zealand and said: *'Do look us up when you come.'*

It had taken slightly longer than expected, but two decades later Chalkie and his wife Jeanie were delighted to see us. Sadly, Chalkie was no longer able to ride his beloved Honda Monkeybike - he was always fascinated by the abilities of the smallest Japanese machines. He was now 79 and the previous year had suffered a stroke which had left him unable to coordinate fully. Having been out with friends for the day he was tired, said Jeanie protectively, after we'd chatted for an hour. Could we please come back in the morning, asked Chalkie, so that he could show us around?

Chalkie had always loved motorcycles. At 18 he joined the Royal Armoured Corps in order to ride bikes, but a few years later was sent to war - not on two wheels, but in a tank. He survived action in Egypt, France, Belgium and Holland before being shot in the head by a sniper in Germany in 1945.

The bullet passed through the top of Chalkie's skull, through his brain and exited from his jaw. Miraculously, this didn't kill him and he was flown to Oxford where he recovered quickly, overcame a slight lingering paralysis, and was soon back in service in Haifa, Palestine.

By 1947 Chalkie was back in civvy street, married, needing a job and still longing to ride motorbikes. He landed the perfect career with the Metropolitan Police Force, riding a Triumph 500cc Speed Twin. Ten years of patrolling the capital's streets were enough and, for a complete change, he took his wife and son to peaceful Bideford in Devon to run a dairy farm. But the country idyll was shattered when his wife was diagnosed with Multiple Sclerosis. As her condition deteriorated she spent her last days in a Cheshire home, so Chalkie gave up the dairy farm to work for Leonard Cheshire in order to be near her.

In the years following her death, Chalkie met Jeanie and they decided to start a new life in New Zealand, where he was able to combine his passion for motorised two-wheelers with his love of the great outdoors. Now, as a journalist, he became fascinated by the immense technical progress being made by Japanese motorcycle manufacturers - especially in small-engined machines - so he taught himself the Japanese language in order to visit the country and see for himself how they did it. This so impressed the Japanese they welcomed him with open arms and several commissions followed.

Now that his riding days were over, Chalkie was delighted to have us to talk to about our respective biking exploits. He'd arranged for his engineer pal Bill Prosser to take us to visit another petrol-head, John Stickney, whose passion for motors had filled a huge garage with wonders: Two Honda 305cc CB77s, identical to the 1965 model I owned when Viv and I were tearaway teenagers back in 1970; a 1961 Honda Benly 125; a Honda CB400 café racer; a Velosolex; three Zundapps and three Suzuki 100cc twins. On four wheels were a Fiat 600 Abarth; Renault Gordini 750; Fiat Topolino; Triumph Spitfire and an Austin Seven Special.

For many years New Zealand imposed restrictions on imports of motor vehicles, with the result that the Kiwis were obliged to keep ancient relics running - often in top-class condition - long after they'd disappeared from British roads. This passion for preservation, tinged with nostalgia for the old country perhaps, continues today and many New Zealanders harbour lovely old vehicles in their garden sheds and garages.

After our trip down memory lane and a pub lunch we were taken to visit a Nelson brewery which produces Aussie-style lagers suitable for antipodean tastebuds. For all their nostalgia for the old country, Kiwis have yet to discover how to make UK-style beers and ales. Late in the afternoon we left Chalkie and Jeanie at their historic South Street home and zoomed two-up back to the Honda shop at Richmond to collect Viv's bike, left there that morning to have its oil leak fixed.

Chapter 3

Maungatapu And Murderers' Rock

Next morning we called on another Nelson resident, Garry Askew, who my brother had assured us would be happy to offer us a cup of tea on our way through town. Garry did better than that. After a drink and introductory chat, he took us to visit his 'bach'. In Kiwi-speak bach (pronounced batch) is short for bachelor - and is the name given to remote country cabins which were traditionally used by single men while away from home on hunting, fishing or gold prospecting trips. The bach is now an institution in a country where holidays are spent getting even closer to nature.

Garry's bach, less than ten kilometres from the bustling heart of Nelson, was exceptional both for its setting and its luxury. Tucked away in a small orchard of exotic fruit and nut trees, this lovely wooden cottage nestled near the end of the sealed road in the steep and wooded Maitai Valley. Behind its wide verandah was a huge open-plan lounge, diner and kitchen, two double bedrooms, washroom, bathroom and fridge room. It even had a separate garage containing a VW Beetle, hidden behind orange, almond and lemon trees.

'Well, there you are,' said Garry. 'Stay as long as you like, and you can use the Veedub while you're here too.'

We protested that we had only called for a cup of tea, we had no intention of stopping, we couldn't possibly etc, etc. But it was all to no avail. Garry wouldn't hear of it. The bach was unoccupied, we could use it as a base while we explored the region and what's more we were invited to dinner with Garry and his wife Philippa that evening, so he could tell us of all the great off-road tracks we really must explore over the coming days.

'The phone's connected so you can call whoever you want,' said Garry. 'There's beer in the fridge and food in the cupboard - just make yourselves at home.'

This kind of hospitality and generosity towards almost total strangers - Garry had met my brother on the ship that brought him from England 35 years earlier - left us lost for words. But it's not uncommon in New Zealand, a country where sheep outnumber people by ten to one and vast areas of land are still unpopulated.

It stems from a time when the early colonists often found themselves remote and cut off from the civilisation they'd left behind in Europe in the mid-1800s. A sheep farmer's wife in the remote hill country was ecstatic, one traveller wrote, to see another woman for the first time in six years. Passers by were begged to stay and were asked: *'How long can you give us?'*

After a walk in the hills opposite the bach we feasted regally at Garry and Philippa's and were treated to a video show of their own 4WD expeditions into the remote bush country. Garry marked our map. There were enough tracks in the vicinity to keep us occupied for a month, but first up would be the Maungatapu Track.

This ancient footpath had long been a route taken by the Maori on their way to collect precious greenstone, the jade-like raw material used for their sacred jewellery and symbolic war clubs. It had then become a pack-horse trail for gold prospectors making their way to Nelson and had finally been upgraded to a 4WD track. It had some dark secrets from a murky past lurking way up in the hills, and it would be moderately challenging for a pair of wobbly grandparents. Maungatapu: It sounded primeval, awesome and scary.

Next morning, while Viv packed lunch, I checked oil and tyre pressures, lubed chains and adjusted clutch cables. The sun was shining, we were ready for the test.

Turning left out of our bach's drive, the tarsealed road soon gave way to gravel and crossed the Maitai River as the steep-sided valley narrowed and climbed into the hills. With the steepening gradient came a change in the track surface and surrounding vegetation. The fine gravel soon gave way to rocks and mud under overhanging fronds of treeferns and trailing lichens. We really felt we were ascending into the wilderness and in places the going got really tough. Several sections required a full-on charge approach, with an open throttle and gritted teeth. The muddy quagmires had our wheels slithering sideways and at one point it all became too much for Viv. I rode her bike through one particularly tricky section while she visibly shook with a mixture of fear and anger. The fear of falling was real enough, but the fear of failure was worse. The anger was with herself for giving up on the hardest bit and needing to be helped. The flood of emotions burst out in tears.

I felt awful. Why had I chosen this difficult route which was making Viv weep with frustration? It was hard enough for me. Was I asking too much of my wife, expecting her to overcome such difficult obstacles with such limited experience and minimal training?

There had been a serious attempt at professional tuition the previous year. I'd booked a one-day off-road riding course and presented it to Viv as a birthday gift, a sneaky way of ensuring she would agree to do it, provided I went along to give her moral support. But instead of teaching her new skills and adding to her confidence, the off-road riding day had left her bruised and less sure of her riding than ever. Within minutes of starting the day's session they launched us up a near-vertical gulley, crisscrossed with tree roots. All but two of the eight trainees fell off on this first slope, and for Viv it was a huge mistake. While the others - all much younger and more experienced - laughed it off and formed teams to carry the bikes to the top of the slope, Viv was badly shaken and asked: *'Is it all going to be like this?'*

The next section had been a deeply rutted track and within 100 metres Viv had crashed again, more heavily this time, bruising her leg and winding her severely. It took a long time to get her back on the bike, and now all her confidence was gone. What followed next was a field of mud - literally up to our handlebars in places - and then an open practice area where instruction was finally provided in a range of useful off-road riding skills.

Too late. By now Viv had no faith in her ability to ride a motorbike on a smooth track, let alone tackle the miniature cliffs, jumps, foot-down sliding turns or anything else. She was ready to give up, go away and nurse her bruised arms and legs and have a private cry. The course that claimed to be *'Ideal for novices and experts alike...'* was anything but. Off road riding ability is all about confidence. After this training day, Viv's was shot to pieces.

I cursed my mistake then, and now, a year on, I was cursing the decision to ride the Maungatapu Track. We had nearly three months ahead of us. There was no need to rush our fences.

But we were at the saddle now, the summit of the track and time for hugs and reassurance, a drink and some quiet meditation. After half an hour Viv gave me a brave smile and said: *'Right. I'm ready for the next bit. I'm going to be okay from now on.'* And so she was. A private watershed had been overcome in her mind and from here on it was all downhill.

The descent towards Pelorus Bridge was much more gentle, a doddle after the ride up to the peak of the pass, with just a couple of small streams to ford on the way down. Immediately after the first of these - Kohuru Creek - we came across Murderers' Rock. It was here in June 1866 that a bunch of desperadoes committed one of the most evil crimes of the fledgling colony.

The Burgess-Kelly gang (actually, Sullivan, Levy, Burgess and Kelly) four ex-convicts who'd made their way to New Zealand from Australia, robbed and murdered gold prospectors on their way to Nelson. Over a number of days they gunned down five unsuspecting gold diggers, using the rock as a lookout point and hiding place from which to pounce upon their victims.

After the prospectors were missed and then their bodies were discovered hidden in the bush a few metres from the Maungatapu Track, the hunt was on for the killers. It didn't take long before one of the gang was picked up in a Nelson oyster bar and he was soon persuaded to squeal on his mates. For turning 'Queen's evidence' he was freed and took the next ship to California, while his three accomplices were hanged.

The thought of the horrors that had occurred in this remote and beautiful place made us shiver, but we saw neither murderers nor Maoris - not a soul, in fact - as we rode down to the gentle plains below and celebrated our conquest of the 39km Maungatapu Track with an early picnic lunch.

After the Maungatapu Track, lovely scenery on the way to Pelorus Bridge

Fabulous holiday home 'bach' near Nelson, NZ hospitality at its best

Feeling elated, we decided to ride to French Pass, a tiny hamlet at the end of a long finger of land pointing north into Cook Strait, the channel between the North and South Islands. A sign at the start of this road warns motorists: 'French Pass 77km - return trip 4 hours'. Which may sound improbable but ignore this at your peril. Nothing can prepare you for the impossibly winding road that carves its wrinkled way along the face of this jagged peninsula. This road has more tight kinks than an Afro hairstyle and at first the riding was fun, constantly changing gear and swooping around the turns at 20kph. But after ten kilometres the constant turns had made us dizzy and disoriented. And then the tarseal ended and we were on loose gravel again. Much as bikers love bendy roads, this was too much. Within a few more kilometres we were bend-drunk and wobbly, longing for a straight road.

Fortunately, there were numerous excuses to pull up and let our heads stop spinning while we took in breathtaking, sumptuous views. Between the massive and elegant fronds of treeferns we could see distant coves and emerald islets, set like jewels in a sparkling azure sea. At every turn there were yet more precipitous drops, rugged headlands and tree-cloaked peaks reflected in the shimmering waters. On and on we rode, past Okiwi Bay and Elaine Bay.

By the time we reached the tiny campsite and grassy park at French Pass it was mid-afternoon and we were just in time to witness a marine phenomenon. The gap between the mainland and nearby D'Urville Island is narrow and funnels the sea to perform impressive contortions as the tide runs strongly here. There was a visible slope on the sea surface where the water was pouring from one level to another. Then, astoundingly, a small coaster appeared travelling at high speed towards the briny waterfall. It was sucked into the gap and spat out the other side like a cork out of a bottle. I'm sure the skipper knew what he was doing, but it looked a decidedly hairy short cut from where we were standing.

Fortified by a healthy apple which Viv had packed and a Cookie Time cookie that I had smuggled into the bottom of the rucksack, we set off for the dizzying two hours of chicanes to return to the main SH6 road. By this time we were overdue a comfort break and stopped at the first café. Unfortunately, like so many in New Zealand, it had no toilet.

This peculiarity of Kiwi roadside eateries was proving more than a little inconvenient. After several hours of riding and stopping for gulps of rehydrating water, the sight of a café promised welcome relief from riding with crossed legs, as well as a cup of coffee and maybe just one more of those scrummy cookies.

By the time we had parked up, removed helmets and gloves, unstrapped the rucksack containing our valuables and struggled inside - we would be fairly bursting for a pee.

'Can we order some coffee and use your toilet please?' It seemed a perfectly reasonable request, even if made in a high-pitched voice.

'Aw no - we don't hiv a toilet, sorry,' said the woman behind the counter.

'What!?' panicky now.

'There's a public toilet down the street, on the other side of the road,' she said.

'Cafés without toilets should be burned, then bulldozed and their proprietors taken out and shot!' I said. But she didn't hear me. I was already waddling urgently down the street, cursing under my breath and crossing the road oblivious of passing traffic.

Back at our Nelson bach, after 225km, much of it over the rock and mud of Maungatapu and the gravelly twists and turns of the French Pass road, we toasted our achievements with a fine bottle of NZ wine and rustled up a fitting feast before collapsing into untroubled sleep for ten hours. Perfect.

The little Serows had behaved faultlessly the previous day, all except for one small glitch. Over the trials and tribulations of the Maungatapu Track the torquey little engines had thumped away strongly, and on the slippery twists and turns to French Pass and back the dual-purpose tyres and positive handling had inspired us with confidence. But my headlamp bulb had failed - or at least half of it had. The dip beam filament had blown, which not only made the bike illegal, but somewhat hazardous to ride after dark. Dipping the light for oncoming traffic rendered me instantly invisible and made the road disappear - not too hot in a strange country with numerous rocks, cracks and dead possums littering its highways, and where the locals didn't have much of a clue how to deal with motorcyclists when they could see them, let alone the Invisible Man and Hell's Granny.

So we phoned the ever-helpful New Zealand Motorcycle Rentals. They would send a replacement bulb by post to Garry and Philippa's house (another good excuse to make use of their exceptional hospitality and stay on at the bach for another couple of days), but in the meantime we could get a bulb from a Nelson bike shop and they'd reimburse us later. What great people to deal with! The attitude of this bike rental company was both refreshing and delightful.

Chapter 4

The Black Prince

There are many reasons why we choose to travel by motorcycle - fun, fresh air, freedom and the joy of being part of the environment instead of cocooned in a tin box, watching the scenery go past like a 3D movie. But it has to be said that convenience is not one of biking's strong points. Every stop requires a complex ballet of disrobing that goes like this.

First pull off the gloves, open the helmet visor, extricate glasses and perch them somewhere they won't fall off. Then unstrap and pull off the crash helmet, putting it somewhere it won't fall off, without knocking the glasses on to the road. Put glasses back on to see to undertake the rest of the operation, and realise the gloves have blown off the seat and are now underneath the bike. Retrieve them and stuff them inside the helmet so they don't get lost. Turn and lock the steering and pocket the ignition key.

If it is dry and sunny, the next stage is to remove, with some urgency, the riding jacket. This is a necessarily large, quilt-like garment with the ability to raise body core temperature by about 1^0C per second once the bike has stopped. Its pockets are bulging with vital items such as wallet, sunglasses, visor spray, spare tissues plus odd tools and bits of wire that I like to keep close to hand. The jacket is held shut by a belt, pop-studs and Velcro from chin to crotch, then a full-length zip, with further pop-stud closures at the sleeve cuffs. All these are designed in a hefty and commodious fashion in the vain hope that they might keep out the rain. They don't of course, but they do add a few excruciatingly sweaty seconds to the process of preparing for a dash to the loo.

If it is raining there may not be the same heat-induced panic - in fact, you may be inclined to keep the jacket on until under some sort of cover - but now the jacket is streaming wet, cold and clammy and has tripled in weight. Not only has the material and its quilt lining soaked up enough water to fill an average domestic bath, but the pockets are also full of water, soggy tissues, a wet wallet and rapidly rusting tools and wire.

And then there are the overtrousers. I won't call them waterproof overtrousers, which is how their makers laughingly describe them, as they patently are not. In 30-odd years of motorcycling, many of those as a journalist road-testing machines and clothing of every description and in every weather for a number of different bike magazines and newspapers, I have only come across one pair of trousers and one jacket that were truly waterproof. They were the first ones I ever owned.

When, at age 16, I bought my first-ever machine - a shiny black 90cc Honda C200 motorcycle - my good friend Ian Grommett told me just where I could buy a shiny black motorcycle riding suit to match. He told me, with the kind of glee that only teenage boys can muster, that the suit was being sold at a giveaway price by the distraught mother of a chap who had recently died. I don't remember now whether his demise had been the result of a motorcycle accident - I think not, as there was not a mark on the jacket or trousers - but that didn't stop Ian taking great delight in retelling the story of how I came to be clad in a dead man's riding suit. Still, I was an impoverished schoolboy, it was ridiculously cheap and I could not resist such a bargain.

Also, much to Ian's amusement, I had then and still have today no real sense of fashion or any kind of dread of looking absurd, provided I am garbed in a good cause. Which was just as well. The suit was called a Belstaff Black Prince and had been designed for the kind of dedicated professional dispatch riders who rode in all weathers and all seasons in the late 1950s and 1960s.

It was made of rubber. Not the kind of flimsy latex you might find in a deep-sea diver's suit, oh no, but the kind of heavy-duty, industrial rubber used to make the lower sections of Wellington boots or floormats for car footwells. It was exceedingly thick and exceptionally heavy. It took two hands, a firm grip and a grunty heave just to hoist the jacket off the ground. Once airborne it was essential to keep the momentum going, and with something in the style of an

Olympic discus thrower, I had to crouch and pivot on one heel, so that the open jacket fell across my shoulders.

From this position, and with a little more effort, it was usually possible to straighten my legs and wriggle my arms into the vast sleeves. Partly because the suit was several sizes too big for me, and partly by design, the colossal triangular sleeves actually started at the collar and at the waist and tapered to a cuff which reached a good six inches beyond my outstretched fingers. After much tugging and stretching, my hand would appear and could be secured in the light of day by strapping up a hefty cuff belt with a steel buckle.

Once both hands were available for duty, it was possible to set about the procedure for closing the front of the Black Prince jacket. Being double-breasted with an overlap of several metres of material, the inner zip started somewhere near my left knee and travelled, in a series of jerks as befitted a corroded metal zipper, up to my left shoulder. The enormous front flap of the jacket then swung across my chest and clanged shut like the bow doors of a cross-channel ferry, only rather more watertight, to be fastened by pop-studs that could easily have held down the roof of a circus big top.

Finally the collar, which came up stiffly past my mouth and lodged under my ears, was held shut by another wide belt and buckle. This jacket could easily have doubled as a restraint for the criminally insane, which several of my friends believed I must be to wear it.

But when the weather turned cold and wet, then snowy and icy as it did in my first two-wheeled winter of 1969-70, I had the last laugh. While others left their bikes at home or lobbied their parents for the cash to buy four wheels - 'It's so dangerous on a motorbike, Mum. I'd be much safer in a car.' - I happily buzzed around south Lincolnshire through snow, slush, rain, hail and sleet with a manic grin frozen on my face (these were the days before full-face helmets). My Belstaff Black Prince jacket was utterly rainproof, windproof and bulletproof. Its few seams were overlapped and vulcanised like the ribs of an inflatable dinghy. There was just no way in for water and, because of the jacket's thickness, it had a remarkable safety aspect too.

A year or so later I fell from my third motorcycle, a 305cc Honda CB77, when leaking oil slicked the rear tyre. I spun down the road on my back rather like one of those crash-landed flying beetles, and got up without a scratch and barely a mark on the jacket either.

But I digress. I must tell you about the Belstaff Black Prince trousers. These were made in the same style and gauge of material as the jacket and, rather like full-length waders, came up snugly beneath my armpits, held aloft by braces. There was no front opening, instead a one-piece fold of material unpopped to allow you to climb in from the top, with room enough to invite in several friends, if the mood so took you. Again, hefty overlapped and welded seams, a double-thickness bum section and belted leg cuff closures kept out the weather, if not the cackles and sniggers of girls on the pavement.

I have to admit that the trousers were so vast and ungainly that I was unable to feel the bike's petrol tank with my knees. This, and the lack of any front opening should there be a call of nature, meant I often rode in light rain without my Black Prince trousers. There was hardly any uncovered leg to get wet, thanks to the jacket reaching my knees and my jackboots - but more of them later. Suffice it to say that, when fully attired, there was nothing much that could threaten my person. And this probably inspired Belstaff's chief designer to name the garment Black Prince, since all that was needed was a horse and lance to be equipped for a medieval duel.

Sadly, my Black Prince suit is no more. When I turned up for my first motorcycle journalist job at Motor Cycle News and the other staff members all fell off their chairs laughing, I realised it was time for my rubber bondage period to end. Unaccountably, Belstaff no longer produces the Black Prince suit, more's the pity, and I have yet to find anything so wonderfully, completely waterproof.

As for modern overtrousers, which is where I believe this diversion began, these simply redirect falling rain and road spray to a point where an inadequately sealed and straining crotch seam allows it to pour in unchecked. Just a few minutes in a heavy downpour will have your trousers and underpants sodden and, after an hour of modest precipitation, the water will be running down your legs into your boots and wicking, via your shirt and jumper, up to the higher reaches of your body. Consequently, when you do stop for the loo and peel off your outer garments, you look for all the world as if this pitstop came too late.

If there is any motorcycle clothing manufacturer out there willing to rise to the challenge, I will gladly pay good money - maybe even more than the fifteen shillings I gave for my Black Prince suit - for a garment that is *truly* waterproof. On condition I get a full refund at the first drop of water that sneaks in.

And it's not just the clothing that makes motorcycling slightly more challenging than driving a car. Luggage that you would normally pop into your car boot and forget about until you reach your hotel must, on a motorcycle, remain displayed for all the world to see and help themselves to. The alternatives are to spend a further sweaty quarter-hour unstrapping and unclipping the bulging panniers, then lugging them to your café table. Or park the bikes where you can keep a constant eye on them while you slurp, rest and chew. Which is why we normally parked on the pavement outside the café window and muscled little old ladies out of their seats so we had a clear view. You see, people think motorcyclists are anti-social for no good reason. It's not true - we just want to keep an eye on our luggage.

So, if it's all so much trouble, why do we bother? Why not join the fleets of motorhome travellers seeing New Zealand from behind a glass windscreen in air-conditioned comfort? I can do no better than borrow the words of Sam Manicom, published in Motorcycle Voyager magazine:

> 'Would you like five good reasons to head off on that big trip by bike? Are there only five? Of course not, the list is probably endless, but we'll start with five and end with a bag of oranges. Let me explain.
> 'When I was first planning to ride across Africa, most people couldn't understand why I wanted to go by bike. Plenty understood that I'd been bitten by the travel bug, but thought that doing it by motorcycle was nuts. Looking back, I can understand why - I'd never ridden a bike before.

'Which brings us to the first reason to do that big trip - mental attitude. Mine was that you can do anything if you put your mind to it. Australians used to be particularly famous for their attitude of 'She'll be right' and 'We can fix it'. Take that philosophy with you, and you're already on to a winner. Essentially, doing the big trip by bike gives you the chance to become a positive optimist.

'Second reason. We spend a lot of time being told that the developing world sucks. The people there are always fighting wars, burning down rainforests and generally causing trouble. Just read the papers. But a bike helps you prove otherwise - it's the best form of icebreaker there is. With a backpack you're stuffed in with the rest of humanity. On two wheels you're an individual, an oddity. The very fact that you're not surrounded by metal and glass means that you are open to adventure, you've nothing to hide behind. People will recognise this and come to you. Your bike will always be a focal point, the start of some of the most amazing conversations you'll ever have.

'Reason number three. There's something special about being out on a bike. I could rattle on about the ever-changing sounds and scents of the country you're passing through, or the feeling of being open to the environment and the people. But just think of the pleasures of a ride through English countryside, then multiply them, because most of what you see travelling the world is bigger, bolder and less familiar. You will only get the true impact of this experience by being out there on a bike.

'The fourth reason is inner calm. It comes from being free. Travelling by bike, you're your own boss. You can start the day when you want, make it as long as you please and take the time to look at whatever you choose. I remember once on a narrow coastal road, stopping to look at the view: a pale blue sky and sea, so perfectly matched I couldn't tell where one started and the other ended. It was as if the world was floating in forget-me-not. I couldn't have stopped if I was in a car - the road was too narrow. In a bus, I probably wouldn't have noticed. But on the bike I just flipped out the sidestand, sat down and stared at the view for hours. Inner calm.

'Fifth and finally, it's when things inevitably go wrong and the proverbial hits the fan that you discover hidden depths to yourself. People are often far more resilient and resourceful than they think they are - many underestimate themselves simply because they haven't been tested. And when things look hopeless, a solution is usually just around the corner.

'Take this example - struggling along a bad road in the back of beyond, I was dehydrated because my main water tank had punctured. I'd already had two tyre punctures that day and fallen off ten times. And despite 40-degree heat, I'd picked up a stinker of a cold. I also knew there wasn't another village for miles, so things looked pretty bad.

'Then, rounding a corner, I saw a dust-covered, battered old truck, its driver brewing up under the shade of an acacia tree. Tea never tasted so good, and Rojan invited me to stay at his house that night. Better still, his mate was a biker and was bound to have a spare inner tube. He was a welder too, and could repair my water tank. Oh, and among the load on Rojan's truck was a bag of fresh oranges, which did a lot for my cold.

'There's lots of reasons to go travelling by bike. Do it - it's a great world out there.'

Following our host Garry Askew's advice we set off west around Tasman Bay to Motueka and then, via another ridiculously twisty road, to Kaiteriteri and Marahau. After the wiggly road to French Pass the day before, this stretch of tortuous tarmac set me thinking. Did the NZ Government's highways department have several thousand kilometres-worth of spare tarmac they didn't know what to do with? Why else would they lay 30km of zig-zig roadway

43

to get just five kilometres as the crow flies, with so many tight bends one after another that 15 kph was the maximum safe speed?

But then we stopped to let our spinning heads unwind and I glanced along the steep hillside to which the road was precariously attached. It had more wrinkles than Sid James' face when he smiled. To build a straight road along it would call for dozens of suspended roadbridges across yawning chasms and hundreds of tunnels through countless bluffs. The cost would be prohibitive. So the roads followed the old native tracks weaving around every contour of the landscape, with today's drivers proceeding not much faster than a fit Maori jogging home with a basket of shellfish on his back.

At a café at Marahau we were able to leave our bikes and riding gear while we explored on foot around the estuary and sandbanks of Sandy Bay. This lovely and unspoiled spot, close to the Abel Tasman National Park, was alive with wading seabirds and we came within arm's length of nesting red-breasted plovers, all-black oystercatchers and red-legged avocets - recognisable but subtly different from their northern hemisphere counterparts.

It was hot and sunny, as it had been for the past few days since we arrived in Nelson 'Sunshine Capital of the north' and we supposed that the NZ summer had finally arrived and the cold, rainy days of our first weeks were a seasonal anomaly. We would soon discover this land of contrasts had a few more tricks up its sleeve...

After another blissful night in Garry's bach, drifting off to the sounds of birds, frogs and crickets, we awoke to the din of torrential rain hammering on the roof. A phone call to John and Jill, no more than 200km to the south, revealed that it was dry and 30ºC in Christchurch. Ho hum. We contented ourselves with washing clothes, writing diaries and made a small contribution to our hosts by vacuuming and cleaning the bach.

Staring out of the window at the rain bouncing off the rock-hard seat of my bike I mentioned to Viv that, since the demise of my whoopie-cushion idea, I'd been desperately uncomfortable and was in serious doubt that I could ride all the way round New Zealand without my bum seizing up and falling off.

'Ah, I'd been meaning to talk to you about that,' said Viv. 'I've been devising a sort of bottom-yoga for motorcyclists while I've been riding along and I think you ought to try it. It'll stop you getting a numb bum.'

She even wrote it down for me, and it worked so well I'll repeat it here, so that should you ever ride a motorcycle with a hard seat, or get stiff fingers, arms or legs, you'll know what to do too.

Yoga For Motorcyclists, by Viv Goddard

To keep the blood circulating around the nether regions and help prevent numb bum and other stiff bits, perform the following exercises:

1) Clench buttock muscles. Hold for a count of three then relax. Repeat three more times.

2) Grip the tank with your thighs. Hold for a count of three then relax. Repeat three times.

3) Put some weight through the legs on to the footrests, as if you were about to stand up, but don't! Hold for a count of three then relax. Repeat three times.

4) Change the part of your posterior which is in contact with the seat by tilting the pelvis forward and backward slightly, adding a slight arch in the lower back then a slight rounding of the lower back, making sure you return to the central position. Relax and then repeat three times. This should help with backaches too.

5) Lift feet up on to tiptoes, raising the knees, but keeping contact with the footrests. Hold for a count of three then relax. Repeat three times. This helps prevent the calf muscles seizing up, which can be associated with deep vein thrombosis.

6) Shrug the shoulders up towards the ears, hold for a count of three then relax. Repeat three times.

7) Keeping your thumbs on the handlebars, wiggle your fingers for a few seconds. Then, keeping your

fingers round the bars, move your thumbs in a similar way.
These exercises should only be done on a straight bit of road with minimum traffic. Make sure you keep up concentration on road conditions, traffic, mirrors etc. All these exercises should be repeated regularly and started before you get numb parts!

Heard this morning the sad news that George Harrison had died. He was a man of quiet charm whose great musical talents were largely overshadowed by the other Beatles. But the radio station played his music all day long in tribute, which delighted us. We decided that whatever cloud George has retired to, he will be keeping his neighbours amused as he strums on a celestial sitar.

In the afternoon the downpour had eased to a light drizzle, so we popped in to Nelson to collect photos and do some shopping before returning to the peaceful charm of our temporary wooden country cottage to rustle up a meal and retire early to the steady drumbeat of more rain on the roof.

Chapter 5

The Mighty Maitai

It precipitated persistently all night and was still chucking it down when we woke the next morning. While waiting for the kettle to boil for our morning cuppa, I peered out of the kitchen window and was alarmed to see the garden under water and the fruit trees growing out of their own reflections. Jeez - a flood! I opened the front door and stepped on to the verandah for a better look, and to check that our bikes were still upright - it's all too easy for motorcycle sidestands to sink in to softened ground - and was greeted by a roaring, rushing, thunderous noise that I just couldn't place.

I popped back indoors to pull on my boots, find an umbrella and tell Viv that I was going to investigate what sounded like a cement mixer at the end of the driveway. But as I tiptoed through the water towards the road I could tell that this was nothing man-made. Beyond the tarmac I could see angry brown water boiling past at the speed of an express train - carrying whole trees along with it! Ye gods, this was scary!

When we had arrived at the bach a couple of days before, we'd had to peer down ten metres into the rocky riverbed to see a tiny trickle of water glinting between the boulders. Now the Maitai River was living up to its name. It looked like the whole mountain had melted and was roaring down our valley in a liquid lava-flow. I ventured only 100 metres towards the town before my worst fears were confirmed and I hurried back to tell Viv.

'We're cut off! The river's right over the road and the way it's sluicing down the valley - taking full grown trees with it - there may be no road left soon!' I said, in a slightly breathless, panicky tone.

'Well I refuse to worry about anything until after I've had my breakfast,' said Viv, pouring herself a large bowl of All-Bran. 'A girl's got to stay regular if she's going to deal with a flood of Biblical proportions. Have a cup of tea and relax. I don't suppose

Transformed from a tiny babbling brook,
the Maitai River in flood

*we're in imminent danger of being washed away and we don't
need to go anywhere today, do we?'*

It was true. We had planned to visit Golden Bay at the
northern extremity of the South Island today, but it would
keep.

*'We couldn't be much more dry and comfortable than we are
here,'* she continued, between mouthfuls. *'You could turn on
the radio and see what the local news has to say about the flooding...'*

Good idea. We were just in time to hear the 8am bulletin:
*'...Hivvy overnart rain has caused some minor locarlised flooding
and slups to the north and west of the Richmond Range. The Mit
office is forecasting more rain over the nixt 24 hours...'*

No mention of a pair of British bikers stranded halfway
up the Maitai Valley. But at least they conceded that the rain
was 'hivvy' and there was more to follow. The 'slups' were
predictable too. Even in dry weather, minor landslips rained
stones and soil on to the road below wherever the route was
carved out of a hillside. This sort of rain must have brought
some serious mudslides down on to parts of the region's
roads. It sounded like a day for leaving the bikes well alone

so we decided to undertake a cautious exploration on foot instead.

I say cautious, because NZ has a long and grim history of drowning people who have not treated the country's many rivers and streams - especially those in flood - with due respect. In fact, drowning was so prevalent during the early years of colonisation by the British that it became known as the New Zealand disease. The steep terrain, heavy rainfall and rapid run-off can swell a modest trickle into a raging torrent in minutes. According to Ray Mears, the TV outback survival guru, the trick to crossing streams is to have a long pole to hand. This can be used to gauge the depth - don't cross if the water is fast flowing and above knee deep - and to act as a downstream prop to help prevent you being swept off your feet.

We had neither long pole nor any intention of crossing any streams when we set off towards Nelson later that morning. In fact, if the water on the road got deeper than an inch or so we would have to turn back, since Viv's ancient walking boots were now leaking badly. Protected by a huge sun parasol, which didn't so much stop the big rain drops as reduce them to a fine mist, we walked and waded on and on, gasping at the sound of chunks of bank collapsing and marvelling at yet more trees sailing past us... until we rounded one corner and saw a 200-metre stretch of road submerged beneath the swirling brown waters.

By this time we had squelched two-thirds of the way to Nelson and giving up now would feel a bit like the old joke of the Irish cross-channel swimmer who turned back because he got tired three-quarters of the way across. So I left Viv perched on a piece of high ground and waded gingerly forward. Two minutes later I was sloshing back to tell her: *'It's okay - not more than ankle deep - I'll carry you.'*

'You ARE joking! When was the last time you carried me? I'm not the sylph-like maiden you carried across the threshold in 1972 you know. I've put on a few pounds and your muscles... well, this isn't sensible, you'll do yourself a mischief.'

'Aw, come on now. We've come all this way, we're not giving up just because of a couple of inches of water...' and I turned and assumed a posture like Quick-Draw McGraw.

'You're going to regret this,' she said as she climbed on my back and I staggered off into the brown water. I have to admit, she did feel like a sack of potatoes and my back, legs and arms were soon screaming in disbelief at this sudden stupidity. But I can be remarkably stubborn when both sanity and gallantry are challenged and, eventually, the waters thinned to a film and my creaking knees bent enough to set Viv down on her own two feet again.

'My hero!' she said, 'You can straighten up now - I'm off...'

'Yes, yes, I know... Don't rush me. I rather like it like this,' I hissed back through clenched teeth. 'Could you perhaps put your knee in my back and pull on my shoulders for a minute, please?'

Eventually, I was semi-upright again and we continued into Nelson where we found a pleasant pub which served pints of anaesthetic and hot food. After several hours we were ready for the return trip - so we called a taxi. Well, there's no point in overdoing it, is there?

In the afternoon we phoned to book a ferry crossing to The North Island for Tuesday morning and a motel room for Monday night at Waikawa Bay, just five kilometres from the ferry terminal at Picton. Then, while 'hivvy' rain continued to drum on the bach roof, I decided it was time to employ my bodging skills once more.

A close inspection of Viv's left boot had revealed the source of leakage was at the toe, where part of the rubber moulding had come away from the leather. After wedging a tissue in the gap and leaving the boot to dry thoroughly near a heater for an hour or three, I set about dripping melted wax from a nite-lite candle into the crack. Then, by heating the boot toe over the candle flame, I encouraged the wax to flow into all the crevices. Amazingly, despite the improbable nature of this wax-fix, Viv reported my repair cut leaks by 80 percent. Quite how she measured the improvement this precisely I'm not sure - perhaps only one toe got wet instead of all five - but I was delighted to get a positive result, so I didn't question the details too closely.

After that, a little light reading about Nelson's history revealed that the first European to clap eyes on this beautiful, sunkissed and occasionally monsoonal shoreline, was almost certainly the Dutch explorer/navigator Abel Tasman. In December 1642 he sailed into the protected waters at the northern end of NZ's South Island with two tiny ships, the Heemskerck (60 tons) and Zeehaen (100 tons), and drew the first ever chart - two curving bays and a headland. But after four of his crew were killed by Maori, he named the western inlet 'Murderers' Bay' and sailed away dispirited, without trying to land. Later colonists, perhaps with an eye towards a future tourist industry, renamed it somewhat more attractively 'Golden Bay'.

But the pioneering Dutchman lives on with the second of his two bays, the one in which Nelson nestles so snugly, called Tasman Bay, and the headland between them preserved as the Abel Tasman National Park. And it was Tasman who named the country New Zealand after his native land.

Many years later, in 1769, Captain James Cook, the renowned and celebrated British explorer/cartographer, completed his circumnavigation of NZ and a further 57 years later, in 1826-7, the Tasman Bay coastline was surveyed in detail by the outstanding French navigator Dumont D'Urville whose name remains on the spectacular D'Urville Island - now a scenic reserve - at the top of the Marlborough Sounds.

In the early 1800s sealers used this coast as a base and the first land-based whaling station was established in 1820 on the south coast of Arapawa Island, past which the Interislander Ferry sails to connect the North and South Islands. The first white settler was James MacLaren, who in 1838 was given 150 acres at Croisilles Harbour, past which Viv and I had ridden on our way to French Pass, and had marvelled at its beauty.

The British promptly formed the New Zealand Company to colonise the land and to profit from bringing in settlers, primarily into the North Island. But Captain Arthur Wakefield persuaded Governor Hobson to permit a second colony outside the Auckland area and, in October 1841, Wakefield discovered a natural harbour inside the boulder bank off what is now Nelson. It provided a '...*haven of plenty for many pioneers,'* according to Wakefield, and on February 1st 1842 the barque 'Fifeshire' entered Nelson Haven (no prizes for guessing who this was named after) followed by 'Mary Ann' and 'Lord Auckland', three immigrant ships containing just over 500 settlers.

The New Zealand Company parcelled up Nelson district's 210,000 acres and sold them in 1,000 lots, each consisting of one town acre, 50 suburban acres and 150 rural acres of land. Hence wealthy settlers bought 210 acres of prime NZ land and set to building fine timber houses in the city and using poorer immigrant labour to plant the remaining land. Of the £300,000 the New Zealand Company collected, £130,000 was used to pay the passages of immigrants from the labouring class.

But, as so often with these grand schemes, all was not as rosy as the colony's promoters had painted it. The promised 210,000 acres turned out to be only 60,000 lowland acres - and only 4,000 of that was first class soil - so the pressure was on almost immediately to expand. First to the north west to the Golden Bay area, then south to the Buller River / Murchison area and then east to the Wairau Valley, which led to skirmishes with the Maori, most notably the Wairau Incident in which Wakefield and 21 other whites, plus four Maori were killed.

Monday December 3rd. As we packed up to leave after five nights in Garry and Philippa's idyllic country cabin, rain continued to fall and the radio had bad news: The road we were about to take from Nelson to Picton was closed due to a major 'slup'. We consulted the map and saw the only alternative route - south almost back to Murchison, then an enormous trek east to Blenheim and finally north to Picton - would triple our journey. There are few alternatives in this mountainous country. The Maungatapu Track would be an obvious short cut in good weather, but after all this rain, if mud and rockslides didn't get us, the streams we had forded a few days before would surely sweep us away now.

We really didn't want to make a 270km marathon trip in the rain instead of the 90km dash we had planned. So I called in at the Automobile Association office before leaving

Nelson. I asked if go-anywhere trailie bikes like ours could possibly pass the obstruction on the SH6 road near Rai Saddle.

'We're telling everybody to go around via State Highway 63,' said the AA lady, when I finally got to the front of the queue.

'Yes, I know you are. I heard the radio broadcast. What I'm asking is - can we get through the landslip on off-road motorcycles? We can ride through streams, over rocks - plenty of places a 4WD car can't go. Maybe we don't have to go all that way round?' I pleaded.

'We're telling everybody to go around via State Highway 63,' she repeated, like a recorded message.

'Do I get a more helpful answer if I show you my AA membership card?'

'No, it's the same for everybody.'

'Then I'm pleased I didn't waste my money joining!' and I stomped out to tell Viv what I'd learned.

'I think we might be able to get through,' I lied.

'Did they tell you we could?' asked Viv, suspiciously.

'Well, not exactly. But I think it's worth a ride up there. It's a helluva long way round otherwise...'

So off we rode heading north in heavy rain and headwinds to do battle with the 'slup'. 15km later we were waved off the road by a yellow-jacketed highways agency chappie and my heart sank. We were obviously going to get turned back. My stubborn attitude had simply added another 30km to a long, wet day of riding.

'Any chance we can get through on the bikes?' I shouted through the wind, rain and engine noise as I pulled up alongside him.

'Yeah. No worries, mate. You'll get through okay. Just hiv to wait here 20 minutes or so for stuff coming through the other way.' I guess he thought I was slightly unhinged when I shouted 'YES!' and punched the air.

I turned to Viv and smiled - which was a waste of effort as we were both wearing full-face crash helmets - so I shouted: 'Told you we could get through!' as if I'd never had any doubts. I would feel smug for the rest of the day.

We were soon on our way, in convoy with a dozen other hopefuls in cars, climbing higher on a very twisty road to the Rai Saddle where we came across 300 metres of raging brown water boiling over the road, with mud, sand, gravel and rocks tumbling across under our wheels. It was tricky trying to dodge the biggest boulders and avoid being swept sideways by the deepest parts of the stream, but we both managed to get through without putting a foot down and so kept our boots dry inside.

I was experimenting with another patent modification. We had brought walking boots from Britain to serve double-duty: Firstly as riding boots to keep our feet warm, dry and protected on the thousands of kilometres of roads and trails, and secondly as walking boots for 'tramping' in the bush whenever the mood took us. This arrangement worked very well and our walking boots proved to be surprisingly compatible with the bikes' foot controls. However, being walking boots they didn't reach beyond our ankles, and the cuffs of my overtrousers had an annoying habit of riding up and letting rain and spray in the top of my boots.

So that morning I'd fixed rubber bands to the trouser cuffs' zip pulls and passed them over my toecaps to hold the cuffs down. It may have looked comical, but it worked perfectly - another successful bodge.

The rain got progressively heavier so, by the time the Rai Valley Café appeared between the stair-rods, we were only too pleased to stop and dry out over lunch. We chatted to a Dutchman who was cycling in the opposite direction. He'd been reading his book for two hours hoping for the rain to cease. As we'd had non-stop monsoon for the past three days, we wished him well - especially with pedalling through the torrent of mud and rocks up near the saddle.

On to Havelock where we turned left to follow the Queen Charlotte Drive and finally the clouds parted, the fierce NZ sun made the roads steam and we enjoyed some stunning views over the sparkling waters of the Queen Charlotte Sound. We rode through Picton to Waikawa Bay and the welcoming Sunnyvale Motel where brothers Colin and Barry Lowe showed us to a well-equipped apartment, and Colin's wife Kimoko provided us with freshly-baked cookies and milk for the fridge. All this for just NZ$45 - about £13 for the pair of us! We were so impressed we immediately booked to stay again when we returned from the North Island.

After a refreshing cuppa and a shower, we donned shorts and flip-flops - it was now a hot and sunny evening - for a stroll to the nearest shop to buy provisions for supper. The nearest shop turned out to be at Picton five kilometres away, but the balmy weather and fine views made it an enjoyable walk and a pleasant change from the morning's torrential rain, gale force winds and battling through road hazards on the bikes.

We decided that Waikawa Bay, with its beautiful waters, boats bobbing on their moorings and the surrounding tree-smothered hills, was the perfect place to live. We dined on bread and cheese, beer and apples, sitting at the table thoughtfully provided outside our motel room door, then turned in and fell asleep as the light faded to soothing calls of a bellbird in the garden outside. Lovely.

N

Matakohe

Coromandel
Peninsula

AUCKLAND

Coroglen Track

Thames

Paeroa

Tauranga

Whakatane

Tirau   Te Puke

Ohope Beach

Matawai

L Taupo   Wairakei

Taupo

Mt Ruapehu   Turangi   Wairoa

Gisborne
Tuanui Track

*Tukino
Track*

*Turakina Valley
Track*

Napier
Hastings
Havelock North

Taihape

Hunterville

Dannevirke

Feilding
Palmerston
North

Woodville

Shannon

⌡ - tarsealed road

⌡ - gravel/4WD track

WELLINGTON

Chapter 6

The North Island

We were up bright and early at 6.30am and off to the ferry at Picton, where it had started raining again, making the railway tracks and diesel-slicks of the dockside marshalling yard distinctly dodgy. The efficient ferry office had our tickets waiting for us and we rode into the belly of the Interislander ferry 'Awaroa' where we were left entirely to our own devices by the crew. This suited me just fine, as car ferry staff don't always handle motorcycles with care and understanding. I used four tie-down straps per bike to secure the Serows to the car deck. I'd heard Cook Strait could be very rough and was taking no chances.

There were no other motorcycles travelling with us but, besides the cars and campervans, there were several lorries filled with sheep, whose bleats reverberated around the inside of the steel hull.

The passenger decks were bright, clean and pleasing, with plenty of benches to stretch out on and seats and tables to sit at and eat our lunch while the stunning scenery of the Marlborough Sounds slipped by through the mist and rain outside the windows. In the event, the three-hour trip was a pleasure with no Pacific rollers between the two islands to shake us up. At 1pm we docked at Wellington where we were the last off the ship.

We weren't in any hurry to leave, as outside was a screaming gale and torrential, horizontal rain. Once off the ship we had to wait on the dockside for 20 minutes, lashed by the rain and barely able to hold our bikes upright in fearsome gusts of wind, while a freight train shunted back and forth across the exit road.

Through Wellington the roads were streaming with rain and manic, impatient traffic - as if the wild weather had made everyone frantic to reach their destination before the wind and rain overwhelmed them. Buffeted and battered by the storm, and with rain rattling like machine-gun bullets against our visors, we didn't see the nation's capital in its best light, but the northern suburbs looked like Welsh valleys, with cottages huddled down the hillsides sheltering from the screaming wind and rain.

We pressed on northwards at half-speed, struggling to keep our machines in the slow lane of a rare piece of cheerless, windswept dual carriageway, while cars and lorries hurtled past, oblivious of our plight. At a fuel stop I asked Viv how she was coping and did she want to stop for a coffee.

'God - I never knew it could be so difficult just staying on a motorbike!' she shouted over the tempest. *'But I'm okay. I'd rather keep going for a bit and try to find somewhere less wet and windy. I'm afraid the bikes will blow over if we leave them on their stands in this...'*

As we edged up the coast the rain eased off and within a mile the hurricane winds had blasted the road dry. Then we were away from the coast, moving inland where the wind was less punishing and I realised the tension of riding the stormy road from Wellington had produced aches across my shoulders and a searing hot needle of pain between my shoulder blades. We trundled into Shannon and pulled up outside The Old Plum Duff Tea Rooms, where we had barely prized our aching bodies off our bikes before we were warmly greeted by proprietor Bob Smith. This cheery gent, whose well-upholstered form overflowed his shirt and shorts, was as generous by nature as he was of anatomy. After coffee and muffins and a critical discussion about Wellington and its weather, Bob lent us his phone so we could call Marie Frost, a business associate of mine, who lived in nearby Feilding.

Marie imports magnotherapy products from the company I deal with in the UK, and has sought advice from me via e-mail on various topics over the years. She had kindly offered to put us up for the night when she heard we would be touring NZ, and was now pleased to hear we were only an hour away. Whether she was quite so pleased when two dirty, bedraggled and tired motorcyclists arrived dripping on the doorstep of her palatial ranch-style home, we couldn't tell. Marie's answer to all our apologies for the state we were in was: 'NOT *a problem!*' as she ushered us through to a capacious bedroom and hot showers.

Feeling 100 percent more human, we were then introduced to Marie's lovely daughters, Raili and Hannah, dog Cadbury and cat Webster, and her charming fella Joe, who was busy barbecuing chicken, venison and steak to go with salad, beans and a bottle or three of fine NZ wine for our supper. I vaguely remember slurring my words before Viv apologised and dragged me off to bed.

We slept like the dead until 5am, when Marie's cockerel decided it was time we woke up. Why these incredibly noisy and spiteful birds don't end up on the barbecue the first day they ruin their owner's sleep I've never quite understood. Only peacocks have a more shrill and penetrating call, and it has always baffled me how some people can bear to keep those deafening birds as garden ornaments. They clearly have a different threshold of pain.

Once it became clear that the cockerel was going to shriek its hideous head off until I got up and strangled it, I pulled on T-shirt and trousers and stumbled outside into a gorgeous morning. There, bathed in golden early-morning sunshine beneath an amazingly deep blue sky, were three fluffy lambs, four young cows and a flock of endearing chooks (as chickens are called in NZ) all ambling about in the lush grass of Marie and Joe's fabulous homestead. When the cockerel squawked again it seemed entirely appropriate and I beamed at it in a haze of bucolic happiness.

Viv was soon beside me, calling to the lambs and giving the woolly creatures hugs and cuddles through the fence. Since the last of our three children left home, Viv has developed a deep and slightly worrying affection for sheep and goats. With Cadbury sitting at my feet and Webster rubbing his back against Viv's legs it was easy to guess what was coming next.

'*I want some lambies, just like these,*' crooned Viv. '*Aren't they gorgeous? What do you suppose a place like this would cost?*'

Over a leisurely breakfast, after the girls had gone off to school and Joe had headed for work at his building firm, Marie told us she had bought this five-acre homestead - a 'lifestyle block' - with its enormous single-storey mansion, three-car garage and huge farm shed, for the equivalent of £80,000 a year or so before. And this was in the midst of the country's prime farmland surrounding Palmerston North. Look for something similar in Surrey and you'd be lucky to get change out of a million! There's no wonder Brits come out here for a holiday and never go home. We were severely tempted, and it took Marie no time at all to persuade us to stay a second night.

While our laundry whizzed around in her washing machine, Marie helped us plan our North Island trip. We didn't have long, as we'd promised to be back in Christchurch a couple of days before Christmas, and it was already December 5th. In fact, we'd had to book our return ferry crossing for the 17th as the last few days before the holiday were booked solid with people returning home to their families - or getting away from them - for the festive period.

That done we set off just before noon to explore the rolling farm countryside of the Turakina Valley in the hills above Hunterville, an hour away to the north. Or it would have been an hour away, but we made a lengthy detour around some remote farming communities before I would admit that I'd got us hopelessly lost. By the time we reached Hunterville we needed to top up our fuel tanks and took the opportunity to buy bread and cheese, tomatoes and apples for lunch. It was a scorching day, with not a cloud in the sky and not a hint that it had ever rained or ever would again. For that reason we had left our waterproofs at Marie's house and were rejoicing that summer had finally arrived. We had still not learned that New Zealand is a country with a meteorological sense of humour.

Soon we were having fun on gravel roads again, a 46km loop which followed the Turakina Valley from Pukeroa to Papanui Junction, then a right turn to Koeke Junction, then south again to Pohonui. The dirt track connected a series of tiny hamlets, many consisting of a single farmhouse, nestling in lovely rolling country scored by deeply indented streambeds cut deep into the limestone. We saw cattle and sheep but hardly another human being and no vehicles of any kind.

After a peaceful picnic we pressed on, becoming increasingly confident on the fine gravel as we learned to control the constant slips and slides. Eventually, we were throwing our bikes around the blind bends in the knowledge that we had the place entirely to ourselves. For an hour or so we behaved like a couple of teenagers let loose, careering down the bendy farm road at ever-increasing speed, until the sun and dust and the dry-mouthed exhilaration forced us to pull over on to the grass verge beside the Mangamahoe Stream to take giggly gulps from our bottle of water. Our grins faded as we strained to make out an odd rumbling noise... then a huge gravel lorry hurtled round the bend from the opposite direction. It filled the entire road. Had we still been going hell for leather, we would have hit it head on.

As the noise faded and the dust settled I suddenly felt a cold shiver down my spine. Viv put it into words: *'That was a close call. Perhaps we'd better go a bit steady until we can see what's coming.'*

Riding more like sensible grandparents, we had time to savour the scenery. We stopped to take a few photos before we rode out of the beautiful secret valley to make our way back to Hunterville for a coffee break. Incredibly, out of nowhere, a jet-black cloud appeared and hosed down the road ahead of us. We got slightly damp, but as we sipped our drinks at the café, we could see it moving slowly south - the direction we had to go - with dark curtains of rain blotting out trees and hills in a solid wall of water. We made our coffee last as long as we could, trying to work out if the road back to Marie and Joe's would take us around the deluge. Eventually we had to set off or be seriously late for the meal that Marie was preparing for us. For 20km we dodged the rain, but finally the cloud closed around us, laughed at our lack of waterproofs, then drenched us to the bone.

For the second day in a row we arrived at Marie's looking like we'd just ridden through a river. This time our boots were full, our gloves were swollen with water and dripping red dye as if they were bleeding - even our helmets were wet inside.

'NOT a problem!' said Marie, as she loaded our clothes into her tumble drier again and shooed us through to the

dining room for roast beef, roast pumpkin and kumara, cauliflower and potatoes. Another couple of bottles of Shiraz mysteriously emptied themselves as we told of our day's exploits and learned more about the culture and customs of New Zealand from our generous hosts.

Another blissfully sunny morning greeted us when the cockerel called us from our beds, and by the time we tucked into a hearty farewell breakfast on the patio at 8am we were pleased to be in the shade of the huge sunbrella to escape the searing sun. When we had packed our bags, strapped them on the bikes and pulled on our still-damp jackets, helmets and gloves it was 10.30 and now the sunshine was brilliant and blistering.

Just as we were about to ride off and cool down in the slipstream, a car pulled into the driveway and a white-haired Scottish lady, here to do business with Marie, greeted us warmly and wanted to know all about our journey. Then she proceeded to tell us her life history, that of her late husband - *'Och ay, he died just a wee lad of 65. Dropped down dead from a heart attack and he never drank nor smoked nor chased loose wimmin, so let that be a lesson to ye,'* she said - then went on to tell us of all her children and grandchildren, while the pitiless sun beat down upon us in our riding gear and turned us into two ready-to-serve, boil-in-the-bag meals.

We finally excused ourselves, said our goodbyes to Marie - *'Now you make sure you come and stay with us again on your way back south to Wellington, it's NOT a problem!'* - and rejoiced in the cooling breeze.

We took a back roads route via Colyton, Ashurst and then over the saddle to Woodville. This lovely country road winds up the rugged hills of the Ruahine Range through rich beef and lamb country. In these remote areas we'd become used to raising a hand to wave to anyone - we might be the only human beings they'd see all day - so we weren't surprised when a farmer busy chasing his herd of cattle up a field waved back enthusiastically.

How nice, we thought, to take the trouble to wave like that when he clearly had his hands full with the mob of rampaging animals. Then we rounded the bend, smack into the back of the other half of his herd of young bullocks. We didn't actually run into them, but you'd have thought we had by the way they galloped off down the road in panic at the sight of two helmeted aliens riding noise-and-light-emitting beasts. There was no point in stopping: Farmer Barleymow was now out of his field, preceded by a few dozen more cavorting bullocks, so we trickled forward as the filling in a mobile beef sandwich until the animals ambled into a corral and we got past safely. Phew! There are so few people here that one man must move his cattle across the roads on his own. But there are so few vehicles, this is seldom a problem.

At Woodville we stopped at a pleasant café which had tables and chairs on the pavement beneath a permanent wooden canopy. This meant we could sit in the shade, with our luggage-laden bikes at the kerbside, and chill out while the small town's inhabitants all drifted past doing their shopping and socialising. Viv wandered off in search of alternative riding trousers. Now that the sun had come out with a vengeance, the lined black ski-pants she'd bought in Christchurch were much too hot.

I ended up having a long chat with Sam, Woodville's postie, who passed by on his bicycle and, seeing two motorbikes and a stranger sipping coffee, stopped to find out who we were, where we'd come from and where we were going. In fact Sam was ready to discuss any topic, so long as it kept him out of the scorching sunshine, and we were still yakking contentedly when Viv returned, empty-handed but hot-legged from her quest.

Then she had another idea. Taking a tiny pair of scissors from our emergency pack, she disappeared into the loo (yes, this café had one, hoorah!) and cut out the lining from her trousers. This made them a little cooler, but unbearably tickly, as the inside of the outer material had a peculiar prickly texture. By the time we reached Dannevirke - a bigger town with Viking signs to remind the world it was founded by Scandinavians - Viv was desperate to get out of her hot and prickly modified ski-pants, so we stopped again and Viv soon returned triumphant. She had found a pair of cool cream slacks for NZ$1.50 (about 40p) in an op shop (charity shops

63

are opportunity shops down under) and they were perfect. Her $32 (£9) ski-pants were deposited in the bin. The bargain trousers would perform faultlessly for the next 10,000km.

On through Norsewood (those Vikings get everywhere) before turning off on to SH50 for a quieter route to Hastings and Havelock North via Tikokino and the lush green vineyards of Hawke's Bay. Despite the melting tarmac, we rode on up to Te Mata Peak, an unusual rocky outcrop that towers over the southern edge of Havelock North and provides fantastic views over Hastings, Napier and the broad expanse of Hawke's Bay to the north, and beautiful hilly countryside to the south and west.

In front of the trig point, beyond the safety railings which kept viewers away from the lip of the sheer cliff, were two wooden structures, platforms which followed the contour of the cliff straight over the edge. Painted in large letters on one was 'DANGER - KEEP OFF' and on the other 'GO AHEAD - JUMP OFF' which seemed oddly conflicting advice, until we realised they were launch platforms where thrill-mad Kiwis, armed only with a few ounces of flimsy silk, hurl themselves off and over the vertical drop. As the blustery updraught made us stagger and our hair dance wildly, the thought of anyone deliberately throwing themselves off for fun seemed quite lunatic.

What really takes the biscuit - or in my case, makes me reach for another Cookie Time cookie to ensure a future gust doesn't lift me off my feet - is that many of the people we met in NZ thought our riding motorcycles around their country was the most dangerous thing they could think of! And this in a country that invented bungy-jumping, wire-riding, jet-boating and white-water rafting. I ask you.

We booked in to a tourist flat (like a small motel unit, but without the full kitchen facilities) at Arataki Park, washed our sweaty clothing and hung it to dry in the hot breeze while we walked to Havelock North for supper. On the way back under the stars - Orion's Belt features his sword sticking up in the southern hemisphere, which gave rise to an alternative suggestion from Viv, but modesty prevents me from telling you what it was - we stumbled across a cul-de-sac with several houses dressed up in gaudy Christmas lights. It seemed incongruous in this land of blisteringly fierce sunshine, in the season of blue skies and melting tarmac, to see Santa Claus and his reindeer flashing on a suburban house roof. Very odd.

But if we thought the heatwave was here to last, we were brought back down to earth with a splash. We awoke next morning to torrential rain once again and left reluctantly in a downpour. We had planned to explore the Art Deco architecture of nearby Napier, but the appeal of gazing at buildings rapidly dissolved in the driving rain and we pushed on around Hawke's Bay hoping to catch up with a patch of blue sky we could see on the horizon. As SH2 wriggled up into the hills through Tutira we found the road tricky in places, where melted tar slicks from the previous day were now covered with puddles and were as slippery as greased glass.

After 130km we arrived in Wairoa, the only district in New Zealand to have a majority Maori population, announced by a sign saying 'Wairoa - New Zealand As It Used To Be'. We had not really encountered Maoris so far, or experienced any of the native culture, and we were eager to get a flavour of these proud Polynesian people. Besides, we were ready for lunch and keen to get out of the rain. We stopped beside the broad green Wairoa River, lined with palms and rata trees, and popped into a nearby café.

We were well used to the form with Kiwi cafés by now. The proprietor flashes you a big beaming smile and says, 'Hi, howya goin'?' And after you've replied, 'Goin' good, thanks,' he or she then says, 'Great. Now what can I getcha?' as though they've been waiting all day just to bring a little happiness into your life. It's really quite delightful and part of the reason we made so many coffee stops.

So it came as quite a shock when I approached the middle-aged white man behind the counter with my best smile to be met with a flat stare and an unfriendly 'Yes?'

Slightly taken aback, I stammered, 'Er, we were hoping to have lunch - do you have a menu?'

'What you see is what you can 'ave.' And with that he turned his back to me and commenced wiping the counter-top behind him. I stood open-mouthed for a minute, in a state of shock, half expecting him to turn around again, smile and say, *'Nah, only jokin' mate! Here's the menu - choose whatever you like and I'll bring it over to you.'*

But he didn't. After a full minute of staring at his back, I returned to our table and told Viv I was less than impressed with the café's policy of 'service with a snarl' and thought we should try elsewhere.

Snag was, a move meant putting on our heavy, rain-soaked riding jackets, gathering our dripping overtrousers, gloves and helmets, lugging two hefty sets of panniers and a rucksack back outside and trudging through the rain to find another café. Seemed a lot of trouble to go to, just because the owner had an attitude problem.

While we were considering all this, two other customers came in and were subjected to the same gruff treatment. One was an elderly white man and the other a Maori woman and neither flinched. Maybe this was a feature of Grumpy Jacks, or whatever the café was called, and people came in specially to be maltreated? Whatever the reason, there was no shortage of customers coming and going while we munched a sandwich, sipped a coffee and waited for the rain to stop.

And it wasn't just the café proprietor who had a surly attitude. All the customers, brown, white or shades in between, bore a stony, miserable expression and shuffled to their tables with their drinks and snacks without sharing a single word, smile or any kind of acknowledgement of their neighbours. Very strange.

Eventually the rain had eased to a heavy drizzle and we decided to go, one at a time, on shopping forays while the other guarded our luggage. I was eager to buy a book on New Zealand birds to help us identify the many strange and wonderful species we had seen. Every shop we went into had the same odd, downbeat feel. Nobody gave a smile as they served us and everyone, Maoris and whites alike, wore surly, resentful expressions. The Maori lady at the fuel station as we left town was the glummest of all, and could barely stir herself to take my money.

If Wairoa really is an example of 'New Zealand As It Used To Be' then thank goodness the rest of the country has adopted a friendly, happy disposition. We were more than pleased to be leaving, but as we rode away I remained troubled by the town's gloomy countenance. What had gone wrong here to make the people so dour? It was peculiar and deeply puzzling.

We continued east in intermittent rain towards the Mahia Peninsula at the northeast corner of Hawke's Bay with the intention of picking up a coastal track - the Parity Road - to get our off-road fix for the day. But when we reached Mahanga and the end of the tarmac, we could see the track ran along the beach for the first few kilometres and decided the bikes could do without sand and seawater in their chains, brakes and wheel bearings.

We were just exploring another little track when we met a creaking, rickety, oil-dripping school bus. The Maori driver realised we must be lost, since the track was a dead end, but he kindly climbed down from his decrepit old vehicle, much to the delight of the giggling little faces inside, to give us directions for the Tunanui Road which cuts up and over the hills and through the Wharerata Forest before rejoining the main road north for Gisborne.

This gravel track was steep and slippy and it was tricky to control the bikes with their heavy luggage on board, especially in places where there was wet gooey slime underneath the gravel. But we pressed on slowly and were rewarded with great views over unspoiled hills and, finally, the native trees and amazing tree ferns of the forest.

When we finally pulled into Gisborne, 245 soggy kilometres after leaving Havelock North, we were ready for a hot shower, a hot meal and an early night. Fortunately, the Gisborne Motel (NZ$70 - £20) provided all three - so long as we had something to cook. A short stroll to Woolworth's produced a home-bake pizza and a bottle of wine, so we were soon contented and, shortly after that, fast asleep.

We awoke to the familiar but depressing sound of rain. What a novelty. While Viv cleaned the sticky mud left by yesterday's trail from our bags, boots and trousers, I did my daily round of checks, oilings and adjustments on the bikes, which brought out our landlord Stephen to see what

I was up to. I explained that we'd blown a fuse in his electric heater, trying to dry our boots and socks. Unfazed, he gave us a little local history.

Gisborne, at the northern end of Poverty Bay, was the site of Cook's first landing in New Zealand on October 9th 1769, a visit which ultimately led to British colonisation and changed the nation's destiny. Cook is therefore revered by the European Kiwis and his landing site celebrated with a monument. Among the Maori community, Cook is seen as the ultimate villain and Gisborne the beginning of the end of Polynesian rule.

Stephen also wised us up on the correct pronunciation of Whakatane, the next main town on our route north. It seems the Maori insist on pronouncing Wh as F, with hilarious consequences.

'You mean, this town is really called...' I hesitated.

'Yes, Fuckatani!' said Stephen, earnestly, *'and if you have a look on your map you'll find plenty of other place names that you can have fun pronouncing.'*

And I have to admit, I did find a little light amusement on the dismally wet and windy ride ahead singing to myself, *'It's a long way to Whakatane, it's a long way to roam...'* etc.

By the time we set off from 'Gizzy' it had stopped raining, but we were not going to be fooled this time and had on 'full wets'. As we fought our way up the Waipoa Valley into the teeth of a blustery gale, the rain started in earnest, but we pressed on as we had advice from Stephen that the tiny hamlet of Matawai contained the only café en route. Which answered Viv's question: *'Does it Matawai we stop there?'* - *'Yes, it's the only place with a café!'*

However, it has to be said that the owners of the Matawai Café were either well aware that they had no competition for the custom of passing travellers, or else they were blissfully unaware of the constituents of hot beverages. My hot chocolate turned up as faintly brown water, which had no flavour of any kind, and through which I could see the bottom of the cup. Viv's coffee appeared and tasted as though one chestnut had been boiled in it for perhaps 30 seconds.

These joke drinks had taken so long to be served that we had warmed up and partially dried out, and had enjoyed a good laugh at the feeble and ridiculous local crafts and odd ethnic motifs on display. We couldn't bring ourselves to tell the batty old dear that she'd forgotten to put the main ingredients in our drinks, and so we set off again, giggling about, *'Does it Matawai our coffee has no coffee in it?'* and *'What the Whakatane have we let ourselves in for?'* Little things...

What we'd let ourselves in for was a hurricane screaming out of the 58km long Waioeka Gorge, which we were just about to ride into. We could barely stand up next to the bikes and progress was slow and difficult. Out of the six gears we had to choose from, fourth was the highest our bikes' straining engines could pull against the blast, and sometimes we were down to third gear, flat out at 60kph (37mph)!

Despite the rain and hideous wind, there were astounding views of vertical cliffs and steep hills thickly clad in native bush including the massive treeferns (pongas) and dozens of other exotic species that I promised to look up later. In between the foliage, which was being whipped to a frenzy by the wind, was the raging brown torrent of the Waioeka River which grew ever wider as we descended towards Opotiki.

The road was liberally strewn with rocks and gravel from frequent 'slups' and there were hundreds of streams rushing across the tarmac, but the road crews were out in force and the worst of the falls were being cleared, with only a few places where we had to thread our way between huge rocks. These gave rise to conflicting instincts: We felt the need to go slowly to avoid clouting the biggest boulders - some would need several men to move them - or getting skittled by the smaller debris under our wheels. And yet we dearly wanted to speed up and 'get the hell outa there' as quickly as possible. The knowledge that these rocks had all crashed on to the road in the past hour or so was not at all reassuring, when a glance upward revealed there were hundreds more right above our heads awaiting their chance to fulfil Newton's First Law of Gravity. At times like these our crash helmets felt more like eggshells and we couldn't help riding with our heads tucked into our shoulders.

But nothing hit us and, apart from a few minor skids and wobbles, we emerged from the Waioeka Gorge wind-battered and soaked through but elated to be alive. If the truth is told, both Viv and I felt a little dizzy and drowsy and were feeling slightly secondhand with sore throats and the trots. But the appeal of a warm and dry lunch stop as we pulled into Opotiki soon raised our spirits. This was at an establishment called 'Hot Bread Shop & Café' and was intriguing for the numbers of exceedingly large people who waddled in to buy huge bags of pies and sticky cakes.

We luxuriated over a hot meal and coffee that actually had some coffee in it, and slowly warmed up. For the first time on this trip we had both been really cold due to the rain and the huge chill factor of the storm-force wind, and it took a long time to stop shivering and get blood flowing again to fingers, knees and feet.

By 2pm we were warm, replete and ready to do battle with the elements once more. Which was just as well, because outside the rain had decided to resume full monsoon proportions. But we didn't have far to go now, having decided to call it a day at Ohope Beach, a resort suburb ten kilometres to the east of Whakatane. Unusually, we'd left Gisborne that morning without our next accommodation booked, thinking that if the weather improved and we were feeling a little more hale and hearty we might push on to Tauranga or even Thames further to the north. But it didn't and we weren't, so we splashed in to Ohope Beach in torrential mid-afternoon rain, more than ready to get off our bikes and escape from the crazy weather.

Only snag with this plan was finding a motel with a vacancy. I squelched into the first and stood dripping in reception while the manager took about two seconds to remember he didn't have any rooms free. Strange that, considering it was out of season and no-one in their right mind would come to the beach in this awful weather. We trundled on to the next one - same response - and I got an odd feeling of déjà vu... this was a replay of the welcome we got in Hanmer Springs and I really wasn't in the mood for it. At the third place, Ohope Beach Holiday Park, Amanda at reception was genuinely apologetic.

'I'm really sorry - we're full up. Because of this awful weather all our campers have booked into the cabins,' she explained, then: 'Would you like me to phone for you and find you a motel?' I could have kissed her.

'I'll try the Aquarius Motor Lodge, they've loads of units,' she said, picking up the phone.

'Just been there - fully booked... or so they said,'

'That's strange,' she said, 'considering it's out of season. Who would come to the beach in this weather?'

'My thoughts exactly.'

'No worries - I'll try the Westend Motel for you,' she said pressing the buttons on her phone.

'Hi, it's Amanda here at the Ohope Beach Holiday Park. I have two people here looking for a motel and all our cabins are taken by campers - do you have a unit free? You do... OK... it's $75...' she raised her eyes to me and I nodded enthusiastically, causing more drips to spatter her desk, '...that will be fine. Er... these two people are on motorcycles, is that okay?' she asked, reading my mind. 'It is, fine. I'll send them along to you now.' And she gave directions to the beach front motel and wished us a pleasant stay.

'Amanda, you're such a sweet girl I'd like to take you home with me,' I said. She didn't hear me as I waited until I was outside and muttered it under my breath so that Viv couldn't hear me either. People can so easily misunderstand these things.

The Westend Motel was like a small vision of heaven and the fact that we had to drag our luggage up a windswept, rain-lashed exterior staircase to our first floor apartment didn't dent our relief one jot. Soon the kettle was boiling for our first brew and our clothing was draped around the place which rapidly resembled a Chinese laundry. By now we were old hands at rigging up an interior washing line, strung from curtain rails and light fittings, and getting the heat up to warp factor nine.

This motel room didn't have a heater, but Viv soon had the cooker on with hob aglow, oven door open and warming drawer full of boots and socks and gloves. New Zealand cookers, we discovered, don't come with a UK-style grill compartment, but all feature a heated warming drawer at the bottom, which can be handy for... well... warming things, I suppose.

We dined on toast and jam while we peered out of the windows, squinting through the mist on the inside and rain rattling against the outside, and tried to make out the surf crashing loudly on to the beach only a few metres away. In better weather this would be a fabulous spot.

The apartment was soon filled with an odd assortment of smells. The toast and coffee aromas were quite pleasant, but my jacket had been damp for so long it smelled as though it was decomposing internally and that several rats had died in its pockets. Our boots in the oven ponged fearfully as they hadn't been fully dry in over a week, and gloves and helmets added their own unique fragrances as they gave up their moisture to the sauna-like fug of the room. Our hands and toes were white and wrinkled, as if we'd spent all day in the bath. We both had sore throats, grumbling tums and felt pretty lousy. It was time for a rethink.

'*Do you think we should give it up?*' I asked Viv.

'*Give what up?*'

'*Give up this mad idea of riding around New Zealand on motorbikes. We're soaked through constantly, we're both feeling poorly and if the weather carries on like this we're likely to get pneumonia...*'

'*And do what - pack up and go home?*' she asked.

'*Well no - I mean perhaps we should seriously consider giving the bikes back to the rental company when we get to their Auckland shop in a day or two, and getting a campervan to do the rest of the trip in.*'

Viv was visibly shocked at this suggestion. She sat bolt upright in bed. '*Give up my motorbike for a campervan! I love my bike... aren't you getting on very well with yours?*'

'*Well, yes, my bike's fine too. It's just this weather is ridiculous. I was afraid you might be thinking it's all too much. You know - 'what the Whakatane have we let ourselves in for?' and all that...*'

'*I don't think we ought to give up. A campervan is boring. We ought to wait and see what the weather is like tomorrow. It can't rain forever, the sun might be shining in the morning,*' she concluded optimistically.

So we looked at the map for the next day's journey and soon descended into childish giggles while suggesting possible translations for some of the more risible place names: Hungahunga (feed me, feed me), Pukemoremore (don't order the shellfish), Whareponga (fairy snuff!), Whakapapa (that's illegal, surely?), Whatawhata (so eat fewer cookies), and my personal favourite, Whakamarama (gosh, that's amazing!).

I had good reason to utter my personal favourite again at 5am when we were woken by deafening rain hammering on the roof and clattering against the windows. We buried our heads in the pillows and pulled the covers over our ears. It was 8.30am when we got back on the road in a fine wet drizzle. But we were well prepared this time: I had a split carrier bag fastened under my chin and tucked into my groin to deflect rain from my leaky jacket zip and an old bin liner was stuffed inside Viv's overtrousers to stop the rain soaking through to her trousers and knickers.

Yesterday, at the Hot Bread Shop & Café at Opotiki, Viv confided in me later, she had taken off her wet knickers in order to dry them under the hand dryer in the loos. What she hadn't realised, until a bloke pushed past her, was the hand basins were shared between the gents and ladies and she'd been caught red-handed and with her pants down.

'I did have my overtrousers on, I hasten to add, but when this chap pushed past and looked over my shoulder to see me airing my knickers under the hand dryer, I nearly died of embarrassment,' she said.

Of course, having gone to some trouble with these plastic bag rainproofing arrangements, it promptly stopped raining. After a fuel stop at Whakatane and one last snigger over its name, we headed west around the Bay of Plenty towards blue skies. By the time we reached Te Puke the sun was out, the roads were steaming and as we rode into Mount Maunganui, Tauranga's upmarket seaside resort, it was decidedly hot and we needed to take off the plastic bags and a layer or two. Good excuse for a coffee, so we pulled up at a roadside café where people in shorts were eating breakfast in the sunshine and we felt silly peeling off enough outer clothing to cater for a trip to the South Pole. That's the thing with New Zealand weather - there's rather a lot of it and it can change from winter into summer in the space of half an hour.

Mount Maunganui, incidentally, is named after a conical hump which is perched on the end of a sandy peninsula. And speaking of conical humps, on the way back to the main road I felt obliged to stop and eye up the beach-babes cavorting in the surf.

> *'What have we stopped for?'* asked Viv.
> *'Just checking on the weather, Darling.'*
> *'And what's the verdict?'* she asked in all seriousness.
> *'Perfect weather for bikinis!'* which earned me a thump.

On through the busy port and industrial city of Tauranga we rode to rejoin the Pacific Highway SH2 heading north into the sunshine with the temperature climbing into the 30s. We turned off the rapidly melting main road at Karangahake Gorge and found an idyllic picnic spot on rocks beside a waterfall. Here we were, turning red under a fierce sun, slapping on factor 30 and trying to find shade, when only yesterday we'd been drenched to the bone and suffering from hypothermia. This country's weather is certainly not boring.

'See... told you the sun would come out again,' said Viv between mouthfuls of bread, cheese and tomato. *'Still want to swap the bikes for a campervan?'* And I think I detected a hint of smirk.

Now, lest it appear that our motorcycling had adopted a supercilious attitude or that we rode through the countryside with our noses in the air, let me make it clear that we were fully conscious of the more colourful tourist attractions that beckoned along the way.

Take Te Puke for instance: For a small town of 6,000 inhabitants, Te Puke offers more than a mildly amusing name to encourage passing travellers to stop and part with their cash. It features the Te Puke Vintage Auto Barn *'where older cars are seen and loved'*, with an impressive 90 vintage and classic vehicles on display, and morning and afternoon teas by arrangement.

Nearby is the Comvita Education Tourist Centre, incorporating the International Honey Institute and a live bee display, where you can see honey and pills, potions and lotions being produced.

There's also Hill Hoppers U-Drive 4WD adventure track, plus Longridge Park, a golf course, a variety of gardens, native bush walks, jet boating, horse-riding, clay shooting, swimming, surfing and fishing. What more could a tiny rural town do to thrill and titillate passers by? It could take them for rides in a string of carts made to look like kiwifruit. I kid you not.

As we crested the rise before the run down to Te Puke, I almost fell off my bike at the sight of a gigantic slice of kiwifruit standing on its edge, four stories high, with people leaning out of a window near its top, waving at me. This is Kiwifruit Country, the showpiece of an industry that New Zealand all but gave away when some bright spark decided it would be a good idea to sell kiwifruit plants, as well as their fruits, to every other country around the globe. Despite that commercial shot in the foot, New Zealanders remain justly proud of their furry brown fruits with the tangy green interior.

Just as we wobbled to an open-mouthed standstill at the side of the road, a tiny tractor with brown hemispherical roof came trundling down a track towing three bizarre giant kiwifruits containing human beings, waving and wriggling like gigantic maggots. It was all rather weird and unsettling, just the sort of thing kids would adore.

We rode on, shaking our heads in wonder, without stopping to sample the Kiwifruit Slice Viewing Tower, the Kiwicarts, the orchards, the horticultural theme park or the Magic World playground with its castle and dragon maze. We would have done if we'd had kids. Honest.

Seriously though, for a sparsely-populated country adrift in a vast ocean, thousands of miles from anywhere, New Zealand sports an amazing variety of attractions to woo the tourist. There's an earnestness about the Kiwis' desire to see their visitors have a good time that's really quite endearing. As a general rule Viv and I don't 'do' tourist traps, having no desire to 'ooh' and 'aah' alongside hundreds of others, and in the New Zealand countryside the wildlife and the heart-stopping scenery were all the entertainment we needed. But even we, cynical as we are, couldn't help being impressed at the lengths the locals had gone to to provide entertainment and amusement.

Chapter 7

Coromandel Capers

We rode into Thames early in the afternoon and found the main street shut. It was the day of the town's Christmas parade - which seemed bizarre in blazing sunshine - and everybody and their dog had turned out to take part. The fire engine, police car and ambulance led the civic amble around the town, followed by a marching band, several trucks full of hysterical people who'd obviously got into the Christmas spirit a trifle early, then delivery vans, tractors, the local tyre shop truck and various other motley vehicles. It was a grand turnout and we were delighted we'd arrived just in time to witness this slice of rural revelry, especially when the local flying club buzzed the crowd with a small plane towing a glider in a noisy fly-past.

Thames had a Wild West frontier town feel to it, rather like Murchison, with single-storey wooden shopfronts shaded behind broad verandahs and historical two-storey inns, like the Brian Boru Hotel which has provided beds for guests since 1868. But our accommodation was on the outskirts, where the Brookby Motel nestled by a little stream, a haven of quiet charm. We checked in quickly, unloaded our bikes, changed our clothes and legged it back into town to see the rest of the festivities, but by 2.30pm it was all over except for some riotous cheering and guffawing from one of the street-corner hotels which the revellers had taken over. So we strolled the main street, browsing and picking up a few items of shopping.

In a store called Gemstones we met David Taylor who was an interesting mix of nationalities and was keen to tell us all about himself. His family, as his name suggested, was originally English but after 200 years living in India had become fully assimilated and David looked and sounded very 'Goodness Gracious Me'. He came from near the Afghan border, had served in the RAF on V-bomber duty while stationed in our home county of Norfolk, where he had played hockey for the forces before training in textile manufacture - and he had finally left India to settle in

Auckland and sell gemstones. He had a delightful selection of glittering rocks and crystals, all sourced from Indian mines. Quite fascinating, but he had told us his entire life story twice before we could get away. Phew!

Back on the street the sun was scorching, so we headed back to our motel to wash clothes and make the most of the dry weather and washing line provided outside our back door. Then I sat down with a cuppa to plan the remainder of our North Island trip. We had so few days in which to get a glimpse of this wonderful, but quite different, country. If we tried to see too much it would all pass in a blur, with no time to stop and smell the roses. Then I turned over the card I'd been given when we registered at the Brookby Motel and read aloud:

'Here's how they describe this place - 'A rippling brook, A tranquil scene, A place of rest, A traveller's dream' - what do you reckon, would you agree with that?'

No reply. I looked up to see Viv slouched in her chair, head back, eyes closed, mouth in 'catch fly' mode.

'I'll take that as a yes,' I muttered and sloped off to crash out on the bed, where my snoring would be less likely to wake her. I'm so considerate sometimes.

We both felt decidedly peckish when we woke, which was just as well, as the Thames Chinese Restaurant was offering a smorgasbord that evening. We didn't let this odd clash of national identities, the second of the day, put us off and helped ourselves to more food than was strictly necessary, or good for us. All for NZ$15 (£4.30) each.

After such a splendid feast we felt obliged to walk it off and struck out along a track which headed up the valley behind our motel. The path tiptoed precariously through lavish bush above sheer drops to the stony Karaka Stream riverbed below. It was really quite lovely but, after an hour or so, with fading light increasing the risk of us losing our footing, we retraced our steps and were soon lost in another traveller's dream at the peaceful Brookby Motel

Proprietors Keith and Dawn Newton obligingly stored our luggage in their office next morning while we set off to ride around the Coromandel Peninsula, which pokes northwards from Thames for a further 60km into the Hauraki Gulf. To the east, lies the blue Pacific Ocean..

77

The coast road, curving alongside the waters of the Firth of Thames, was a delight to ride, not least because of the fabulous Pohutukawa trees which light up the whole of this coastline in December with their extraordinary bright red flowers. Many of the trees were so laden with delicate scarlet blossoms their entire crowns were ablaze with vivid colour. We just had to stop to gasp at the spectacle and try to capture it with our camera.

We weren't the only ones who found the flowers attractive. Back on the road, several large bees bounced off our visors, helmets and clothing before one managed to wedge itself inside my collar, and showed its annoyance by stinging me on the neck. After a frantic screech to a halt and fumble to remove the bumble, a dab of Germolene soothed the throbbing and we set off again with collars tightly buttoned up.

At Tapu we turned off the coast road SH25 to ride over the Coromandel Range to Coroglen. The tarmac soon became narrow and bendy, crisscrossing the Tapu River via single lane bridges and providing great views up the gorge to Maumaupaki peak looming above. Soon the 'seal' ended and we were then on a hard gravel road. It might be appropriate here to explain some of the antipodean road signs...:

SEAL ENDS - No, not a Maori delicacy, but notice of a change of road surface. Seal is short for tarseal or tarmacadam road.

METALLED ROAD - No, not an iron or tin surface, but a road finished with loose granite chippings and no tar, which can prove slippery for a motorcycle and will feel like metal if you fall on it.

UNMETALLED ROAD - These were usually our favourites - dirt roads that were often rough, steep and muddy. Many were designated 4WD. In winter, most become impassable.

WASHOUT - No, not an alfresco laundry, but an indication that part of the road has collapsed, usually fallen down a vertical cliff. Keep clear or you'll follow it.

SLIP - Pronounced 'slup', where rocks, mud, gravel and usually water have fallen on to the road to make the going more interesting.

SLUMP - No, not a suggestion that you should slouch in your seat or flop on to your petrol tank, but an indication that the road surface has dropped due to an underground collapse. Hit one of these at speed and you will realign your vertebrae and revisit your breakfast, perhaps simultaneously.

ONE LANE BRIDGE - Just what it says. And whatever the priority indicated, motorcyclists are well advised to give way, as the locals don't slow down at all.

RAIL/ROAD BRIDGE - This is a single lane bridge which you share with trains. Yes, really! And, as if the prospect of a car or train meeting you head-on isn't enough, you have to ride along the railway track too. Keep motorcycle wheels well away from the rails, or you could be pitched into the parapet with fatal results. Fortunately these bridges are very rare, but we did come across them on the west coast of the South Island.

Back on the road from Tapu to Coroglen we were enjoying a stretch of fast, bendy road with a damp and compacted shale surface, a bit like a speedway track. We weren't doing the full Ivan Mauger sideways stuff, but we were slithering and sliding in a semi-controlled sort of way, which felt every bit as exciting to us. This time we were not lulled into a false sense of isolation because oncoming traffic, including the occasional lorry, sped around the bends towards us.

Past the Rapaura Water Gardens we stopped to visit the Square Kauri. This, according to our guide book, was a rare 1,200 year old Kauri tree which had been spared the logger's axe and saw during the late 1800s due to its unusual shape. A hundred metres up the hill from the car park was the start of a forest trail, with 180 steep wooden steps climbing high into the native forest before we came to a boardwalk up among the branches. We followed the boardwalk through the dense green foliage and suddenly we were face to face with the trunk of a HUGE Kauri tree. Despite the height we'd climbed it still towered above us, majestic and magnificent.

*The 1200 year old Square Kauri tree on the trail
from Tapu to Coroglen*

A quirk of nature had caused this tree's trunk to grow in an almost square shape, an oddity which saved its life by general consensus when all its neighbours were felled in the frenzy to cash in on the new colony's bounty. By the time it was realised how precious these trees were and how slowly they grow, it was too late. Almost all had been turned into planks and posts, furniture and fences. Mankind will have to wait one hundred generations before the Kauri saplings planted now will even begin to resemble the fabulous trees that confronted the frontiersmen of the mid-1800s. We just hope the Square Kauri can be left unmolested in its lonely vigil until a tiny fraction of the former Kauri forests re-emerge from the NZ soil.

A noticeboard told us that this Kauri tree contains more than 69 cubic metres of timber, which seems astonishing when you realise how big one cubic metre is, then went on to say that the largest Kauri tree still standing contains 465 cubic metres - seven times as much! These trees truly deserve the Kiwi's most popular adjective - awesome!

After soaking up the views over the track and across the valley to the Camelback Range opposite, we returned to our bikes in a more sober, reflective mood but still enjoyed the remaining 30km of loose track - ideal for our trailie bikes, but don't try it on your Ducati 996.

After rejoining the tarsealed road at Coroglen we turned east on the Pacific Coast Highway for Whenuakite ('Fenoo-ahkey-tay') with eyes peeled for the Colenso Country Café & Shop, our planned coffee stop. This turned out to be a charming place, set among herb gardens and fruit trees, displaying quality NZ art and offering full meals and wine - a cut above your average roadside caff.

With a lot of kilometres still to ride we confined ourselves to delicious coffee and a slice of irresistible cake (thank goodness for those stretchy-waist trousers) then swung our legs back over our Serows for a quick blast to the south. The road became increasingly twisty, with our bikes never upright and some of the bends scraping our footrests on the surface of the tarseal at only 35kph. Fun, but we still had to watch out for local loonies in tricked-up V8 Holdens and logging lorries careering around the bends towing teetering trailers loaded with tons of logs. If just one log slipped, no, don't think about it.

Soon we were blasting alongside the harbour of bustling little town Tairua, looking across the shimmering waters at its posh neighbour Pauanui, an upmarket seaside resort with luxury harbourside holiday homes, golf course and airstrip for those who wish to fly to their weekend retreats in their private planes.

After Hikuai we turned right to climb back over the Coromandel Range, with dozens more swooping turns, some of which I'd swear were more than 360 degrees, up past Kaitarakihi Peak and then down the Kirikiri Valley to Kopu and a short dash back up the west coast to Thames. After the exhilarating morning's ride I was ready for cool beer in the posh Brian Boru Hotel or even 'The Udder Bar' at the Coromandel Backpackers complex. I wanted to find out if this was a topless tavern or whether they simply catered for the local dairy farming community, but Viv sensibly pointed out that we still had to ride to Auckland, 130km north.

We picked up our luggage from the Brookby, thanked Keith and Dawn and booked in for another night in three days time, then sped off to snatch a hasty picnic lunch beside the mangroves of the Waihou River as black clouds loomed overhead and the first fat raindrops splatted on the hot ground.

Following the Pacific Coast Highway SH25 over the marshy flatlands to the south of the Firth of Thames I got my first real fright of the trip. A young girl in a Toyota, chatting to her passengers, waited for the three cars we were following to pass before pulling out of a side road straight across my path. Only a big fistfull of brake and a tyre-squealing swerve saved me from impaling the side of her car. Jeez - what was she thinking? She quite clearly saw all five vehicles travelling in close procession and Viv and I had our headlights on. Whatever she was smoking had evidently altered her perception of time and distance. The experience made me more acutely aware of other road users, which was no bad thing for surviving the Auckland motorway later that same afternoon.

Fortunately, there were almost no other vehicles on the long drag north from Waitakaruru into the teeth of a dry gale that had replaced the brief shower. Down to fourth gear, and third in the gusts, we were making painfully slow progress, so I adopted a tactic I used 30 years before on my low-powered little Honda 90 - I crouched down behind the handlebars to cheat the windblast and reduce the drag factor. It was not ideal, as in this position I couldn't see my rearview mirrors and when I did steal a glance over my shoulder, Viv was trailing way behind, a speck in the distance. I forgot she had missed out on a misspent youth playing boy racers.

After a coffee stop at Kawakawa Bay we plugged on through Clevedon and then got thoroughly lost in Papakura, the most southerly suburb of Auckland. All signs for the city disappeared and we were left floundering in a commercial district with no sense of direction. Eventually I worked out that, as we were in the southern hemisphere, the sun at 4pm should be in the north west, the direction we needed to go, and a few minutes later we had found our first piece of Manic Motorway.

It was the start of the rush hour and I had fondly supposed that most of the traffic would be heading out of the city. Instead, it seemed to me that all of Auckland's one million inhabitants had chosen this exact moment to drive up the Southern Motorway into the city with us. And they were pretty impatient to get there too, with cars and trucks constantly swapping lanes without signalling and cutting each other up fearfully in the process. It was like a gigantic, high-speed game of dodgems - a nightmare after the empty roads we'd become used to - and we suddenly felt very small and very vulnerable.

Riding defensively in tight formation, with Viv tucked behind my left elbow, we stuck to the middle lane to keep clear of traffic leaving and joining via the multi-numerous slip roads. There were no fewer than twenty six - yes, twenty six! - junctions on our northbound carriageway alone between Papakura on the outskirts and the Auckland Harbour Bridge, which we had to cross. We rode with fingers on brake levers and eyes everywhere.

Viv grabs a snack at Kawakawa Bay.
It's the waterproof trousers that make her irresistible!

As the great heaving, writhing morass of traffic edged closer to the city centre, another peculiarity of the Auckland motorway system began to impress itself upon my fevered brain: Ridiculous Road Signs! On the outskirts, the big green motorway signs had usefully said 'Takanini & Manurewa' before the turnoff to Takanini and Manurewa, and 'Manakau Airport' before the turnoff for Manakau Airport. No problem so far. Then I noticed a sign for 'Green Lane East' with no indication that it led to Remuera, followed in quick succession by 'Market Road', 'Khyber Pass Road' (Jeez - did this *really* go to the Khyber Pass?) 'Symonds Street & Wellesley Street' but not a single clue which suburbs they went to.

A moment of panic swept over me. There was absolutely no chance of consulting a map. In a car you can coolly ask your passenger to navigate, or if you are on the M25 orbital road around London you can read the map yourself while driving. I'm not sure if this is compulsory, but I've noticed that most drivers do this while simultaneously talking on their mobile phone. However on a bike, whatever country you are in or motorway you are on, map reading means stopping and the scary, honking, swerving, deathwish river of steel we were in precluded even slowing down without first leaving the motorway altogether.

Why, oh why, do they tell you the name of the street, not where it goes to? If you're a local and *know* that 'Khyber Pass Road' leads to Newmarket and Mt Eden, you hardly need a road sign at all. Direction signs, surely, are provided for the benefit of those people who *don't* know the names of the roads, only where they want to get to. Telling them the name of the street is about as helpful as a poke in the eye with a burnt stick. Auckland's motorway planners need a jolly good slapping.

And they're not alone. In my home county of Norfolk, back in England, the highways department has removed thousands of signs which told motorists which road led to what village, and replaced them with others which say 'Shortthorn Road' or 'Parish Road'. The reason is obvious. They hope that if they don't tell motorists where some of these minor roads go to, people won't use them and this will save the council having to spend money maintaining and repairing them. What actually happens is motorists do twice as many miles on these little back lanes getting lost and frustrated before asking the locals - me, usually - for directions. Yes, Norfolk County Highways planners need a jolly good slapping too.

Back on Auckland's Southern Motorway, we were now descending towards the city centre and could see the huge spindly arches of the Auckland Harbour Bridge in the distance. I knew we had to cross it and then turn left for the suburb of Birkenhead, but which of the many turns led there I had no idea. Suddenly we were on the bridge where either side stretched sparkling water and a forest of yacht masts, but my eyes were fully occupied trying to pick out the upcoming road signs.

'Stafford Road' - where did that go, for God's sake? 'Onewa Road' - oh, this is impossible! Then, as we were almost past it, a tiny brown sign for Birkenhead. I swung out my left arm, almost slapping Viv in the face, and swerved up Onewa Road... straight into a torrential downpour. We pulled over in the residential street so I could have a look at my scribbled directions to our motel, but the rain was so heavy I got only one quick glance before the ink ran off the page and the paper disintegrated. We had got so hot and sweaty coping with the motorway madness that we decided to leave off the waterproofs we had removed in the steamy back streets of Papakura, and rode the last five kilometres to our accommodation absorbing several gallons of rainwater.

Bush Glen Motel had been chosen because it sounded quiet and leafy, and because it was cheap, our standard selection criteria. In fact, we thought it was decidedly seedy and rundown, but our unit had the most fabulous treetop balcony overlooking wild bush and gardens. Within minutes of arriving and stripping off our dripping clothes we were struck dumb by the sight of a gorgeous parrot (actually an eastern rosella) sitting on the telephone wire right outside our kitchen window. Then we spotted two colourful Barbary doves in the top branches of a tree just alongside our balcony, followed by three tuis in a big pine tree, a bellbird, several little waxeyes and a dancing fantail. The birdsong was wonderful, with the bellbird's liquid, bell-like tones ringing out at dusk like someone playing a xylophone very skilfully. After a long and stressful day, we slipped into a blissful, uninterrupted sleep and woke at dawn to the bellbird's morning chorus.

Despite its peeling paint and a cronky cooker, we decided to stay put at Bush Glen for a second night, as we had business to attend to in Auckland. First up was a ride back across the spectacular harbour bridge to New Zealand Motorcycle Rentals' Auckland headquarters for the bikes to be serviced, while we took a walk along the waterfront, photographed the bridge and I got a top-class haircut for NZ$12 (£3.50) from a cute Chinese lady called Karen.

Then I caught the shuttle bus to the airport to meet a business colleague, Paul Garland, who had flown in from Australia for a meeting with me and Marie Frost, who'd driven up from Fielding to discuss strategy for expansion of their businesses in Australia and New Zealand. Viv, meanwhile, treated herself to a picnic in the park and some leisurely shopping. We regrouped at the bike rental shop just before they shut for the day to pick up our freshly-fettled Serows.

Back at our birdsong motel, we did a quick change before setting out on foot under Viv's newly-acquired umbrella (yup, raining again) to find the home of my long-lost cousin Robin Purllant. He had heard we were in town and had invited us to supper with his wife Helen and daughter Saskia. Robin and I had a bit of catching up to do. The last time we'd met, at my childhood home in the Fens of Lincolnshire before Robin emigrated, I had been just two years old and a lot had happened to us and our families in the intervening 47 years.

Next morning both Viv and I had sore throats and felt a little groggy. Nothing to do with the excellent wine-lubricated conversation of the night before, more likely a result of the past weeks of being alternately drenched and scorched, chilled and boiled. But our spirits rose as we left behind the frantic pace of Auckland and slipped through ever more leafy suburbs, then open country to the north en route for Matakohe and a charming little wooden cabin that was to be our home for the night. Its location was even more idyllic than the Bush Glen Motel: Perched on a low hill thrust into the estuary of the Arapaoa River and surrounded on three sides by water. We'd chosen the Matakohe Motor Camp because it was a short walk from the Matakohe Kauri Museum, and that's where we headed after we'd soaked up the views and the calm of this lovely spot.

We spent the whole afternoon, and could easily have spent a full day, at the Kauri museum. I had Joni Mitchell's classic song 'Big Yellow Taxi' reverberating around my head: *They took all the trees and put 'em in a tree museum, and charged all the people a dollar and a half just to see 'em.'* In fact, they charged us $7 (£2) each just to see 'em, and it was well worth it.

The museum was wonderful. Its exhibits and photos told the story of the early years of the European settlement of New Zealand and how the Kauri forests of the North Island were cleared to provide pasture land for sheep and cows. The trees were the pioneers' first cash crop, but since the ancient Kauris were vast they took some felling, cutting and shifting. The exhibits told of the amazing feats of engineering that were required to move these enormous lumps of wood. Here's a brief outline of what was required:

A large tree might take a team of men several days to cut through and topple, since there were no chain saws in the late 1800s. The fallen tree could weigh several hundred tons, so the next task would be to reduce it to 30-ton sections so it could be moved. To give some idea of scale, your car weighs one ton. Imagine 30 cars welded together and then try to shift them in one piece.

When they had measured and calculated a 30-ton length, two men would set about cutting it off with a handsaw. First step was to dig a tunnel under the tree and excavate a pit where one man would spend the next few days while he operated the lower end of the pit-saw. Can you imagine it? Standing in a dark, wet, six-foot hole beneath a vast tree in the steamy semi-tropical jungle, pushing and pulling on the handles of an enormous saw blade under a constant rain of sawdust. His partner, meantime, had constructed a platform on top of the trunk from which to push and pull his end of the colossal saw. After an eternity of mind-numbing, back-breaking, push-pulling of the steel blade the trunk would be severed and the relief the men felt would be tempered with the knowledge that they could now move down a few feet and start all over again.

Meanwhile, the first 30-ton log needed moving. Using screw jacks, wedges and props, one man could gradually roll the vast bulk laboriously, inch-by-painful-inch, to a position where it could be hauled away by a team of oxen. Often as many as 16 or 18 oxen would be needed to haul a single log. Or sometimes the men would construct a makeshift railway and mount the log on a trolley, with a man lying *underneath* the log to operate a rudimentary brake to prevent the colossal load running away on the downhill course.

More commonly the logs were rolled into a streambed and then, when enough logs had accumulated, a Heath-Robinson dam would be unleashed so that a rush of water could wash the gigantic logs down to the river and thence to the sawmills. Sometimes streams, creeks and rivers would be choked with logs for three or four years while they waited for sufficient rainfall to build up behind the dam to float them downstream.

Needless to say, it was all incredibly heavy, arduous and dangerous work, but in the threadbare economy of the young colony it paid just enough to help a man keep his family fed. And, as the Kauri forests disappeared, the value of the wood multiplied. A single log of Kauri worth $24 in 1909 was worth $15,000 in 1990. And with good reason: Kauri wood is amazingly useful stuff. It was used for buildings, ships, furniture - almost anything in fact, as it is immensely strong and durable, surprisingly elastic and resists rot and attack from wood-boring insects. It is also very beautiful. When polished it has a wonderful glowing golden grain and shines as if lit internally giving the impression of a hologram. Consequently it became much prized for furniture and ornaments. Some of the examples in the museum are jaw-droppingly gorgeous.

Despite the mammoth effort required to drag it out of the inhospitable wilderness, it was soon nearly all cut down, sawn up, shipped and sold. And then people started to realise just what they'd lost. As Joni sang: *'Don't it always seem to go that we don't know what we've got 'til it's gone...'* Almost all the magnificent Kauri trees, many of them thousands of years old - gigantic, silent, defenceless - had been destroyed. Just a few precious acres, less than five percent of the original forest, were saved when the young NZ government came to its senses and banned the felling of live Kauris.

Then the resourceful loggers realised that they could earn a living from digging up the remains of long-dead trees from the swamps. Amazingly, this wood was as good or better than the new stuff, despite having been buried under mud and water for up to 300,000 years! How's that for durability?

At the same time that the true worth of Kauri wood was beginning to be appreciated, the value of gum - the resin from the Kauri trees - was also on the rise. For hundreds of years it had been collected by the Maori because it burned very well. They used gum to light their huts and fishing boats, but the Europeans had many other applications. It could be used in the manufacture of linoleum, varnish and a hundred other commodities and the finer pieces of amber were turned into jewellery and ornaments. Demand gave rise to another breed of pioneers - gum diggers - who searched the swamps with 20-foot long metal spikes to locate and retrieve the 'Kauri gold'. Many of them earned more than the gold-diggers who preceded them. A wonderful collection of some of the amber they found is on display in the museum's Gum Room.

Then the museum was closing and we realised the whole afternoon had vanished in this absorbing place. We stumbled out, blinking in the late afternoon sunlight, and realised we had no food or plans for supper. The Matakohe House B&B and Café next door was shut, but the charming lady proprietor spotted us with noses pressed to the glass and took pity on us.

'I'm only slightly closed' she said. *'If you need something immediately I can make you a sandwich. Or if you'd like to come back at 7pm you can have a full cooked meal with us.'*

We saved our hunger and were rewarded with a superb meal, fine wine and sparkling conversation with the other evening guests.

Chapter 8

Heading South

We called in briefly at the Kauri Museum shop next morning to buy some gifts for our family back home - small items only, as they all had to fit within our already bulging luggage. Then back on the road again, south to Auckland and another unpleasant journey on the teeming motorway before getting lost once more in the southern suburbs.

This time I figured out where I was going wrong. My usually reliable sense of direction was being shunted 180 degrees out of whack by the sun being in the wrong part of the sky. Having lived in the northern hemisphere for almost 50 years, I had grown so used to the sun crossing the sky from left to right when facing south, I used it as a subliminal direction indicator. Here the sun crosses from right to left when you're facing north, so if I just followed my instincts, which I often do on unfamiliar roads, I ended up heading in the opposite direction to the way we wanted to go.

Fortunately, Viv had no such problems. She freely admits to having no sense of direction so she is a bit more attentive to road signs. Not for the first time she pulled up alongside as I was consulting the map and muttering darkly, to enquire sweetly why we had turned left ten kilometres back, when the sign to our destination pointed to the right?

'*Sign! What sign?*' I said angrily. Gratitude and humility don't come easily to me when I'm lost.

'*At that last T-junction. It was a bit hidden in the bushes, but it pointed right for Clevedon. I presumed you must know a better route when you turned left,*' she said.

'*But it CAN'T be! We need to go south.*' I said squinting up at the sun and checking my watch.

'*It IS be!*' she said, '*And I think you'll find we're heading north.*'

'*Oh poo! I forgot the stupid sun's in the stupid north in this stupid country. Sorry!*'

Viv never let on that it was neither the sun nor the country that appeared stupid from where she was sitting. Back in the peace and tranquillity of Kawakawa Bay we stopped for a picnic lunch and then rode on to Thames and the 'travellers dream' Brookby Motel.

We were up, packed and off by 8.30am for our longest day's ride so far, 300km from Thames to Turangi, at the southern tip of lake Taupo. Fortunately, the sun shone, the roads were dry and we had a following wind - an important consideration for our underpowered and overloaded Serows - so we made excellent progress. And as we rode along I sang a little song to myself in an effort to recalibrate my mental sundial. It went: *'The sun has got his hat on, hip hip hip hooray! The sun has got his hat on and he's in the north today!'* It wouldn't make the Top Ten, but it did keep us pointing in the right direction.

Our route took us due south down the middle of the North Island through Paeroa, Te Aroha and Matamata, where we stopped briefly for fuel, then Tirau, a tiny town dominated by a huge sheep and a gigantic sheepdog.

These gargantuan animals turned out to be buildings, constructed to celebrate the region's sheep-rearing heritage and to attract passing tourists. It worked. We felt compelled to walk in and look around these unlikely-looking 'cultural centres' which were actually overblown giftshops, selling every possible commodity and trinket imaginable on the sheep theme - plus many more items that were clearly the products of a fevered mind, or possibly a cross-breeding experiment between sheep and humans.

Despite their best endeavours we weren't tempted to buy a pair of 'lambswool nipple-warmers' or any of the other goods of questionable taste, but we did make use of their excellent loos before crossing the road to enjoy a fine cup of coffee and slice of cake, seated at the pavement table of a pleasant café. The reason the amazing buildings and their equally jaw-dropping array of commodities didn't persuade us to part with our money was, we told ourselves, because we didn't have room for anything else in our bags - not even a pair of nipple-warmers. But before we left town we blew that theory by popping in to The Jade Shop next door and buying gifts made from jade, paua shell and ponga, the treefern wood.

Now on SH1, we pressed on southwards through Putaruru and Tokoroa and were approaching Taupo near midday when we were tempted off course by a sign announcing Wairakei Thermal Valley. We had missed the top tourist attraction of Rotorua, with its spouting geysers, bubbling mud pools and other volcanic delights, partly because we couldn't fit it in to our tight schedule and partly because we didn't fancy joining vast crowds of sightseers. But this little geothermal valley was low-key and nearly deserted.

After a happy hour spent wandering around its active vents, steaming ground, mudpools and craters, we made friends with a fat and friendly sheep, aptly named Porridge, plus a noisy gaggle of Guinea fowl and other exotic birds before grabbing a bite to eat at the valley's 'Rustic Café'. The lack of customers allowed the jokey proprietor to regale us with tales of his past career as a mechanic for UK motorcycle racers and to try out his favourite party trick.

This involved inviting us to open a piece of folded paper which, he claimed, contained the eggs of the weta, New Zealand's famous giant insect. I suspected a booby-trap and only jumped a few inches off the ground when the paper wriggled violently in my fingers. It contained two paperclips wound up by a rubber band. His next victim, an elderly lady, almost weta-self! She was not amused, assaulting him both physically and verbally for playing such an evil trick on: 'an old lady in poor health'. Seeing the way she whacked him with her handbag, I dread to think what damage she could have done if she'd been young and fit.

We rode through Taupo - beautiful, with its stunning lake backdrop, despite the crowds and bumper-to-bumper traffic - and then the scenic lakeside ride to Turangi and Creel Lodge, our motel for the night. We'd picked this one, not because it was cheapest, but because it promised 'supreme serenity - the only motel backing on to the Tongariro River, with the quietest location'. And it was true. After a riverside walk and a modest supper rustled up in our cabin's kitchen, we heard nothing until the tuis and bellbirds called us from our slumber next morning.

With the wind still from the north we set off at a good lick on SH1 which, at this point is also called the Volcanic

Loop, since it joins up with SHs 49, 4 and 47 to circumnavigate active volcanoes Tongariro, Ngauruhoe and Ruapehu in the Tongariro National Park. As if it needed a third name, this stretch of highway is also called The Desert Road, which puzzled me as it passes through the centre of a lush green country with enough rainfall to make the Sahara bloom.

Then suddenly we were riding through a barren landscape alongside Mt Ruapehu. Of course, this was the mountain that last erupted in September 1995, when it rained volcanic rock, ash and steam over the surrounding countryside, plus slurries of rock, ash, soil and water, in a series of explosive emissions. Less spectacular, but far more devastating, had been a massive flood from Ruapehu's crater lake on Christmas Eve 1953. The water level had risen dramatically over preceding years after eruptions blocked the lake's normal overflow. When the lake finally burst free the resulting torrent tore down the mountain and swept away a railway bridge just before a crowded train arrived. One hundred and fifty three people were killed in the crash.

So it was with some trepidation that we turned off the Desert Road on to what my map showed as 'Tukino Road (4WD)' leading to the Tukino Ski Area, just below the rumbling mountain's crater lake. In fact, it was not a road at all, but a barely perceptible set of wheel tracks through deep sand, gravel, streambeds, rocks and other volcanic debris. The soft volcanic sand, in particular, was very difficult to ride through on our heavily laden bikes. We'd wobbled only a hundred metres off the highway when we came across dozens of vehicles, including several lorries, and scores of people milling around a weird looking building.

It turned out to be a film crew shooting a TV commercial for an Indonesian internet company, and the weird hut amid the volcanic scenery was supposed to be a cybercafé on Mars. I was kinda hoping the guys would say it was too dangerous to proceed further, or that we would be somehow interfering with their film shoot, but in typical Kiwi fashion they said: *'Yeah, no worries mate!'* and urged us to carry on up the side of the desolate mountain to the heart of the volcano.

After a few wobbly, foot-down moments in the sandy streambeds, we worked our way carefully on to higher slopes littered with brightly coloured rocks of orange, blue, red and yellow. The higher we went, the steeper the track, the stronger the wind and the colder it got. Eventually we reached a locked gate and stopped to survey the surreal lunar landscape below us and the cloud-covered peaks above. Clearly visible sweeping down from the north was a grey curtain of rain and we'd barely tucked the camera back in its bag when the first cold stabs of water hit our faces. So we pulled on helmets and gloves and set off back down the slippery slope while we could still see which way to go.

It was ten kilometres back through the desolation before we reached the main road again and I, for one, was pleased to be off the mountain that had a real brooding quality to it. Fast road carried us to Taihape (Tie-happy), which proudly announced itself as the 'Gum Boot Capital Of New Zealand'. This seemed a good enough reason to stop for lunch, so we entered a roadside café called Gumboot Lodge, where the staff gave us a miniature Wellington boot with a number on when we placed our order.

It hadn't entirely escaped our notice that there was something of a theme going on here, so we asked the staff why. They had no idea. No, really - the staff of Gumboot Lodge, in 'The Gum Boot Capital Of New Zealand', having just handed us a numbered gumboot to stand on our table - they really had no idea why. We were speechless. Well, almost.

'*Do they make gumboots here then?*' I asked.

'*No.*'

'*Is this a major wholesale depot for gumboots perhaps?*'

'*No.*'

'*So why is it called 'Gumboot Capital' and why have you just given me one with a number on?*'

'*I don't know. I think it's just a gimmick. You know, something to give the place an identity sort of thing,*' she said, with disarming Kiwi frankness.

And she was right. However, Taihape now hosts the NZ National Gumboot Throwing Championships and the town's kids get to learn 'gummy throwing' as part of their school

Dakota aircraft café at Mangaweka

curriculum, so maybe the gimmick has gone slightly to their heads. If you're a lifetime fan of gumboots, you could die happy in Taihape.

Just a few kilometres down the road at Mangaweka, the townsfolk were clearly trying to go one better. They had a Dakota aircraft, painted end-to-end in lurid Cookie Time cookies livery, parked beside the road and serving as a café. It certainly stopped the traffic, in our case for no more than a photo, since we were still gummied up after Taihape, but we were agog.

What a great, barmy, lovely country this is. If someone suggested parking a large aircraft in a small rural English town, painting it to look like a biscuit and calling it a café, there'd be public outcry of indignation, signed petitions from Friends of The Earth, a storm of planning protests and MPs lobbied to prevent such a blot on the landscape. In New Zealand they say *'No worries, mate - She'll be right,'* and have a bit of fun in order to boost local trade. How refreshing.

By 4pm we were back in Feilding for a lovely welcome from Marie, Joe and family - for the first time we didn't arrive dripping - and soon we were tucking in to a great barbecue and putting the world to rights. Hearing that our gift-buying and acquisition of maps, books and leaflets had seriously overwhelmed our luggage capacity, Marie kindly offered to lighten our load by mailing a boxful of non-essential items on to Christchurch for us. What nice people.

For our final farewell breakfast Marie pushed the boat out with bacon, eggy French toast, cooked bananas and maple syrup (a favourite with Raili and Hannah), eaten on the patio in blistering sunshine at 9am. So bright, in fact, that I developed a migraine and had to go back to bed for an hour before setting off for Wellington. En route we stopped off again at Shannon to greet our old friend Bob Smith at The Old Plum Duff Tearooms and to meet 'The Boss', his cheerful and smiley wife.

After a long chat and leisurely lunch sitting outside watching the town's Christmas parade we set off for the last 100km to Wellington, and encountered queues of holiday traffic, melting tarmac and police speed traps before rolling up at Newlands Court Motel in sweltering heat. There's something sublime about taking a cold shower after being boiled alive in riding jacket, helmet and gloves for several hours. After an afternoon snooze, followed by cheese on toast for supper, we took a stroll around the suburbs and turned in for an early night. To tell the truth, we were both knackered and felt less like intrepid explorers and more like a pair of grandparents who'd perhaps bitten off more than they could point a stick at.

More mixed and muddled metaphors crowded my dreams until the all-too familiar sound of torrential rain intruded and told us that morning had arrived, wet and windy. Ah yes, that was more like the Wellington we remembered.

Back on the slick and streaming roads of the capital, buffeted by the wind and drenched by the rain, we filtered into nose-to-tail commuter traffic at 8.30am and, despite taking a wrong turning due to poor signage (not my fault, obviously, as the sun wasn't visible) we were in time to be first on the ferry. We were busy unloading luggage and tying down the bikes when a BMW R80RT turned up carrying Mark, a seismologist on his way to Kaikoura for a conference on predicting earthquakes.

I met up with Viv - she had been drying her knickers in the ladies loo yet again during my first couple of laps around the passenger decks, it really had been that wet - and we settled down to chat to Mark about riding bikes on some of the off-road tracks we were planning to tackle in the South Island. He reckoned we would have no problem riding The Rainbow Road, our next big wild road project. He'd even ridden the Maungatapu Track on a 500cc four-cylinder Honda roadster, he told us, but it had nearly ended in disaster. It had been very hot and the bike's engine had overheated. When he dropped the machine on one of the steep, rocky climbs, fuel spilled from the tank and ignited on the hot engine! He managed to put out the fire and get the bike upright again, so he wasn't left stranded on the lonely trail. On another occasion on his BMW he'd holed the crankcase on a rock and lost all his engine oil. Fortunately, he was near the top of the track with only downhill to go, so was able to coast down to civilisation with a dead engine.

In the midst of these great tales of derring-do, we spotted pilot whales in Wellington Harbour and dolphins diving under the ferry in Cook Strait, where the sea was mercifully flat calm again. We were soon slipping between the tree-smothered, mist-shrouded slopes of Marlborough Sounds and docking at Picton where it was still raining.

Despite arriving before lunch and turning up dripping and bedraggled, Sunnyvale's Colin Lowe greeted us like long-lost friends and readily agreed to extend our special discount rate (it was now high season and we should have been paying $10 more per night) for a further two nights. Then Kimoko, sensing that someone had arrived unfashionably early, appeared with a plate of freshly home-baked cookies and a carton of milk. What service!

We'd decided to stay here for three nights because we needed a break from the daily dash of packing up, travelling and unpacking again. We both had sore throats and felt decidedly off colour. Besides, lovely Waikawa Bay and the welcome from the Lowes made Sunnyvale an ideal base for exploring the rugged, unspoiled fingers of land that reach out into the blue waters of Marlborough Sounds. And Colin was happy to spend an hour advising us where we could go on our bikes and making photocopies of large-scale local maps to help us find our way.

By mid-afternoon the rain had stopped and hazy sunshine tempted us out for a walk around the bay to inspect the posh yachts at Waikawa Marina and dream of sailing around the beautiful Sounds. Well it was my dream anyway. Viv regards sailing with equal measures of fear and loathing and would be very happy if she never again set foot on any type of floating conveyance. For her, ferries are a necessary evil and sailing boats a hideous form of torture, but I grew up with boats and relish any opportunity to get out on the water. As with all successful marriages, we've reached a compromise on the issue: we don't go sailing, but I'm allowed to dream all I like.

Actually, that's grossly unfair, as I do go off sailing on my own from time to time. And besides, rough seas make me seasick, so dreaming of sailing across oceans is infinitely more practical than the real thing. The yachts looked nice though.

After our walk and plenty of fresh sea air we were both ready for a slap-up meal. Over the past few days we'd existed on bread and cheese, or for an exciting change, cheese on toast. So I was despatched to Picton's One-Stop grocery store on my Yamaha to choose something delicious, nourishing and filling to cook in our motel kitchen, plus a bottle of wine to help it down. When I returned with an enormous, square, oven-ready pizza strapped on my motorcycle rack Viv made no comment about my lack of imagination, or this meal's patent similarity to the bread and cheese/cheese on toast that we'd subsisted on for much of the past week or so. It wasn't until I was slouched in an armchair in an alcoholic haze, hands nursing a swollen stomach, that I realised I'd made a cock-up on the catering front. Doh! She may not like sailing, but Viv is wonderfully forgiving of my constant stupidity. I think I'll keep her.

Next day the weather was drizzly and Viv was weepy. We'd been away from home for over a month and we were missing our children. Viv was especially sad that the previous day our youngest son, Michael, had turned 19 and we'd not managed to get through to him on the phone to wish him happy birthday. Then I had a bright idea: Here in NZ we were 12 hours ahead of the UK. As it was only 9am, back home it would be 9pm on the previous day. Mike would be getting ready to go out with his pals - there was still time to wish him happy birthday!

We zoomed up to Picton to make the call... but couldn't get through again, which left Viv distraught. We sent e-mails instead, but it was a poor substitute for hearing our 'baby' son's voice on his birthday. It was the low point of our trip and together with the persistent rain and our sore throats, it was hard to lift our spirits. We went to bed early, determined to wake up cheerful and make the most of our last day at Waikawa Bay by going on a motorcycle off-road adventure.

'It's still raining,' said Viv next morning, as she handed me a cup of tea in bed, 'but it's not so heavy and the sky's brighter - I think it's going to be a better day.'

It's true what they say. A positive mental attitude can part the darkest clouds and as we rode south the rain did stop. Even finding the alpaca farm at Koromiko closed after I'd promised Viv a stroke of these lovable creatures did not dampen her mood. At Tuamarina we turned left on to a minor road to Rarangi then headed back north on a steep and winding climb along the coast with the picturesque inlet of Port Underwood glittering in the morning sunshine below us.

The tarseal soon gave way to a gravel road which continued its sinuous weave high above the water with great views of the rugged peninsula to the east. As we came alongside Hakahaka Bay we turned right to make a steep descent on a very crumbly clay road, chewed into deep furrows by massive logging lorries. On past Whangataura Bay, Opihi Bay and beyond the long, jagged finger tipped by Separation Point which divides the top end of the broad inlet, following the ever-narrower and more grass-covered Tumbledown Bay Road to its end at Jordans Bay.

Apart from an empty bach, there was no sign of civilisation here and we felt as if we'd ridden to the end of

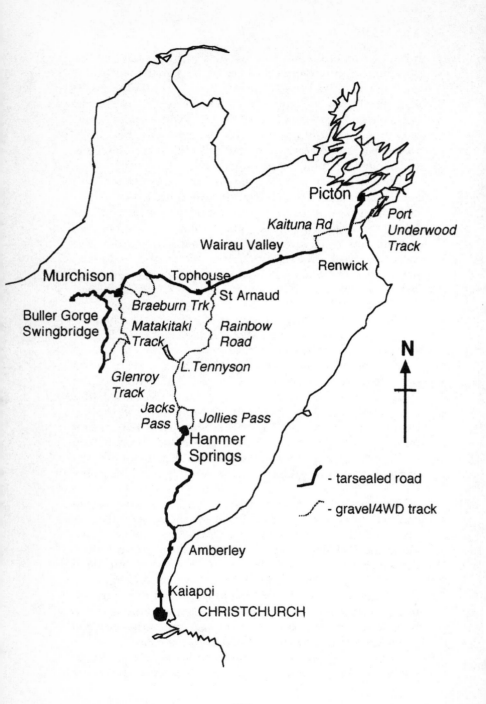

*Bob's Serow slips and slides along the wet shale
of the Port Underwood Track*

the known world. It was perfect, blissfully unspoiled and
filled with exotic birdsong. We parked the bikes, stripped
off our riding gear and walked down to a stony beach where
tuis and bellbirds serenaded us and hopped through nearby
branches as if fearless of man in this remote Eden. Within

minutes we'd also identified a grey heron and a white-faced heron wading through the shallows before us, plus a tomtit - a colourful ball of black and yellow fluff - flitting through the bushes beside us.

Then, as we sat munching apples, a chubby brown bird walked boldly out of the undergrowth and past our feet. We'd never seen anything like it before and, for one excited second, I thought it was a kiwi. Then I realised it was another flightless native of New Zealand - a weka.

By now the sun was burning away the misty remnants of the morning's clouds as it reached the top of the sky. We rode back, getting bolder and faster on the now-familiar road until Viv overcooked it on one bend in deep gravel. She lost both wheels, the bike went down and she yelled *'Arggh!'* - then the bike miraculously came back upright again with Viv still on board and undamaged. This experience slowed her down for the next few kilometres, but gave Viv increased confidence in her Serow's ability to save her from disaster.

When we rejoined the rutted Port Underwood road we turned right for a great ride to Karaka Point and then down again to Waikawa Bay and reached our motel by 3pm. After borrowing Colin's hosepipe to wash the trail's mud from our bikes, Viv popped into Picton to collect another batch of photos we'd had printed, while I checked out the inside of my eyelids. We dined on 'fush 'n' chups' then walked off our supper around the bay, each of us choosing our favourite bach.

Next morning as we settled up and said our goodbyes, Colin refused payment for a wineglass we'd broken during washing up. Despite having had only half a sunny day here, we were sorry to be leaving Waikawa Bay and friendly Sunnyvale Motel, and promised ourselves we would return to explore the extraordinary Marlborough Sounds region more fully one day.

Back through Koromiko - the alpacas were still being shy - to Tuamarina once again, where we stopped to read the plaque at the site of the Wairau Incident. Here in 1843 a dispute over land claims by European settlers led to 22 whites and 4 Maoris being killed, a bit of a setback in relations between the colonists and the locals.

We turned right at this point, seeking the quiet riverside Kaituna Road (confusingly signed Bush Road) and found ourselves riding along a lovely winding country track giving great views of the ice-blue waters of the Wairau River swirling between polished grey boulders. Surrounded by such startling beauty, we could understand why the Maori had been reluctant to give it all away to the newly-arrived whites. They could not have known that the land to the south of the Wairau would one day become the country's prime grape-growing region, as Blenheim's sprawling vineyards reached further along the broad Wairau Valley to keep pace with the nation's thirst.

After we crossed the river heading for Renwick, we passed through many newly-planted vineyards, all very neat and tidy with their regimented rows of posts and wires. There were many signs inviting us to stop for wine-tastings, tours and lunches, but wine and motorcycles don't mix, so we sped by with only the occasional silent sob.

In Renwick we stopped for fuel and had a chat with the locals. Everyone we met wanted to know where we were going, where we had been and many - young and old, male and female - wished they could walk out of their job right then and come with us. It seems there is a magic about travellers on motorcycles riding off towards distant unknown adventures. It's the classic Easy Rider story, where Jack Nicholson joins Peter Fonda and Dennis Hopper on their choppers for a riskier, more exciting life on the road. We were hoping our trip would have a different ending.

Now we were on SH63 heading west, through countless acres of vineyards stretching from the mighty Wairau River on our right to the foothills of the Kaikoura Mountains on our left. It was a long, straight and somewhat boring road, only slightly enlivened when we nearly rode at top speed into a thousand sheep that appeared out of the distant heat haze as a shimmering white mirage and suddenly solidified into a heaving sea of woolly bodies. We'd passed from wine country back into sheep country again and got the full lanolin-pong treatment as we stopped and the huge flock poured around us, urged on by two shepherds on quad bikes and a trio of flat-eared, industrious collies.

We stopped at the next hamlet, Wairau Valley, which consisted of a fuel station, a few houses and the Wairau Valley Tavern. When I searched around the back of the latter and found the proprietress she said it was closed, but she would gladly make coffee for two thirsty travellers, no problem. Two young lads from the house next door were delighted to find a pair of motorcycles stopped in their remote rural neighbourhood and came over to check us out. One proudly displayed a wild boar's jawbone. He shot the animal himself, he said, while out hunting with his dad in the bush below the Fishtail Mountain, which he pointed out among the jagged teeth of the Richmond Range to the north.

With our hot jackets removed, the mid-morning sun burned into our bare arms. The sky in New Zealand can be astonishingly clear and dark blue overhead, as though you are staring straight into space. So we drank up and made to leave, but I couldn't find the lady again. She was upstairs in her rambling inn with music blaring and a vacuum cleaner wheezing. So I put $4 into one of the empty mugs and we struggled back into our hot and sweaty jackets and helmets and were just swinging legs over our machines when she reappeared to say goodbye. I indicated the money in the mug but she refused any payment, thrust the coins back into my gloved hand and ignored my plea to pay her! Now I ask you: What pub owner in the UK would gladly make you coffee when the place is closed and then refuse payment? We were impressed once again by NZ's big-hearted hospitality.

After St Arnaud we decided to take the back-country route to Murchison, where we planned to stay once again at the Kiwi Park Motel. At Gowanbridge we turned off SH6 on to a trail leading to the Tutaki Conservation area and stopped beside the pretty Gowan River for a picnic lunch. Lake Rotoroa, a few kilometres further south, was infested with biting insects, so we didn't dally and took the gravel road to Tutaki, Mangles Valley and Longford.

The Braeburn Track, as this is called, was a delightful gravel and dirt road, pleasantly hard-packed for motorcycle wheels and narrow and twisty to keep the ride fun. We rode through dense stands of trees, between fields and through four stream crossings. These fords were not too taxing, but deep enough to soak our trousers and boots if taken at more than walking pace. The latter part of the Braeburn was on wide and slippery gravel farm roads past fields of sheep and cows before rejoining the main road, now SH6, just before Murchison.

We were welcomed once again at Kiwi Park by Maurice Horner, but we were somewhat startled by his appearance. Maurice is a rootin', tootin', huntin' 'n' fishin' sort of chap - a grizzly bear with a wicked grin and a sense of humour to match - so we were a little taken aback when he appeared behind the office counter dressed only in a fluffy pink towel. He'd been 'chillin' out' in the park's modest outdoor swimming pool. He'd promised his wife Christine that he'd be properly dressed and on duty when she went off to work after lunch - she's a nurse at the local hospital - but it was a hot afternoon, the pool was great, and nobody would turn up before 3pm, surely!

Fast gravel farm roads before the twisty Braeburn Track

He tossed us the keys to unit 13, the 'tourist flat', give us a carton of milk and told us to make ourselves at home. No problem. This was the same comfy cabin we'd had before, which Maurice told us was: *'Like the motel, but $10 cheaper and without Sky TV and the Swedish blonde!'* Viv assured him I didn't need either and bundled me off to unpack.

Maurice was right. It really was a baking hot afternoon. We stripped off our riding gear, hopped into swimming cozzies and headed back for the pool. The water was too cool for Viv, who prefers it to be a steamy 30 degrees, but I soaked away the heat of the day for ten minutes, until Maurice's son and friends decided I needed livening up with a few bombs and torpedo dives.

The tui sang in the trees outside while we unpacked, washed clothes and then... yes you guessed it... it rained. What is it with this country's weather? Still, it cooled things down and the pavements had dried before we walked into town for supper at the Mid-West Café for just NZ$12 (£3.50) each. A stroll down to the mighty Buller River took us past two great old 19th century buildings, the Murchison Theatre and Commercial Stables, and feeling suitably nostalgic we stopped for coffee at the Commercial Tavern, which has its history from 1880 displayed on the walls in photographs.

It had turned into a balmy evening, so we walked back down Fairfax Street, past the Kiwi Park, to see if the guy in the last bungalow on the right was still playing his guitar. He'd delighted us with his music last time we were in Murchison and it sounded like he was getting even better. But his dad obviously didn't think so. While we were loitering beyond the fence a door slammed, an engine revved and a middle aged man roared out of the gate in a Land Rover and gunned it down the street.

The last of the day's sunshine lit up the surrounding hills and created a fabulously bright rainbow over to the east, where we would be riding the Rainbow Road in two days time. It seemed like a good omen.

Friday December 21st. It was the shortest day in the northern hemisphere and the longest day here in New Zealand. We packed in brilliant sunshine but left our bags with Maurice while we rode off to explore the Matakitaki Track to the south. After a few kilometres the tarseal gave way to a twisty metalled road with rock hard surface and fine, dusty gravel on top, which made it very slippery. In fact, I thought my front wheel would skid from underneath me at every turn and was going so slowly that Viv wondered what was troubling me, as she wasn't finding the surface a problem at all.

'Well obviously,' I said, 'your bike's steering, handling and roadholding must be better than mine.'

So we swapped, Viv went in front on my bike and promptly disappeared into the distance while I continued to flounder on the dodgy gravel on hers. Well poo! I reluctantly had to admit that Viv had become the faster, more confident rider on these loose surface roads. While she, in her usual self-effacing way, said she probably didn't realise she was about to crash.

The track took us through dark forest with glimpses between the trees of the beautiful blue Matakitaki River, and on to open fast stretches. Past Six Mile, the site of New Zealand's oldest hydro-power scheme and down to Horse Terrace Bridge, where the old Mammoth Hotel used to stand when 2,000 Chinamen lived here in the gold rush days. Now the gold and the Chinamen are long gone and just a farmstead remains. The bridge itself spans a narrow rocky gorge where the restricted waters of the Matakitaki boil through below.

After the bridge the rough road doubles back on the other side of the river, but we decided to take a detour and diverted south down the Glenroy Track. This quiet, narrow farm track twists for about ten kilometres through lovely pasture land, past fields of grazing cows and alongside the startlingly opal-blue Glenroy River into the heart of New Zealand hill farm country. Like most roads in these remote areas, the Glenroy Track is a dead-end road, reaching deep into picture-postcard countryside to provide access for a homestead. But no-one minds you riding your motorbike down them. No irate farmers waving shotguns, as you might get in parts of Britain. In fact, folk are genuinely pleased to see you.

Back at the Matakitaki River, we turned left to pick up the trail to the Maruia Saddle Road. This was very different, a narrow, winding, bumpy track which climbed steadily between trees and alongside precipitous drops to our left. We noticed that the path was strewn with tiny red leaves, undisturbed before we arrived, so few vehicles pass this way. We hadn't see one since leaving Murchison.

In places the track carved a tunnel beneath huge overhangs where grass and tree roots supported a ceiling of loose rock above our heads, and the trail became even more narrow, rocky and bumpy as we reached the saddle. The descent forded six streams, three of them quite deep and one fairly tricky with soft sand and boulders, before we reached three homesteads at Frog Flat and the hamlet of Burnbrae, where we picked up SH65 for the ride back north towards Murchison.

We decided that Maurice could babysit our luggage a little while longer and detoured to the 'Buller Gorge Swingbridge - Adventure & Heritage Park'. The Adventure consisted of a mildly daunting but impressively long swingbridge (a swingbridge in New Zealand is a wobbly, wire-suspended bridge, unlike the British swing bridge, which pivots to allow ships to pass), followed by the 'Comet Line', a wire ride back across the swirling waters and rocks of the Buller river. We didn't feel the need to strap ourselves into a harness and hurtle across the gorge dangling from a thin wire, and instead indulged in the Heritage part of the park instead.

On the far side of the swingbridge lies the site of White's Creek Faultline, epicentre of the 1929 Murchison Earthquake in which the ground rose 4 metres, plus the shafts of old mine workings. Having read that the Buller still has gold in its sediment I dug in the coarse sand by the water's edge and found some sparkly flecks, which helped justify the bites from large black sandflies which I collected at the same time.

Back at the little cafeteria we discovered Viv's helmet had lost one of its visor locking buttons, leaving the visor flapping free and useless. This was a disaster. Without it the visor would have to be removed completely, limiting Viv to half-speed riding. It could have fallen off absolutely anywhere, but on a hunch I returned to the carpark with fingers and toes crossed, and found the button beneath Viv's bike. Deep joy!

It was now early afternoon and the sun had been growing steadily more ferocious, melting the tar of the road on our way back to Murchison. There we collected our luggage from Maurice, who thankfully had his clothes on this time, before heading east for St Arnaud. The sun was blindingly bright, even behind sunglasses, and the sky spotless navy blue. But as we approached St Arnaud, in the distance ahead was a single black cloud with a solid black curtain beneath it which blotted out the landscape. As we drew closer it became obvious we couldn't avoid this seriously scary-looking lump of weather, so we stopped to put on waterproofs.

One kilometre later we rode into a solid wall of water quite unlike anything we had ever seen before. Barely able to see through the deluge, we puttered into St Arnaud on roads awash with water up to a foot deep to find most of the population sheltering under the canopy of the village fuel station-cum-store. The noise of the rain hammering on the frail roof prevented speech - I couldn't even hear my motorbike engine running - but within ten minutes the monsoon had passed and the waterfall stopped abruptly, as if God had turned off the tap.

We were soaked through, of course. We couldn't have been any wetter if we'd jumped into the Buller on the way. But there was only another five kilometres to go to Tophouse, our accommodation for the night. Mac and Gladys Hollick ignored our sodden, dishevelled state and showed us to one of their 'Cosyview Cottages', four modern wooden cabins behind their historic 1887 hotel where they provide B&B, restaurant and tearooms.

We declined their invitation to join their other guests for a meal in the restaurant, as we had food with us which was now more than a little damp and unlikely to survive another day of bouncing around inside a hot pannier. But we did join the Hollicks and their guests for coffee and a chat later, plus a guided tour of the old building and a resumé of its colourful history - most notably a double murder and suicide in 1903.

Then I made the mistake of asking Mac if, after the recent rain, he thought it would be okay for us to tackle the Rainbow Road, our off-road riding epic planned for the next day. He said it was unlikely that even 4WD vehicles would be able to get through for a few days, as the rivers were all up and more rain was forecast overnight. Viv, bless her cotton socks, replied bravely that we were looking for a challenge, but I have to admit that his comments - especially coming from a local who ran the closest guest accommodation to the Rainbow Road - had unnerved me.

Chapter 9

The Rainbow Road

I struggled to find sleep, what with the sound of rain drumming on the thin cabin roof and disturbing visions of swollen, raging torrents looking much like Nelson's Maitai River in spate.

Riding the Rainbow Road had long been planned as our major wilderness expedition for this first part of our travels. It consists of approximately 100km of farm track, most of it designated 4WD-only, through some of the most remote and deserted land of the South Island. From St Arnaud in the north it runs alongside the headwaters of the Wairau River, the same Wairau we'd crossed near Renwick two days earlier, through a gorge, over the Island Saddle at its mid-point and then along the Clarence River valley to Jollies Pass and Hanmer Springs. Apart from a farmhouse near the start, where we were told we would pay to be allowed past a locked gate, there were no houses, no people and no help should we get into difficulties. This was what we'd come for, the long wild roads of New Zealand, a venture into the unknown. I just hoped I hadn't overestimated our abilities.

I had two main concerns: The first was the numerous river crossings we'd have to tackle. If we didn't drown, there was a very real risk of one of the fully-laden bikes toppling over in a stream and ingesting water or soaking the electrics, either of which would leave us stranded. The one remaining bike could not carry two loads of luggage and two people.

The other worry was petrol. We'd filled up in Murchison, but that was 75km back. We were perhaps five kilometres from the start of the Rainbow, and it was approximately 100km long. It was hard to tell from the map. One person had told me it was 115km. Our bikes could do about 180km to a tankful on the road, but would they use more fuel in low gear over rough going? I didn't know. If we ran out before we reached Hanmer Springs we were stuck. The sensible thing to do was back-track to St Arnaud and top up the tanks at the fuel station there, but something stopped me going.

The stupid thing was, there were two plastic fuel cans strapped to the rack of Viv's bike - both empty. I had this fleeting image of a NZ Wilderness Rescue vehicle pulled up next to two rusting motorcycles and two piles of bones. One Ranger was saying to the other: *'Jeez mate, they rode out here into the bush carrying two impty fuel cans. How stupid can you git?'*

Sleep eventually shut down my lurid imagination and we woke to a damp and misty morning, but no rain. Across the valley echoed the haunting cry of the New Zealand magpie, a *'quardle, oodle, ardle, wardle'* song that sounds like two birds singing in harmony. We decided it was a another good omen for the day's mission ahead.

As the clouds lifted up the mountains and a watery sun lit up distant peaks, Viv packed all our luggage for the umpteenth time and I gave our bikes a thorough check over. Viv's Serow had already lost one machine screw from its exhaust cover, so I tightened all nuts, bolts and screws using the bike's tiny toolkit, then topped up the oils and lubed the chains. After more than 3,500km of roads, tracks and trails since we set off from Christchurch almost a month before, the bikes were still in great shape.

I wished I could say the same for myself. My sore throat had diminished slightly, but now I had the trots and a sore bum - not ideal for spending a day bouncing over potholed tracks on a hard, narrow motorcycle seat. If Viv felt less than 100 percent she wouldn't admit it. The discovery the previous day that she was the faster off-road rider, despite my 30-plus years of biking experience, had put an extra twinkle in her eye, and she couldn't wait to get started on the Rainbow Road.

I went to settle up with the Hollicks and was somewhat dischuffed to be charged $90 (£26) after being quoted $80 (£23) when I booked two days previously.

'Oh no, it's $90 now, $80 is our low season rate, sorry,' said Gladys.

Frankly this was a bit steep for a rather basic cabin that was none too clean inside and in need of maintenance for its seized up windows and cranky loo. But at that precise moment my grumbling tummy told me that this was not the time to stand and argue, so I paid up grudgingly and trotted back swiftly to use up the rest of the toilet roll. That showed 'em!

The first 17km of the Rainbow Road were undulating tarseal through pine forest, but at the turnoff for the Rainbow Skifield the hard surface ended with a sign warning that the road ahead was suitable for 4WD vehicles only. Ignoring the fact that we had only one wheel drive vehicles, we continued over a gravelly metalled surface, dodging deep potholes hidden in the shadows of the trees, and on through shallow fords, with no sign of the raging flood waters Mac had predicted.

Eventually we came to a gate, a house and people! This was the Rainbow Station, where Mrs Graham and her children relieved us of $10 (£2.85) per bike for the use of their road (it's $20 for cars, ha, ha). At the same time a chap in a hefty 4WD pickup was coming through from the other direction and reported the streams were all passable, although there were many potholes and washouts to look out for. I think this latter comment was directed at Mrs Graham, as he'd just paid $20 for the privilege of being jolted and shaken senseless on her road. But while potholes are a nuisance for most vehicle drivers on a single track road, they don't bother us bikers, as we can usually go around or between them, or stand up on the footrests to let the bike bounce without shortening our spines.

The knowledge that a vehicle had just come through allowed some of my worries to evaporate. There was just the small matter of fuel. Our trip counters now read 107km since the last fill and I estimated Hanmer Springs must be another 90km to the south. Let's see now - 197km on a 180km fuel tank range? Mmm, interesting!

As we set off Mrs Graham shouted that we might see two cyclists who went through the previous day. Well, blimey, if cyclists could do it, we should have no problems, surely?

Rattling along beside the Wairau, the scenery became more hilly and the vegetation more scrubby. By noon we had crossed the river's crystal blue waters via a long and half-rotten wooden bridge, seeing dark shapes of trout dart away from our shadows between the rattly planks. The road was ideal for our bikes, not too gravelly, and wound ever higher into steeper mountains and more sparse vegetation. At the Wairau Gorge the river had cut a deep and narrow cleft into the rock and our track twisted under rocky overhangs, slimming dramatically in places where washouts had dropped half the road into the swirling waters below.

There were more fords through smaller streams, but these were mostly shallow, if rocky, and could be tackled with confidence after a pre-splash recce. Bridges carried us across the river twice more, the last crossing of the rapidly dwindling Wairau letting the road double back and climb towards the Island Saddle nestling between Mt Dora (2,202 metres) and Mt Sebastopol (2,013 metres). The air was thinner and cooler here, but the long straights allowed us to tackle the climb confidently at 50kph with only the occasional big pothole to watch out for.

It was possible to spot these holes early by a change in colour, the yellow clay being visible where wheels had bashed through the darker gravel surface. It also helped to stand up on the footrests, as the extra elevation enabled us to see where the deepest holes were and then weave around them. This was also a good excuse for me to ease my sore backside.

On the way down from the saddle we caught up with one of the cyclists, a very slender girl on a mountain bike, well laden with camping gear. I slowed and called over:

'Hi, howya goin'?' (I was really getting into the local dialect by now).

She was relieved to be on a downgrade after the long and arduous climb to the saddle, she said. Her boyfriend was up ahead and they planned to stop at Lake Tennyson overnight. I told her we would be there for lunch and perhaps they'd join us? Then I raced on to catch up with her fella. He was about five kilometres ahead, off his bike and waiting at the turnoff for the lake.

I pulled up alongside him and said, 'Hiya! Are you waiting for a girl on a bicycle?'

'Yeah, she's right behind me I think,' he said, stretching his neck and peering back up the trail.

'Well, I've got bad news,' I said, 'She's five kilometres back there with a broken wheel. Can't even push her bike as the wheel's jammed in the frame. I said I'd come and let you know she's stranded.'

'Oh Jeez!' he said, and started to turn his cycle around for the long climb back up the hill. I steadied him with a hand on his shoulder.

'Nah. I'm only joking - she's fine! She'll be along in a few minutes. Just winding you up mate.'

Now he could see me laughing inside my helmet and broke into a big smile himself.

'Oh, right. Nice one! You had me goin' for a minute there.'

'We're stopping by the lake for lunch. I hope you'll come and join us so I can apologise properly,' I said. And they did.

Ted Lewis and Shelley Trevaskis were from Australia and were cycling around New Zealand with no time limit, they told us. They were both thin as rakes and had massive appetites due to the million or so calories they each burned off every day cycling up impossible mountains. Snag is, you can only carry so much food on a bicycle when you also have to bring your tent, sleeping bag, clothes, cooking equipment etc. We gave them our spare loaf of bread and apples, since it would be 36 hours before they reached civilisation and we would be there by tea-time. They ravenously stoked up with sandwiches thickly spread with peanut butter, slices of banana and drizzled with honey. High energy food for high energy people.

Ted said they were hoping to catch a trout from the lake for their supper. What do they eat, I wondered to myself as I opened a triple-choc Cookie Time cookie, if they don't catch one? Beats me, I decided, as I munched away. Well, you've got to draw the line somewhere and handing over my cookie could cause me sleepless nights, trembling of the extremities and severe depression. Better not take the risk, I reckoned.

Despite these moral dilemmas, we had a great time with our new friends, who'd forgiven me for the broken wheel joke, if not the cookie, and we left them and headed off at 3pm alongside the Clarence River. The track here was very dry and dusty, and Viv, who insisted on riding behind me, quickly looked like a ghost. I speeded up to put some distance between us, so the dust might not choke her quite so much, but Viv knew she could match or better my speed, so she speeded up too. I speeded up, she speeded up. Soon we were hurtling along at 80kph along the loose and lumpy track as it weaved through the barren and rugged landscape.

There were cattle grazing along the thin strip of vegetation near the riverbed and an Australasian Hawk circling overhead, fingertip feathers outstretched and white tail flashing. The young calves had obviously never seen a motorcycle before, and stood in the road transfixed by the noisy plume of dust approaching, with a flickering headlight at the front and strange helmet-head above. At 20 metres off they suddenly took fright and dashed for the safety of their mum's wall-like flanks, peering from beneath her neck with furry faces of wonderment.

At Duncan's Creek we were faced with a choice: There was both bridge and ford. The bridge seemed a bit sissy, so I wobbled through the ford, which was wider, deeper and rockier than the others we'd crossed that day. Viv, with an 'anything you can do' expression, followed, but hesitated mid-stream and ended up paddling in the deep water which filled her boots. We flopped on to the grass to laugh and dry out her socks in the sun. The giggles turned to snores and we woke up ten minutes later with bright red and tender faces. Despite the thin cloud up high, the sun in New Zealand takes no prisoners, and we were both mildly burned.

Back on track we made short work of the fast and straight dirt road for the next ten kilometres before we joined the deeply-gravelled Jacks Pass road near the Amuri Skifield. This was really slippery and unnerving, so I decided we'd take the un-metalled Jollies Pass around Mt Isobel. This was a mistake, as by now Viv was too tired to summon up the concentration and confidence needed to tackle this steep, rutted and rocky climb. She made it to the saddle okay, but when I stopped at the top to admire the view, she pulled alongside in tears.

'It's *too difficult!*' she sobbed, '*I can't do it any more!*' and pulled off her helmet so the tears could flow freely.

I was really sorry. I had no idea this difficult climb would prove too much at the end of a long day's riding. But words were useless. All I could do was hug her until the sobbing and shaking had stopped. I was cross with myself. Viv had done so well today - at least 95km of gravel tracks, loose shale, potholes and streams. She'd ridden so faultlessly and confidently, it was easy to forget she was also a middle-aged mother of three, a grandmother, and only started riding three years before. I must not ask too much of her again, I decided.

I suddenly realised that I was feeling wiped out too. I'd ridden almost all of the Rainbow Road standing up. Partly to avoid the worst of the bumps and holes, partly to ease my sore and blistered backside. Now that we'd stopped for five minutes my legs were trembling, my arms felt like lead and my shoulders ached.

'I'm okay. I'm okay now,' said Viv huskily, as she fished in her jacket pocket for another tissue to blow her nose.

'Well, we're almost in Hanmer Springs now, Sweetheart,' I said. *'It's steep and a bit bumpy going down the hill, but if we stay in first gear and go really slowly, I'm sure you'll be all right.'*

Actually, there was not much choice: Ride down or spend the night on the top of Jollie's Pass. By the time we rolled into the Forest Peak Motel and climbed wearily off the bikes it was 6pm. We were both dog tired and very dusty. I checked in and got the key for our unit, but as I lifted the heavy panniers off the bikes I felt ashamed at the thick layers of dust on them and decided I ought to try to beat the worst of it off before carrying them into the clean and carpeted lounge.

A quick hunt for a suitable implement turned up a magazine beneath the TV. Rolled up it made an ideal luggage-beater and I was well into bashing clouds of dust off the second set of panniers when the motel owner's wife walked past. I looked up and smiled in mid-beat, hoping she would be impressed to see I was trying to keep the dust outside her neat motel room.

'Is that my Sky book?' she asked, icily.

I looked down at the shredded remnants of the magazine in my fist and unrolled it.

'Er, I think it's a TV magazine,' I answered, stupidly.

'*Yeah! My Sky book,*' she repeated, testily. '*Don't you spoil it or I'll get you to buy a new one!*' And she turned on her heel and stormed off.

'*Well, bugger me!*' I said under my breath, as Viv came out in her socks to see what the altercation was all about.

'*Try to do the woman a favour by keeping the dust out of her motel room, and she tells me off for creasing her sodding TV magazine,*' I spluttered.

'*There's no pleasing some people,*' said Viv with a smile, quoting one of our favourite lines from 'The Life of Brian' film.

Like most other children, I don't much care for being told off, even when I'm in the wrong, as I clearly was in this case. So I consoled myself by making up childish jokes about the lady and her husband. This wasn't too difficult, as their names were Janet and John. By the time we had showered and changed and were ready to hit the bright lights of Hanmer Springs, we'd misappropriated nearly every innocent lesson from the famous Early Reader Books of the same name. And felt much better.

Actually, bright lights were notable by their absence in town that evening, so we plumped for PJ's Pizza Place and enjoyed our BYO wines and their superb gourmet pizzas. In fact, I was so impressed with the economy of the BYO concept that I was experimenting with the theory that enough wine poured in one end must surely anaesthetise the extremely sore parts at the other. So far all I'd noticed was that my lips had gone slightly numb and seemed to be stuck in the silly grin position.

But hey, I thought, give it time and peristalsis should ensure a smile at the other end too. It was at this moment, just as I was giggling over yet more Janet and John jokes, but couldn't remember them long enough to tell them to Viv, that she noticed that a couple we'd chatted to over coffee at Tophouse the night before had just walked into the restaurant. We invited them to join us and I so impressed them with my wit and repartee that Viv soon explained that it was way past my bedtime and she had to take me back to the motel in order to beat me over the head with a rolled up TV magazine.

Getting used to the bikes,
just off Summit Road, Banks Peninsula

Yamaha XT225 Serows loaded up and ready to roll in Christchurch.

Maungatapu Track.
Bob fords a stream on the way to Pelorus Bridge.

Pohutukawa trees on the Coromandel Peninsula.

Charming wooden cabin at the Matakohe Motor Camp.

Crossing the Wairau River on the Rainbow Road.

Ice-blue Wairau River seen from the Kaituna Road near Renwick

Ted Lewis and Shelley Trevaskis met on the Rainbow Road

Early Kiwi campervan spotted at Mount Somers

1866 Chinese gold miner's stone cottage, Moa Creek.

View from Moa Creek cottage door.

The blue Clutha River at Alexandra.

Waiting to board the TSS Earnslaw at Queenstown.

*No footprints in the golden sand at
Horseshoe Bay, Stewart Island.*

*Viv at Lee Bay, Stewart Island at the start of the Garden
Mound Track.*

Well, that's what it felt like next morning anyway. And my sore bum didn't appear to have responded too well to the anaesthesia treatment either. In fact, the thought of getting back on my motorbike made it quite easy to keep a straight face when I went to pay Janet and John.

Viv was determined not the leave Hanmer Springs this time without first trying out the famous hot spa pools. I sat outside the Log Cabin café keeping an eye on the bikes and luggage, while she went for a steamy soak and swim. While Viv was turning white and wrinkly I met Jari Karjalainen and Katri Tolonen who turned up on a Suzuki 1200 Bandit. As their names might suggest, Jari and Katri are Finnish, but they had been living in Wellington for seven months, Jari working for TAB bookmakers and Katri at university, and they had no intention of returning to Finland again.

New Zealand welcomes young, skilled or educated people and applying for citizenship had been no problem, they said. I watched their bike and luggage while they too went for a dip, and then advised Jari to jack up his bike's rear suspension when he complained that it weaved in bends with the extra weight of their luggage on board.

Satisfied that I'd done my good deed for the day to make up for yesterday's misdemeanours, we mounted up and headed south for Christchurch. As we rode out of Hanmer Springs the first right hand bend had a great long trail of diesel spilled and splashed over the tarseal in a long weaving ribbon of disaster. I spotted it, moved to the centreline and pointed down at the road, hoping Viv would see it too. A check in my mirrors - she did, good girl!

Diesel spills can skittle a motorcycle without warning, so it was essential to keep our tyres away from the lubricant fuel. Every right hand bend was the same. Some dumb truck driver had left the filler cap off his fuel tank. We were especially careful on the last twisty bends before the one-way bridge over the gorge high above the Hanmer River. The bridge itself needs treating with extreme caution by motorcyclists, as it is both narrow and long, and has obscuring bends at both ends. A British biker who had right of way was killed in a head-on collision with a van on a similar one-way bridge while we were in Nelson. It reminded me of the little poem Dad taught me when I was first learning to drive:

Here lies the body of Paddy O'Shea
Who died defending his right of way
He was right, dead right all along
But he's just as dead as if he'd been wrong

In our first month on antipodean roads we'd twice had to pull up sharply to avoid collision with a vehicle which had ignored a Give Way sign. I don't think Kiwi drivers have any murderous intent. More likely they see so few other vehicles on their roads they're not used to having to make allowances for them.

After Britain's crowded roads, New Zealand's wonderfully empty blacktop is a delight (Auckland excepted, of course), but we learned to be doubly cautious when we did meet another vehicle, or when one came up behind us, as they frequently didn't have any idea how to manoeuvre or overtake safely.

The diesel slick preceded us all the way through Culverden until it trailed into the verge. Had the driver realised his mistake, or had he been pulled over by another motorist or the police? No matter, the danger was past and we could enjoy the lovely sweeping curves after Hurunui that were designated 75kph on their warning signs, and which we took flat out at 100kph on our little bikes - great fun.

Through Weka Pass, past Frog Rock and other unusual limestone rock formations, we rejoined SH1 at Waipara and found lots of holiday traffic heading south for Christmas. Lunch was a picnic sitting on pebbles in the almost-dry Kowai River bed, while 4WDs, quad bikes and lads in a cut-down Ford Escort blasted past. I checked on my map. Sure enough, the Kowai River is classed as a 4WD track and, with the water as low as this, there's plenty of room for Kiwis to do their thing on a Sunday afternoon.

At 3pm we rolled down the driveway of John and Jill's hillside home to a huge welcome of hugs and smiles and excited chatter. It was time to take a Christmas break from our travels and I for one (and my bum in particular) was looking forward to having a rest from motorcycling for a few days.

We'd slept in 20 different beds, covered 4,000 kilometres, witnessed stunning scenery, met some lovely people and experienced extraordinary weather in the past month. Some of that weather was still in Viv's boots, which had never dried out completely since the first monsoon we ran into in the North Island. My bodge with the melted candle wax couldn't hide the fact that these boots were fit for slinging. On Christmas Eve we rode into the city and while NZ Motorcycle Rentals serviced the Yamahas we shopped for a few last-minute Christmas pressies, and I treated Viv to a new pair of boots.

Christmas shopping in the middle of summer seemed weird to us, with 'Jingle Bells' ringing out down the streets while shoppers in shorts and T-shirts tried to keep out of the fierce midday sun. The fake snow and dancing Santas in shop windows sat between surfboards, bikinis and snorkels and the North Pole seemed half a world away.

One poor soul had drawn the short straw and was dressed in full Father Christmas costume, complete with long white beard and red floppy hat, and was handing out shop fliers in the centre of Cathedral Square. How many minutes he'd last in the 30 degree heat before the paramedics were called we didn't wait to find out. We had to get back 'home' to pack sunhats and swimming cozzies for a unique Christmas holiday with John and Jill in the heart of Banks Peninsula.

For the next two days and nights we stayed at the harbourside bach of Jill's cousins, Richard and Philippa. At this peaceful retreat we had stunning views across the sparkling blue waters to Akaroa, with dolphins swimming past, exhilarating climbs to the peaks of the ancient volcanic rim above us, and in between times feasted royally thanks to Jill's exemplary culinary skills.

On Christmas morning we attended a wonderful service in the tiny wooden church at Wainui, singing hymns and Christmas Carols, and after we finished up with 'Little Donkey' I walked out into the sunshine with a lump in my throat. We'd got the festive spirit easily enough and now we felt that special Christmas magic too.

Among the other side trips and explorations we managed to pack in to our two-day holiday, was a glimpse into a tiny slice of New Zealand's history when we drove to Peraki Bay, where Jill's great-grandfather, Frederick Anson had lived and farmed from 1876 to 1905.

Due to the rugged nature of the volcanic slopes which formed Peraki Valley and the impenetrable native bush which filled its upper half, Anson and his working partner Francis Snow had to be landed from a sailing ship on the beach at Peraki Bay.

Over the years Anson and Snow hacked a zig-zag road out of the dense forest at the head of their valley so they could reach the ridge high above them, and following that great endeavour they cut another road down to Wainui on the Akaroa Harbour shoreline, so they could get their livestock to the market and obtain supplies more easily. The roads they made, Peraki Road and Jubilee Road (so named because they completed it during Queen Victoria's jubilee year) were the roads we drove down to reach this peaceful homestead, with its broad beach still littered with enormous whalebones, testament to an even earlier time, when ships used Peraki Bay as a whaling station before the colonisation began.

That's the thing with New Zealand's history. It's all recent, accessible and tangible. The fact that you can touch it - even smell and taste it in places - makes it all the more colourful and vibrant.

Next day, back in Christchurch, I could not put off any longer a trip to see the doctor. I still had something amiss in the pants department. I won't go into detail - for all I know you might be planning to eat later - but it had to do with a ring of fire which had erupted right where the sun don't shine.

This was going to prove less than ideal for the long days ahead spent bouncing and wriggling around on a hard and narrow motorcycle seat. No matter how well developed your thigh muscles, you can't ride standing up on the footrests forever. Something had to be done.

In my experience, developing an affliction of a deeply personal and sensitive nature while abroad provides an ideal

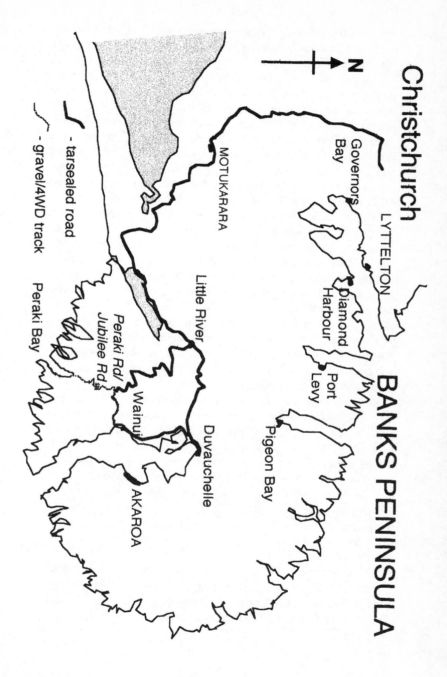

Christchurch

BANKS PENINSULA

N

— tarsealed road

— gravel/4WD track

LYTTELTON

Governors Bay

Diamond Harbour

Port Levy

Pigeon Bay

MOTUKARARA

Little River

Peraki Rd/ Jubilee Rd

Peraki Bay

Wainui

Duvauchelle

AKAROA

opportunity for acute embarrassment or deep hilarity, depending which side of the dispensing counter you're standing.

Many years ago, after a long and gruelling drive with three large children in a very small car to my sister's house in the Dordogne, I arrived to find I had developed haemorrhoids. Not being especially gifted when it comes to speaking French, and harbouring serious doubts about my ability to get the message across to a local doctor - he might misunderstand and take my leg off or something - I was prepared to spend our week-long visit moaning and wincing and standing up a lot.

But sister Sue would have none of it. In her no-nonsense, school headmistress manner, she bustled me off to the 'farmacie' in the next town. As we entered the door my heart sank. This was clearly the preferred meeting place for most of the female population. There were at least a dozen in there, all gossiping about their families' and neighbours' latest medical minutiae, no doubt.

The door closed with a jingling bell, the conversation stopped and all eyes turned to the strangers who'd just stepped in. The white-coated lady pharmacist, who was deep in conversation with three women at the counter, looked up and said: *'Oui?'* I could have, easily.

If I'd been on my own, I'd have replied: *'Non!'* and bolted. But Sue's hand between my shoulder-blades propelled me up to the counter, where I stood panic-stricken and paralysed. My mouth had gone dry, my face bright red and I was struck dumb. There was no way I could summon up from my schoolboy French the words to describe what was wrong with my bottom. A fevered vision of me dropping my trousers and pointing to the problem was just flashing through my mind when Sue spoke up loudly:

'Avez vous une quelque chose pour les 'emerrroids pour mon frére ici?'

I swear that all the ladies took a step closer. I could have died. At this point the pharmacist could have spared me further humiliation. She could have simply reached for the most expensive pile treatment, doubled the price with a

Gallic smirk, then had an uproarious laugh with all the women the second we'd gone.

But no, there was to be no easy escape from this torment. Instead she picked up half a dozen different tubs, tubes and packets from the shelf behind her and arranged them on the counter. The ladies all took another step closer and craned their heads to see. I was surrounded. I couldn't escape a further, vicious twist of this agony.

She spoke to my sister who translated for my benefit and for the amusement of all present. Did I want an ointment, a cream or a gel? Did I want to apply it externally or internally? To illustrate her point, she withdrew a long tube from one of the boxes and held it up like an instrument of torture. Or would I like to go for *'les suppositoires'*?

My mind was reeling. I swear I could hear the sound of blood boiling in my ears. I couldn't for the life of me think what *'les suppositoires'* meant until Sue jogged my memory with vigorous upward jabbing motions with her extended index finger.

I tried to speak, but nothing decipherable in either English or French would come out. The women all shuffled closer - then a younger one spoke up:

'Ze English don't like suppositoires,' she said. Then, switching to a perfect imitation of mid-Essex English: *'Zey say - 'Oh no! I don't want it up me bum!''*

Sue and I burst out laughing and all the tension evaporated. It's perfectly true of course. As a nation, we Brits are disinclined to adopt the continental habit of administering our medications anally. We've all heard that an innuendo is an Italian suppository, but we don't wish to try it, thank you very much. Clearly this French lady had witnessed our funny Anglic ano-phobia first hand. I had an image of an exchange student from Brentwood uttering the exact words she had just repeated, laced with shock and revulsion. There was only one choice now. I bought the suppositories. And very tasty they were too.

Back in Christchurch, I was determined not to let my current ring of fire cause me similar embarrassment. I submitted to an examination by a young doctor and purchased the prescribed ointment without blushing. Within a couple of days I was able to walk without imitating John Wayne and ride without tears. Sheer bliss.

Chapter 10

The Big Crash

It's Friday December 28th. The bikes have been serviced and fettled, my nether regions are on the mend, we've eaten all John and Jill's food - must be time to get back on the road again!

In return for all the gastronomic delights Jill had created for us over the past few days, we had responded the previous evening the only way we knew how - with takeaway pizzas. What these lacked in subtlety they made up for in quantity. In fact Jill had announced she was *'totally stonkered'* before she had barely made a dent in her dustbin-lid sized pizza, and with blueberry custard crumble and ice cream to follow, the rest of us left large slices of first course too.

This enabled Viv to fulfil one of her more wacky ambitions when we set off next day: to ride a motorcycle with a pizza on the back. She didn't play the role of pizza-delivery biker for long, however, as our first day's journey was to include a very long off-road expedition and after the close run thing on the Rainbow Road, when we coasted into Hanmer on little more than fumes, I was determined to carry spare fuel.

The empty fuel cans, for some strange reason, always got strapped to the rack of Viv's bike, while the big rucksack seemed to fit better on mine. After both fuel cans were filled up along with our bikes' tanks that morning, the pizza box was transferred to my rack, underneath the rucksack and the now heavy fuel cans were strapped securely to Viv's bike. It seemed like a good idea at the time, but would have unfortunate consequences before the day was over.

For this second expedition we planned to explore the South Island's West Coast, which promised wild and spectacular scenery, with glaciers tumbling down from the snow-capped Southern Alps to the sea. There were fewer dirt and gravel trails for us to ride once we crossed over the

great jagged spine of the country, we were told, so at the suggestion of John and Jill, we had cooked up a circular route over unpaved farm roads to get our off-road fix on the first day.

This was no regular trail frequented by adventurous 4WDrivers or even astonishingly-fit Australian cyclists. In fact, part of the track we hoped to ride didn't appear on any of our maps, although Jill assured us it existed. She'd walked a part of it with her tramping club friends, she said, but it would mean getting permission to pass through locked gates on remote sheep stations. So she phoned the two Todhunter families who own Glenfalloch and Upper Lake Heron homesteads, deep in the rugged foothills of the Alps to get their approval. Lambing was now over, even in this high country, and they had no objection to two quiet motorcycles passing through their land. We had to report to the two station farmhouses, tell them who we were, and they'd let us through.

It was about midday by the time we'd covered the 100km heading due west across the Canterbury Plain from Christchurch and crossed the Rakaia Gorge Bridge. Soon after this we found the turn off that would lead us alongside the Rakaia's vast, boulder-strewn upper reaches for 60km or so to reach Glenfalloch Homestead, tucked underneath the Ragged Range with views up the valley to the Lyell and Ramsay Glaciers.

Within ten kilometres the tarseal surface came to an end and the road was then metalled with a deep layer of large granite chippings over a rocky surface. It was treacherous going and our spindly wheels skittered and slithered alarmingly. I was wrestling the handlebars to keep my bike upright when I noticed a large 4WD pickup truck coming the other way at speed, kicking up a cloud of dust. Between us was a bend which was no place to meet an oncoming vehicle, be blinded by dust and showered with flying chunks of granite. So I wobbled to the side of the road, as did Viv 30 metres behind me, and waited until the vehicle had passed and the dust subsided.

Then I got under way again, gunning my little Serow for what I hoped was the shallowest layer of gravel in the bend

131

ahead. Cornering on a bike in deep and loose gravel is a fraught, heart-in-the-mouth experience at the best of times. The trick, in my experience, is to aim for the wheel tracks where the gravel has been pushed aside by car tyres and there's little more than dust covering the hard stone surface.

And keep the throttle open. This latter tactic might sound like a recipe for disaster, but a motorcycle steers much better when accelerating. The front wheel goes light and will lift over bumps and irregularities without being deflected, and the bike can be nudged in the direction you wish to go. Conversely, shutting the throttle transfers weight forward, loads the front wheel, makes steering heavy and risks a horrible front wheel skid.

With this in mind I approached the long, wide bend doing about 30kph and accelerated all the way around it, doing perhaps 50kph by the time the road straightened, where the wheel tracks crisscrossed and ridges of deep gravel could not be avoided. It was a real struggle to keep the bike upright and pointing the right way as both wheels skittered sideways in the deeper piles of chippings, and it was another 100 metres before I found wheel tracks again and dared steal a glance in my mirrors. To my horror, there in a heap lay Viv, trapped beneath her bike.

I turned as quickly as I could on the horrible surface, ploughing through foot-deep mounds of the evil blue lumps of stone, and roared back to help. Viv's left leg was trapped between the rock surface and her overladen bike. I had to unstrap the panniers and remove the two full cans of petrol from the rack before I could heave the Yamaha off the ground and she was able to crawl out and limp painfully to the grass verge.

'*Are you hurt?*' stupid question.

'*I'll be all right in a minute,*' she gasped, taking deep breaths. '*I just need to sit down - I feel dizzy and nauseous.*'

Oh shit. I'd broken bones several times in my early biking career and every time a wave of dizziness and nausea had been the tell-tale sign that something had snapped. My mind started racing with how to raise the alarm, fetch help and get an ambulance to carry her to hospital. Once again we were in the middle of nowhere, with the nearest house at least 20km away.

Lying on her back in the grass, the colour started to return to Viv's face and she assured me I could leave her side for a few seconds while I dragged her bike, panniers and fuel cans out of the roadway. The pickup could come hurtling back down the track at any moment and I had visions of an even bigger disaster unfolding.

As I lifted the two cans of petrol on to the grass I realised just how heavy they were. These two great lumps, strapped far back and high up on Viv's bike's rack, would have upset the normally sweet-handling Serow. Remembering how my bike had twitched and wriggled over the horrible gravel, I could see how this weight would have caused Viv's bike to slew from side to side until she was pitched off. Her crash was my fault. I felt sick too.

By now she was sitting up and after a sip of water said she was ready to get her trousers off and inspect the damage. I unlaced her brand new boots and eased them off her feet. The left boot bore deep gouges on both sides where it had been wedged between the bike's metal footrest and the rocky road. It had undoubtedly saved her ankle and foot from serious injury.

Next off were the overtrousers, holed at the knee where a sharp rock in the road surface had punched through them, then the thin slacks to reveal a bloody hole in her shin just below the knee and ominous dark blue bruising. It looked a very nasty injury to me.

'I don't think I've broken anything,' said Viv, as she gingerly tried to bend the knee. 'But it's very painful.'

We spent the next hour bathing and bandaging the wound. Fortunately we had a small first-aid kit for just such an emergency and were able to apply antiseptic cream, a wound dressing secured with surgical tape, followed by a crepe bandage and finally, held in place by an elastic Tubigrip sleeve, a Bioflow Boost. This last item is a magnotherapy unit produced by the Cornish company I work with. Its four big magnetic modules produce a surprisingly rapid pain-killing effect and we always carry one to treat minor aches and pains. Despite our natural scepticism over such things, we've found this really does work and we wouldn't travel without it.

Fully patched up, Viv tried standing and then a tentative step. She was very sore and stiff, but could hobble a few paces. Apart from the inevitable rash of bruises, now beginning to blossom on her hip, arm, hand, elbow and shoulder, all fairly minor thankfully - she had survived a hefty crash on to a rocky road surface surprisingly well. It was just that leg that really worried me.

Time to inspect her bike and gear. The Serow was a bit scratched and scraped and the nearside indicator lens was broken off but quickly refixed with surgical tape, a repair which would last the next 7,000 kilometres. I was able to straighten out the twisted front forks in the time-honoured fashion, by holding the front wheel between my feet and knees and heaving on the handlebars. After repositioning the clutch lever and mirror and cleaning off the muck and dust, it hardly looked like it had been crashed at all.

Which is more than could be said for Viv's helmet. Its visor was deeply gouged and scraped across the left hand side where it had borne the brunt of Viv's head's contact with the ground. And to think we had planned to wear open face helmets until persuaded to go for full face ones by the bike rental company. An open face helmet, judging by the state of the visor, would have left Viv with a severe facial injury, a thought which made me shudder.

The panniers had come off worst. All the fastenings which attached the bags to the metal frame on the bike had been torn out and one of the broad straps which cross the seat and hold the panniers together had been wrenched off by the impact. I rooted around in the rucksack to find the four extra bungy-straps we'd been carrying since mid-November and was pleased to find they held the panniers on the bike reasonably securely. Knew they'd come in handy one day.

'How do you feel about a slice of cold pizza?' I ventured.

'Mmm, that'd be lovely. This crashing business gives you quite an appetite, doesn't it?' she said cheerfully.

So we polished off the substantial remains of last night's meal, followed by Jill's Christmas cake, biscuits and apricots. And then we felt a lot better. We were even cracking schoolboy jokes of the *"ave a crash mate?' 'No thanks, just 'ad one!'* variety. I reassured Viv that she was now a 'proper' biker, since you can't call yourself a real motorcyclist until you've had a major get off, but secretly I was worried about that leg. I knew from personal experience that being able to bend or even stand on an injured leg is no proof that bones are not broken.

Undeterred, Viv was upright again and testing her leg with hobbling steps. She could walk, after a fashion, and thought she could ride, but bending her knee made the overtrousers press painfully on the injury. Time for another bodge. Out came my penknife to cut down the pizza box lid to make an articulated knee and shin protector. After a few minor adjustments it fitted inside the overtrousers and did a grand job of holding the stretched material away from the knee.

Viv could now sit on her bike, raise her foot up to the footrest and operate the controls. Continuing with our day's off-road mission was out of the question, of course, and understandably she had no desire to ride on the god-awful gravel again. So while she hobbled the half-kilometre back to the tarsealed road I rode her bike there and walked back to fetch my own machine.

Tentatively and slowly we made our way back to the main road. Viv was coping with the reduced-speed riding okay and firmly refused my suggestion that we find a hospital or doctor. So we headed south 30km to Mount Somers where our accommodation had been booked for the night... in a caravan.

The Mount Somers Holiday Park was slightly chaotic and crowded with tents, cabins, motorhomes and a funny old 14-foot touring caravan which was to be our home for the night. Viv was delighted with it and we soon had the kettle whistling for a reviving cuppa.

An inspection of the leg showed blood had soaked through the dressing so it was replaced before we set off to look around the village, Viv limping along gamely holding on to my arm. The quaint village shop had an odd mixture of modern supplies and ancient relics on its old fashioned shelves, in a sort of rustic museum meets trading post style. There was even a traditional nativity scene in the shop

Mt Somers Holiday Park.
After her crash, Viv puts on a brave face... and the kettle

window, spoiled only by baby Jesus holding a miniature ice cream cone. Near the shop was an amazing early motor caravan - a lorry with a shed on its back, complete with pitched corrugated tin roof and wooden shutters.

We treated ourselves to an excellent supper at the Mount Somers Tavern but when we got up to leave, Viv's leg had stiffened alarmingly and it was a slow and painful hobble back to our caravan. The only night Viv could not walk unaided was the only night our toilet was in a block 100 metres away. Our midnight three-legged hop to the loo in the moonlight was as hilarious as it was inconvenient.

Viv's leg was stiff but slightly less painful as we did our wounded soldier routine over to the shower block next morning. I offered to go in and rub her down with a soapy sponge, but she insisted she could manage and thought the other lady campers might misunderstand my innocent intentions.

By 9.30 we were back on the road again to make our agreed rendezvous with John and Jill at Hinds. They would lead us to Coldstream where Jill's cousin Joe and his wife Sue run a 1,000 acre sheep farm. It was fascinating to get a glimpse into the life of this hardy and intrepid couple, whose property included a public library and church. Each of these consisted of a small room: The library containing a table, chairs and a few shelves of books plus a catalogue of the library contents dated 1929!

You might wonder what a library is doing on a remote sheep station, but with the region consisting of single homesteads and no town for miles, a source of literary diversion and social contact is vital. A few days earlier the tiny church next door had been packed with 38 neighbours for the Christmas day service.

Joe showed us around his woolshed which had been cleverly designed so that five shearers can trim 1,200 sheep per day. The contract shearing crew slept in a block of cabins and ate at a communal cookhouse near the woolshed during their annual stint.

Over a marvellous lunch (lamb, naturally) back at the farmhouse, Joe and Sue patiently answered our questions about their life and the history of Coldstream. The homestead had been temporary residence for the Queen's Equerry in 1953 when Elizabeth II and Prince Phillip toured New Zealand on their honeymoon, but mostly their lives revolved around their sheep.

By 3pm it was just starting to rain - what a novelty! - as we set off for the short ride to Geraldine and then Fairlie where we stayed at the Aorangi Motel. Our helpful host Kathy Cassie found Viv two sterile dressings to help patch up her still-bleeding leg.

We left Fairlie in sunshine next day to ride through Burkes Pass, where the roadside verges were ablaze with colourful lupins and blue borage, then on to Lake Tekapo. There's nothing much here but a tiny stone church overlooking the lake, but busloads of Japanese tourists, cameras clicking, whirring and flashing, swarmed over the Church of the Good Shepherd, star of a million publicity photos.

Leaving Tekapo to the masses, we rode on to Lake Pukaki which is a spectacular light creamy blue, the milky water looking like freshly stirred duck-egg blue emulsion paint. The lake stretched away to the shimmering white peak of Mount Cook 80km to the north. After fuel and coffee in

Twizel we headed north alongside the impossibly coloured Pukaki to Mount Cook, or rather to The Hermitage, a climber-tramper resort nestling under the ice and snow-covered peaks. This is the closest you can get by road to the country's highest mountain, the spiritual peak of the nation's rugged outdoor psyche.

Just before we got there, however, I spotted a gravel road leading off to the Tasman Glacier and pulled over to consult Viv. She was feeling really brave, she said. Only two days after her big crash she was ready to ride again on a slippery gravel surface, provided the gravel wasn't too deep and we took it slowly. After a longish ride we came to the tourist car park, but carried on through this and on up a rocky and increasingly steep 4WD track for a further four kilometres until finally the going got too tough. We stopped and clambered on to a rocky ledge for our lunch.

Towering above us, between where we sat and where we supposed the glacier to be, was an extremely steep bank made up of huge boulders. I guessed this was lateral moraine, the rubble left at the side of a glacier as it gouges its way down the valley, and I wanted to see what was on the other side. Leaving Viv perched on a rock, I climbed slowly to the top, where I came upon the most amazing landscape I've ever seen.

Malte Brun (3155m) towers over Tasman Glacier wasteland

If I thought the climb up had been steep, the other face of the moraine bank was almost vertical and fell perhaps 500 metres or more to the valley bottom below. Instead of the white glacier I had been expecting, the broad valley floor was dark brown with rubble and boulders that looked more like sand due to the distance involved. This surreal moonscape stretched at least five kilometres to the scoured edge of the mountains opposite, with a few deep, crater-like holes puncturing the surface. These contained muddy lakes, the largest perhaps a kilometre across, and were highly unstable. As I stood on the ridge I could hear the distant rumble and splash as rocks fell from the sides into the water of the nearest one.

Then I made out another noise, the distant drone of a small aircraft. I searched the sky but couldn't see it. Then my eye caught a movement, a tiny speck crawling up the centre of the valley below me. It looked like a gnat hovering over the immensity of the weird landscape and I watched it slowly disappear into infinity in the clear air further up the valley where, 20km to the north, the bright white ice of the glacier was visible.

A rock dislodged by my foot fell noisily in leaps and bounds down the near-sheer face of the ridge I was standing on. It took a long time before its final clatter rose up to me from the valley floor and reminded me how precarious my perch was. Time to climb back down.

At The Hermitage we had a breather and took photos of the magnificent Mount Cook, which beckons Kiwis on to its slopes to attempt to reach its shining summit. But its beauty belies a treacherous nature. It is one of the most dangerous mountains in the world and has already claimed more than 138 lives, among them our nephew Nicholas.

John and Jill's son loved the mountains and lived for the moment he would be climbing them again. When he fell to his death in 1995 he was just 20. The loss of one so young and lovely is still too painful to dwell upon. We gave each other a long hug, then remounted and headed south again, this time passing through Omarama where we had another unusual night's accommodation lined up.

The Glenburn Holiday Park, eight kilometres east of town and overlooking Lake Benmore, was really a campsite. But like most camping grounds in New Zealand, also offered a few cabins. The one we were allocated (NZ$38 plus $10 for linen - £14) was not much larger than a chicken hutch with barely room for two bunk beds. But it did have the luxury of a tiny toilet and shower cubicle at one end.

After nearly 300km and lots of stops to ogle and photograph the breathtaking lakes, mountains and glaciers, we were more than ready for a hot meal. So we dropped our bags and rode back into Omarama to find food. By the time we returned to our hutch I'd developed a screaming migraine and remained horizontal until morning, while Viv consoled herself with a mug of hot chocolate and a packet of biscuits.

Following breakfast in the communal kitchen and a little light motorcycle maintenance, with my eyes carefully shielded from the sun as my head was still very delicate, we rode back through Omarama and over the Lindis Pass on SH8. At Tarras we found a shop-cum-café which provided delicious coffee and scones and a few minutes of idle browsing. Among the Merino wool products - yup, more nipple warmers - was a section well stocked with children's books. We were looking for something suitable for our 15-month-old granddaughter when my eye was caught by a slim volume entitled 'The Possum Hunt'. This picture-story book described in words and colour photos how Daddy took his two small children out after dark to teach them how to trap and shoot possums. It even included photos of possums bleeding to death from daddy's gunshot wounds and being strangled to death in the little boy's 'kill trap'. The little girl, who caught a mummy possum with a baby on its back, elected to release hers back into the wild. The end.

I found it a really shocking and gory example of New Zealand's love/hate relationship with the possum. This creature was introduced from Australia in the 1840s to provide fur, which they continue to do in abundance as there are approximately 70 million of them now, despite the nation's vigorous attempts to exterminate them. The government spends millions of dollars each year providing poisons and, as a result, the countryside is liberally strewn with pellets of 1080, a poison banned in every other country and responsible for deaths of cattle and native birds. Trapping and shooting possums is a national pastime and many New Zealanders will swerve deliberately to run these animals down if they see them on the road.

The excuse for all this barbaric behaviour? Possums like to eat the flowers and leaves of certain trees, and in some cases may kill a tree. Man has destroyed 95 percent of all the country's trees in the past 150 years and decimated New Zealand's native woodlands, so we've nothing to feel superior about. Sick possums may spread bovine TB to cattle, but this doesn't excuse killing possums on sheep farms, which is more often the case.

The usual defence is: *'Possums are not native. They're a modern import and very destructive.'* However, this argument overlooks the fact that possums arrived at the same time as Europeans who are every bit as modern and infinitely more destructive. Perhaps the Kiwi Government should be handing out poison pellets to curb the human population too? And all this from a country which prides itself on being a whiter shade of green and a shining example of environmental political correctness for the world.

I know we've all gone soft in Europe and especially in the UK, where there's now a public outcry if a fly gets swatted. But publishing kiddies' picture books with lurid photos of shot, bleeding and strangulated possums is a bit much, surely? I put the book back on the shelf and found something more suitable as bedtime reading for Annabel.

Chapter 11

Madness In Wanaka

Next stop was Wanaka where we had two plans: The first to visit the Fighter Pilot Museum at Wanaka Airport (we'd been asked to check it out and report back to Viv's dad, who is a WWII aircraft buff), and then to pop in to town to get cash, food and fuel before heading high into the Southern Alps for the night.

The museum was excellent, with great planes, displays and stories of Kiwi wartime exploits. But when we returned to collect our luggage from the office and mentioned to the friendly staff that we were heading into Wanaka town, they looked horrified and said: *'Don't go there!'* It was New Year's Eve, they said, and Wanaka was a great magnet for people determined to see in the New Year with as much alcohol, noise and riotous behaviour as possible.

That would explain why we had seen a queue of people loading up their cars with dozens of cases of beer yesterday in Twizel. They were ensuring that even if Wanaka ran dry before the festivities were over, they'd have sufficient supplies to get completely rat-arsed and then some. The tradition, apparently, is to get totally wrecked and then trash everything in sight. Marvellous!

So we rode into Wanaka wide awake and alert to danger. There was a lot of it about. The town was heaving with youths staggering along the pavements - each clutching the obligatory can and with a six-pack or two under the other arm - screaming and yelling at passing cars. These were no ordinary cars. Most were open topped, sported raucous exhausts and were either accelerating and braking violently every 50 metres, or swerving wildly from side to side. All were overflowing with leering, jeering, shouting occupants and there were frequent exchanges of cans, mostly half-full and hurled with feeling, between those on the pavements and those in the cars. We suspected that some of these people may have been drinking already.

Among the thousands of drunken drivers and yelling yobs, one species was conspicuously absent. We saw no policemen in Wanaka where a little law and order was sorely needed. One could not help comparing the millions devoted by the Government to eradicating the possum, with the apparent absence of any resources spent on controlling these infinitely more antisocial and dangerous creatures.

At the first sign of a bank we pulled off the road and left our bikes as far out of harm's way as we could manage, parked protectively between cars. I stayed near them, cowering in the shade of a shop doorway to keep an eye on our belongings while Viv quickly extracted money from the bank, food from a store and the location of a fuel station from a shop assistant.

It was hideously hot and Wanaka seemed to be building up a head of steam for the midnight madness to come. We wanted to be as far away as possible when it was finally unleashed. Until we were far out of town and well on our way towards the empty mountains, we were more fearful for our lives than on the Auckland motorway in rush-hour.

On the 80km ride to Makarora, SH6 took us alongside Lake Hawea which was beautiful, serene and sufficiently distant from Wanaka for us to stop and breathe a sigh of relief. Two more bikes - a BMW R1100RT and a Honda Hornet - pulled in carrying a French couple and their two daughters aged six and nine. Renaud Biscarrat and his family live in Japan, he told me, and the bikes were ideal for a week-long dash around New Zealand. They had just come down the West Coast and had seen no rain so far, which was music to our ears as that was where we were headed tomorrow, and we'd been soaked sufficiently to last us a lifetime.

I suggested I take a photo of the biker family and they readily agreed, Mme Biscarrat calling: 'Les lunettes, les lunettes!' to her precocious daughters who, in their sexy leather jackets and sunglasses, struck a pose worthy of a bike shop poster.

Compared to the French family's powerful motos, our little Serows felt positively puny as we slogged uphill into a

A-frame chalet at Makarora near Haast Pass

fierce headwind. Climbing higher and higher into the Southern Alps we finally reached Makarora, which consisted of a shop, a DOC (Dept of Conservation) office and the Makarora Tourist Centre, offering camping ground, cabins and A-frame chalets, one of which we'd booked for the night. It was palatial after the chicken hutch cabin we'd dossed in the night before and after the various excitements of the day we were ready for a little peace and comfort.

Our cabin backed on to native forest, a part of the Mount Aspiring National Park, so after a rest and a bite to eat we went for a bush walk in the dusk before bedtime. The silent serenity of the trees and melodic calls of the tuis were a marked contrast to the screaming humanity down in Wanaka. We pitied the townsfolk who must endure this night of hell each year, but were grateful we were far from it.

The year 2002 dawned wet and windy. It must be us. The rain seemed to be following us around the country. Maybe this was God's idea of a joke - a long-term immersion test - but frankly, it was wearing a little thin. Perhaps we could dodge it by staying put today and letting the rain clouds pass by? But a quick dash through the deluge to the office knocked that idea on the head. All the motels and cabins were already booked for the night.

'Never mind,' I told Viv. 'If it's raining up here in the mountains, chances are it will be dry down on the coast where we're headed.'

'Is that a scientific fact, or just Bob's wishful thinking?' she asked with a smile.

Viv wasn't easily fooled. Only a couple of days earlier I had been reading to her a passage from our guide book. It said the moist winds from the Tasman Sea meeting the steep west coast mountains of the South Island deposit up to SEVEN METRES of rainfall per year. That's almost 12 times the precipitation we're used to back home. Seven metres is 23 feet for goodness sake! If five chaps my height stood on each other's shoulders, the top one would be barely able to poke his nose above the water. No wonder they call it the Wet Coast. An early visitor wrote:

It rained and rained and rained
The average fall was well maintained

And when the tracks were simply bogs
It started raining cats and dogs
After a drought of half an hour
We had a most refreshing shower
And then the most curious thing of all
A gentle rain began to fall
Next day also was fairly dry
Save for a deluge from the sky
Which wetted the party to the skin
And after that the rain set in

It didn't sound like the ideal motorcycling climate, but we
had been promised spectacular scenery, with glaciers
tumbling down almost to the sea, so we felt we had to go.
Having made ourselves and our luggage as water-resistant
as we could, we set off rather reluctantly for the Haast Pass
in heavy rain.

It was not only wet, but also windy and decidedly chilly
up there. So cold, in fact, that our visors misted up instantly,
and raising mine a fraction to try to clear it resulted in water
droplets being blown up inside in a fine spray. Within a
couple of kilometres my glasses and visor were covered in
water droplets inside and out. It's quite impossible to see
through four layers of rain drops, so I raised the visor and
was treated to a stinging blast of wind-driven rain-pellets
which hurt so much I was forced to keep below 50kph. The
upside of this pain was that I could more easily ignore the
steady river of cold water running down my neck and inside
my jacket.

Not that my jacket would have kept much out anyway.
By the time we'd battled the 15km to crest the pass and start
our tortuous descent, I could feel icy water running down
my chest and around my back, soaking into my underpants
and running down my legs into my boots. I was tempted,
not for the first time, to wonder just what it was that made
us ride motorbikes. On a day like this it was certainly not
the thrill of being at one with nature or enjoying
uninterrupted views of the scenery.

Had it been possible to see anything through the curtains
of rain, or past my bespeckled glasses, I would not have
dared to look up from the patch of streaming tarseal

immediately in front of my wheels. The road was not only awash with falling rainwater to a depth of some inches, but frequent waterfalls also fell from the cliffs beside the road and gushed as trainee rivers across the surface, carrying gravel and rocks with them. All around we could hear the crash of waterfalls and the thunder of swollen streams.

Under different circumstances we might have been delighted to see the Fantail Falls or Thunder Creek Falls promised by the map, but the road twisted alarmingly in its narrow gorge, frequently reduced to half-width at dozens of one-way bridges, and it was all we could do to stay on the bikes and keep them on the road. Another celebrated scenic delight named The Gates of Haast seemed more like The Gates of Hell, and as we gradually splashed our way down the mountain beside the tumultuous roaring of the Haast River, the rain - unbelievably - got even heavier.

The raindrops were now so big, and hurled at us with such vengeance, that I could actually feel individual drops hitting my helmet and the hammering needles of water stung even through my thick jacket and the layers of sodden clothing beneath it. If anyone claims to make waterproof clothing, this is where they should come to prove it. The hurricane-force wind whistling up the valley was forcing water uphill - I could see ripples of water being blown back *up* the road in places - and of course it blew torrents under our cuffs, inside flaps, through zips, past seals and seams.

By the time we reached the tiny hamlet of Haast Village, we were absolutely drenched and shivering from the wind-chill induced cold. We pulled up at the only café with the kind of relief that a dying man in the desert greets an oasis. For the first time we left our luggage strapped on our bikes out of sight. If anyone was mad enough to stand out in this monsoon and unstrap it all, they could take it! We squelched inside to try to find some warmth. We had been cold before and we had been wet before, but we'd never been *this* cold and *this* wet at the same time - ever! It had taken two hours to cover the 80km from Makarora.

With numb and shaking fingers we slowly pulled off gloves and unstrapped helmets. Viv's fingers were blue. Mine would have been, but once again the dye had run and my gloves had coloured my hands with bright blotches of red. I took our gloves off to the loo to wring pints of water out of them. There was no point in removing our riding jackets and overtrousers - everything beneath them was saturated and Viv's knickers-under-the-hand-dryer trick was pointless. We sat in our soaking clothes, sipping hot coffee and eating a succession of hot foot items until our shivering stopped and the trapped water next to our skin started to warm up. Were we mad? We agreed that if madness is an inability to protect oneself from the elements, we were certifiable. We had to laugh or we'd have cried.

The Fantail Café slowly filled up with passing tourists, well soaked from the dash from their parked cars, as it was still hammering down outside. After an hour and a half we'd worked our way through half the menu and three coffees apiece and felt almost human again. The café was now bursting with trippers looking for somewhere to sit, so we gave up our dripping seats, pulled on our soggy, clammy helmets and stepped outside again.

For a few blissful minutes the rain reduced to a heavy drizzle, which made it possible to refuel at the Haast garage

Drying out and writing letters home, Lake Paringa Motel

without getting too much water in our tanks. Then we set off up the West Coast road SH6 with our visors down. After much drying and polishing and treating of my glasses and visor with anti-misting spray during our lengthy café-halt, I was now able to keep the mist on the inside down to an acceptable level, provided I only exhaled downwards out of my mouth, like Mr Bean.

Then, within ten kilometres, the rain was back at full volume, pelting down with such ferocity that the road became a lake cratered with huge exploding raindrops. Despite staring hard at the road to ensure we stayed on it, I couldn't help noticing the astonishingly lush vegetation on each side. So this was rain forest? I hoped the deluge might ease up enough for us to see some of it later.

It was now mid afternoon and it wasn't only the weather that was worrying me. We hadn't got anywhere to stay. The phone box at Makarora had been out of order, so we'd set out with no accommodation booked. This was now the height of the holiday season and accommodation was reportedly sparse on the West Coast. Maybe the weather would have discouraged others who might be marginally less keen than ourselves on hypothermia and drowning?

Eventually we sploshed into the Lake Paringa café and motel and they had a unit free, thank goodness. We booked for two nights, figuring it would take more than a day to dry out, and began the process of peeling off the sodden layers, pouring water out of our boots and unpacking our soggy luggage. We soon had strings crisscrossing the lounge, kitchen and shower, with items in various states of sogginess dripping or steaming gently in the fug produced by the cooker and room heater. Despite the advice against it, we were forced to place our saturated gloves and boots over the heater to speed up the drying process, otherwise we'd have webbed feet and fingers by the end of the week. It reminded me of the watertight promise I'd received when I bought my first pair of motorcycle boots, way back in 1969.

Delighted as I was with my Belstaff Black Prince suit, I was still on the hunt for biking gear to cover my extremities. Ian gave me the word that just the kind of thing I was looking for, at a bargain price, could be found at Butters pawn shop

149

in nearby Spalding, an eight mile ride from my Fenland home,

'*Motorcycling boots?*' said a slightly puzzled Mr Butters, '*Ah, you must mean our German Ja...er... army boots,*' as he pointed to half a dozen pairs of hideously large and lumpy, knee-length, black leather boots on a shelf behind him.

'*Best boots in the world these are,*' he said, warming to the task of parting a gullible youngster from his pocket-money. '*Top quality leather and German craftsmanship. Allowed the German army to march right across Europe to Russia and back. What size are you?*'

'*Well, I don't have a seven-and-a-half. Nearest I can do is a nine, which will be perfect if you want them for motorcycling - you can wear a couple of extra pairs of socks and keep your feet warm as toast in the winter.*'

And he passed me, one at a time, two huge lumps of leather that looked for all the world as if they'd been modelled in clay as a first practice exercise by a pottery class novice. And felt like it too. Lead diving boots could hardly have weighed more. I was aghast, but Mr Butters was insistent.

'*Get your feet in there and feel how solid they are. You can stand in a stream, up to your ankles in water all day long and not a drop will leak in. Course, they're not new, but they've got years of good service in them.*'

Solid wasn't the word for it. I tried a tentative step and nearly fell over. My feet moved but the boots didn't. And then, as I stared down in disbelief at my skinny sixteen-year-old legs sprouting like saplings from two huge flowerpots, he delivered the coup de grâce

'*A pair of motorcycle boots from Biggadike's,*' he said, nodding towards the bike dealer further up the street, '*will knock you back ten quid at least. I can let you have these for one pound ten shillings...*'

There was no contest. I earned 18 shillings and sixpence a week doing a full-day Saturday job on a bread round with the local baker's shop. I handed over my hard-earned cash, stuffed my shoes inside my Black Prince jacket and clumped out of the shop like Herman Munster.

My little Honda 90, waiting patiently beside the pavement, didn't know what it was in for. First problem, after I had summoned up the energy and momentum to swing my leaden right leg over the seat, was how to operate the kickstarter. I normally flicked out the kickstart lever with my right toe, gave it a deft prod to fire up the little 90cc motor, then folded it away again with a tap from my shoe's instep.

After a minute's fumbling, which felt rather like trying to sew on a button while wearing boxing gloves, I gave up and let my right boot crash to the road surface, my leg exhausted from the effort of holding it aloft. I reached over and folded out the kickstart lever by hand, hoisted my boot above it and let gravity do the rest.

Operating the gear lever presented a similar problem. It was impossible to get the bulbous boot toe underneath the lever for up changes. Fortunately, Mr Honda had seen fit to equip this little machine with a toe-and-heel rocker pedal so, in theory at least, all I had to do was press with my toe for down changes and with my heel for up changes. Only problem was, there was no perceptible articulation in the ankle region of the boot. When I pressed down with my toe the whole boot flopped forward against my calf, and gaped at the front, and lifting my toe made the solid top of the boot crack against my shin below the knee. It was quite distressing.

Still, I could get under way, and I was keen to be gone from the pawn shop's kerbside, where my every move was being watched by the smiling, nodding Mr Butters. I'm sure that through the glass I could see him mouthing the words: *'There's one born every minute.'*

On the move, several other amusing features of my German jackboots made themselves known. Firstly, if I lapsed concentration with my left foot for a moment, either the toe or heel would press against a part of the gear lever and shift me into another gear, or neutral, neither of which was particularly handy. And if I relaxed my right shin muscles, which were keeping my right toes pressed against the cavernous roof of the foot cavity of the right boot, the weight of the boot pressing on the rear brake lever applied an unwanted servo effect which locked the back wheel with a squeal.

After a little trial and error - well, quite a lot of error, actually - I discovered that the way around this impromptu gear-changing and braking was to perch the boot heels on the footrests and angle the boot toes outward so they couldn't interfere with the control pedals unbidden. While this gave an improvement in control, the extra windage knocked around ten miles per hour off the little bike's top speed and the protruding boots doubled the effective width of the bike. The upside was that other traffic generally gave me a wide berth, and I discovered the delights of toe-scraping in bends about 20 years before it became fashionable with sportsbike riders.

When I rode back into Holbeach, there was Ian with a couple of mates, waiting for my return by practising goosestep marching and Heil Hitler salutes, a routine that would keep them falling about laughing for weeks. In addition, Ian could now inform everyone we met that I not only wore the riding suit of a dead motorcyclist, but also jackboots snatched from the legs of a dead German soldier. Such things provide endless humour among lads of that age and even today, 34 years later, Ian needs little encouragement to recount my lack of teenage cool with snorts of laughter.

Chapter 12

Sandflies And Floods

Meanwhile, back at Lake Paringa, the rain was now hammering down with such ferocity that the run-off from the motel units' roofs was threatening to inundate their doors. The owner's teenage sons were still on their Christmas holiday from school, which is all the excuse most parents need to dream up a succession of highly unpleasant jobs. These poor lads were each given a spade and despatched into the deluge to deal with the water.

We watched through the streaming windows as they jabbed at the yard in an attempt to dig channels to redirect the flood into the lake.

'Aw NO! This is crazy. We're gonna git soaked!' and other dark mutterings of a patricidal nature, were soon followed by shrieks and giggles. Within a minute they were drenched to the skin and having a great time chucking shovelfuls of muddy water at each other. Kids, eh?

Thunder crashed, the roar of the rain on the tin roof was deafening. Wow, it really <u>does</u> rain here! We considered our meal options: The nearest shop was 50km to the south at Haast; the nearest restaurant 92km north at Franz Josef. There are no other roads here: To the east are the towering mountains of the Southern Alps and to the west the Tasman sea. We didn't take too long to decide to eat in the Lake Paringa Café, after which we crashed out, warm and dry at last, to a lullaby of rain and thunder. Between the rumbles we could hear the distinctive *'Morepork'* cry of the New Zealand owl. Frankly, on a night like this I would plump for staying in my tree hollow with a packet of pork scratchings.

The rain had eased to a light drizzle next morning, so at midday we decided to venture out for a ride back to Haast and lunch at the Haast Heritage Hotel, where we were pleasantly surprised to park next to three other trail bikes -

two Yamaha XT600s and a Honda 650 Dominator. So there *were* some other mad/brave souls after all.

Inside we found the three riders were women: An ex-pat Brit whose partner runs 'Enduro Tours' providing on/off-road trips for trailie bikers, plus a Kiwi and a Swiss. After a brief chat and a delightfully imaginative meal for an unpretentious hotel in the middle of nowhere, we rode on a further 50km to Jackson Bay, the end of the road and the limit of civilisation on the southern West Coast. Beyond lay the vast wilderness of Fiordland, impenetrable and largely unexplored.

It's doubtful that Jackson Bay would exist at all but for a wildly ambitious project to set up a major port and town here in 1875. Migrants from half a dozen European countries were shipped in to start the settlement, but they soon found existence all but impossible in the desperately wet and remote outpost. Most abandoned Jackson Bay for a more bearable life elsewhere, but a few hardy souls remained to scrape a living from fishing.

The only facility for visitors here is The Cray Pot, a café made from a converted railway carriage standing beside the road and splashed by the spray from the sea. Proprietor Lisa

Craypot Café at Jackson Bay,
most southerly point on the West Coast Highway

Rodger provides a welcome refuge from the weather and sandflies and also serves up hearty fried fish meals and great steaming mugs of tea together with lively banter. She told us her husband Geoffrey helped support their young family by hunting from a helicopter flown by his pal Barry Guise, who lived at Lake Paringa, right behind our motel. It seemed like a hard but happy existence.

Sandflies are a menace all along the West Coast, but nowhere more so than at Jackson Bay. We'd learned to keep our helmets and gloves on until we got indoors in this part of the country and consequently only suffered bites around our cheeks and noses where the determined little varmints had sneaked in under our helmet visors. A young German couple sitting beside us in The Cray Pot's intimate dining room were counting their bites and plucking up the courage to use the basic outdoor privy opposite, where the dropping of pants provides an irresistible target for the little blighters.

New Zealand sandflies are tiny, silent, inconspicuous and insignificant - until they sink their fangs into your flesh, which is about one second after any piece of skin is uncovered. They are a source of endless amusement on the West Coast where they are most prevalent. You don't tend to notice the one that is about to bite your knee, elbow or neck until it has raised the usual response: 'Oww!' Slap! 'Oh, you little brute!' But your partner can see it loitering with intent, so we took to swatting each other's sandflies. This gave rise to countless slaps - not all received with the gratitude they deserved - and occasional misunderstandings. Viv killed one of my freckles 13 times before she finally accepted it wasn't a sandfly. Tourists who stepped off coaches unprepared and wearing only shorts and T-shirts were soon doing a passable impression of a Swiss village mountain dance, with much hopping, skipping, leg slapping and yodelling.

Deet-based insect repellants are effective, but only if you reapply them frequently and in sufficient quantity to produce a haze of evaporating solvent. Which is why most West Coast travellers had that slitty-eyed, glue-sniffer look about them. Taking copious quantities of vitamin B1 is also claimed to put the sandflies off too, but the pong also acts as an effective deterrent for other humans, so this might not be the ideal solution for everyone. Perhaps the Kiwi Government could redirect some of the millions it spends on poisons for the poor old possum and research a means of control for the sandfly instead. There can't be many people who would object to a bit of Government-sponsored sandfly strangling. It might even make bedtime reading for kids.

If sandflies bite you in the daytime, you can be sure that mosquitoes are not far away, waiting to get you as it starts to get dark. In fact, the onset of dusk is the most tricky time because the day shift are eager for one last meal before they clock off, and the incoming night shift are fresh and eager to make a good impression.

Back at Haast we stocked up with groceries and fuel before returning to our Lake Paringa motel for supper before our evening bushwalk. It was raining steadily as we picked our way through the vegetation alongside Jamie Creek, but it was worth another wetting to see the amazingly lush rainforest of ferns and pongas dripping with mosses and lichens.

By the time we got back to our cabin it was almost dark and the weather had closed in again, with solid cloud only 20 metres off the lake outside our window. So we were surprised to hear a small helicopter clatter over our roof and disappear across the lake in the gloom, then return a few minutes later with two deer dangling below it. This must be Barry Guise, we figured, working late to bring home the kill in conditions clearly unsuitable for flying. When the diminutive chopper flew back again for a second trip across the lake, we were seriously concerned for the pilot's safety and breathed a sigh of relief when the little aircraft returned in the dark.

Throughout the night we were woken repeatedly by lightning which illuminated our room through the thin curtains, followed almost immediately by huge bangs and crashes, then more distant rumbles of thunder and the ever-present drumbeat of rain on the roof. No hoots from the morepork owl tonight. We reckoned he was staying tucked up in his nest and banking on a bacon sandwich for breakfast.

Next morning it was still pouring but now it was blowing a gale too, the gusts shaking our motel roof. We only had 92km to ride to reach Franz Josef today, but it was right into the teeth of this northerly gale, ideal conditions for another wet-knicker day. During the night of fitful sleep I had been dreaming up some rain-cheating ideas and, despite Viv's sniggering, I was determined to try them out.

First up were two pairs of instant handlebar-muffs, carrier bags attached to the bar ends to deflect the rain. Okay, so they looked silly and would undoubtedly flap about madly, but they might just work. Next was a full-length bib made from a heavy gauge polythene bag slit along both sides and held in place by a string tied around my neck. This really got Viv giggling, but I was convinced it would keep the water from pouring through my jacket's atrociously leaky front zip.

I'd also purchased five large black bin-liners from our landlady when I settled up that morning - four of them to provide an additional water-resisting layer inside our panniers and the fifth to stuff down inside Viv's overtrousers. The holes in the left knee resulting from her crash were letting rain pour though and we figured the plastic might just keep trousers, socks and boots dry.

By lunchtime we'd survived the wind and rain-lashed journey and negotiated one washout and a muddy 'slup' to reach Franz Josef's Glowworm Cottages and a warm welcome. My rain-beating bodges had been surprisingly successful. No water had got past my plastic bib and through my jacket zip, so for the first time in a while I arrived with a dry shirt and pants. The plastic handlebar muffs had kept most of the rain off my gloves, but had made it tricky to get hands back on to the handlebars after attending to my visor en route. Viv had given up on hers early on because of the fumble to regain the controls, and both her boots were wet inside, so a rethink was needed here. She agreed reluctantly that overtrouser cuff restraints, like the rubber bands that I used to keep my boot-tops covered, would be a good idea in future.

The Blue Ice Café served us delicious pizzas and sticky toffee-pudding for supper and the waitress was very friendly and efficient, so we tipped her. Tipping is unusual in New Zealand - it's not expected and rarely done - so it was nice to reward someone for exemplary service, rather than feel obliged to pay somebody a financial compliment when you really don't mean it, as is the quirky fashion in most of Europe.

In case it appears that our dining out consisted of an unending succession of pizzas, I should perhaps explain that we happen to be pizza fans. Ever since 1977 when Viv discovered a little book by Peter Boizot, the founder of Pizza Express, we've been experimenting with home-made pizzas and sampling the better restaurant varieties with relish. But I wouldn't want you to think we ate nothing else: We frequently rang the changes with cheese and tomato on toast, or even bread, tomato and cheese for picnic lunches. To ensure we got a healthy and balanced diet I maintained a regular intake of Cookie Time cookies while Viv chomped Anzac biscuits and we'd round it off with an occasional nutritious ice-cream. Inexplicably, the stretchy waistband trousers I'd bought in Christchurch now seemed permanently near their limit of expansion. Perhaps the wet weather had shrunk them?

Waiho Bridge to Franz Josef reopens after speedy repair.
Half a metre of rain fell in 36 hours

Our Glowworm Cottage, we realised, was more suitable for glowworms than human inhabitants. It was ridiculously tiny - entirely filled by a double bed, with the 'kitchen' arranged on a couple of small shelves in an alcove, the 'dining room' being another slender shelf with diminutive stools underneath and the miniscule toilet and shower room featured a handbasin that was too small to get more than one hand in at once. It was like a dolls' house but very cosy and all the more welcome because there was no other accommodation vacant anywhere between Haast and Hokitika, a 283km stretch of coast road. We took the precaution of booking our motel in Hokitika for two nights ahead before settling down for another night of West Coast rainbeat-assisted slumber.

Unbeknown to us, a drama was unfolding as we slept. Sheryl, a cheery soul who lived in the cabin opposite when not taking bookings for one of the scenic flight companies in town, had set out around midnight with a friend to visit a pub in Fox, 25km to the south. On their way out of Franz Josef they screeched to a halt just metres from the Waiho Bridge when one of them noticed something wasn't quite right. In the light of their car's headlamps they could now see the problem - the raging brown torrent of the flood-swollen river had washed away the road and the end of the bridge was waving up and down unsupported! A few more metres and Sheryl and friend's car would have been in the water and tumbling rapidly out to sea.

Sheryl sent her friend running back into town to raise the alarm (Sheryl, by her own admission, is comfortably well-upholstered and unsuited to running, even in an emergency) while she stayed with the car to stop any traffic. Good job she did too, as ten minutes later lights appeared coming across the 300 metre single-track bridge as a tourist campervan approached. Sheryl leaped up and down in front of her car's headlights to warn the oncoming driver and finally - a short distance from the yawning chasm and disaster - the campervan halted. The driver climbed out and walked forward to inspect the churning waters where the road ought to be, then shouted a faint 'Thank you!' over the roar of the river before reversing all 300 metres back across what remained of the bridge to warn others from the far end.

Sheryl would recount this tale to us later in the day. The first we knew about it was on the local radio news programme at 7 o'clock next morning: *'The West Coast highway is closed at Franz Josef this morning following a washout at the Waiho Bridge. The Highways Department expects the road to be open by 9am.'*

We gulped our breakfast and legged it down the road, along with everyone else in town, to see overgrown Tonka toys dumping enormous rocks into the raging chasm. And sure enough, by 9 o'clock the traffic was flowing again. Amazing. Had this happened in the UK, the road would have been closed for a month while surveyors declared the bridge unfit and local and central government squabbled over budgets to rebuild it. In New Zealand they hurl in a few rocks, pour some gravel, flatten it with a 'dozer and say: *'She'll be right, mate'.* Marvellous! It has to be said that the Kiwis' pragmatic approach is borne out of necessity. Flash floods wash away bridges with alarming regularity here, and there is no other road to the west of the mountains. If a bridge is out the whole West Coast comes to a standstill.

By 11am we were riding tentatively across the bridge ourselves, trying to dodge the spray thrown up by the surging floodwaters hitting the bridge's slim support struts and spurting ten metres into the air. We were on our way to view the Franz Josef glacier, but we couldn't get very near because the swollen river had closed the walk to the ice face. It looked impressive enough in the distance from Sentinel Rock before increasing rain and sandfly bites drove us back into our helmets and on to our bikes.

There's not a fat lot to do in Franz Josef when it's pouring with rain, which for us was most of the time, so we mooched around the shops, trying out the furry nipple-warmers for size, until it was time for the town's film show. This was a movie entitled 'Flowing West' screened at The Alpine Adventure Centre and was promoted in lavish terms by a spectacular colour brochure. It would be shown on a: *'Giant 'Helimax' Screen, with especially composed music and dynamic digital sound... a huge sensory movie journey through glacier country...'* The film was directed, we were told, by *'World Acclaimed environmental film maker Michael Single. PREPARE TO BE ENCHANTED'* . We could hardly contain our excitement until the curtains slid back at 3pm.

What we got for our NZ$20 (£6) was 20 minutes of helicopter-shot, lurching, sick-making and much-speeded-up footage of racing waves and snow and ice. With no commentary. Much of the racing and flickering footage was so nausea-inducing we had to close our eyes and grip tightly to our seats. Even then there was no escape from the almost equally nauseating 'especially composed' music which assaulted our eardrums at something approaching 200 decibels. Those with a predisposition towards migraine or epilepsy might do well to give this film a miss.

We could have been disappointed that the film show lasted only 20 minutes, but we were immensely relieved to stagger outside, clutching our reeling heads and churning stomachs, at the earliest opportunity. To be fair to the film, anyone who enjoys big-dipper fairground rides combined with the sort of audio-visual apocalypse you might get in a rave disco, would probably find it right up their street. For a pair of crusty old grandparents, it was a disaster movie.

After supper we took ourselves off for a more gentle and soothing form of entertainment - a visit to the nearby glowworm dell. After stumbling in the dark through the forest for a while, we caught up with a group of people on a guided walk. It was so dark that nobody knew we weren't bone fide members of the paid-up party, and so enjoyed a full commentary and saw some great glowworms. Much more to our liking, and much better value for money.

To our surprise and delight, Saturday dawned bright, sunny and DRY! It was a pleasure to ride out of Franz on rain-free roads, heading north on SH6 through Whataroa and Harihari, little country villages with a couple of stores and a dairy, past pretty Lake Ianthe and through dense rainforest to Pukekura (pronounced Pukey-cure-a).

Here we were lured to a halt by a sandfly. Not your average miniscule midge, but a monster sandfly model hanging outside The Bushman's Centre Museum. We took only a brief look around this odd display - there was rather

161

too much emphasis on strangling possums for our taste - and, instead, crossed the road for coffee at the Puke Pub. Viv was feeling a touch queasy this morning, so this seemed entirely appropriate, and the break gave us time to chuckle quietly at some of the West Coast's wilder claims to fame. Such as the: 'World Acclaimed' film maker, who we thought might be world acclaimed throughout his home village, and the 'Internationally Known' Bushman's Centre Museum. This label could be attached equally well to any attraction, shop or roadside layby that has been passed by a person from another country, which means everything and everywhere in New Zealand. *'Oh yeah. Me uncle Bruce from Sydney's heard of us, so we're Internationally Known!'*. They try hard, these Kiwis, for their share of the tourist dollar, and mostly they deserve it.

From Pukekura it was a short hop to Ross, which fully lived up to its claim to be a Historic Gold Town. It was here in 1909 that New Zealand's largest ever gold nugget, the 99oz 'Honourable Roddy' was discovered. After leaving our jackets, bags and helmets with the helpful lady in the Ross Information Centre, which occupies the 1870-built premises of the Bank of New South Wales, we set off on a charming walkway past mining sites and relics and through fabulous native bush. En route we passed by the town's cemetery for the Irish, Scots and English lads who died young here in the 1890s. The gravestones told some tragic stories - such as the father from Dorset who died, aged 40, leaving a widow and two sons, the younger of whom drowned a few years later and the older son shortly after that, leaving the poor woman all alone in this far distant land.

After the excellent boardwalks and bridges we came to the public gold panning area of Jones Creek, where I couldn't resist jumping into the streambed and fossicking around in the sand and gravel. I came away with three sparkly flakes, which could have been anything, but pleased me enormously. Several couples have spent anything from three days to three weeks panning and digging in the riverbed here to produce enough gold to make a pair of wedding rings. Some might consider them romantic fools, but we thought that spending up to three weeks of back-breaking work in a

162

sandfly-infested river would be a good test of matrimonial suitability.

Over lunch sitting outside The Roddy Nugget tavern, we chatted to a Norton Commando rider from Wellington who had ridden in sunshine all the way around the South Islandwithout getting even slightly damp once! We were still spitting feathers as his sweet rumbling exhaust note disappeared into the distance. Still, the sun was shining now and we made the most of it on our ride up to Hokitika and the Kiwi Motor Lodge, the best equipped motel we had encountered so far. In addition to the usual comprehensive motel inventory, these apartments all came with electric blankets, hair driers, irons and ironing boards. Michael and Suzanne Milne were friendly, helpful and hospitable, and the first to give us a full tour of the rooms and facilities and provide guide books and advice. No cookies though. Perhaps they noticed my trousers' straining seams and hid the biscuits.

We woke to sunshine again - hoorah! Sun two days running, we were getting spoiled. Among the many leaflets we'd picked up was one for Hokitika Aero Club. My plans for a scenic flight over the glaciers at Franz Josef had been scuppered by the weather and, although we were some distance from the more spectacular snow-covered peaks, I still fancied seeing a bit of New Zealand from the air. Ray Leach offered a trial lesson in the club's Ranz microlight aircraft for just NZ$80 (£23) per hour. This compared very favourably with $200 (£57) for a half-hour scenic flight. And I'd get to fly the plane, brill! We arranged to meet at Hokitika

At 2pm there was not a soul at the aero club and it was gone 3pm before Ray turned up, apologised, and put me straight into the co-pilot's seat. Gulp! The plane was a RANZ Coyote II S6S Super, a US-designed, NZ-built microlight aircraft powered by an 85hp 912 Rotax 4-stroke engine. Ray ran through the controls and instruments while the engine warmed up, then we took an incredibly short run up to reach 50kph and the little plane positively hopped into the air.

As the ground dropped away and we climbed over Hokitika with great views of the river and coast, Ray handed over control of the aircraft to me. It took about ten minutes

163

of wobbling about all over the sky before I had a rough grasp of how to keep it flying level and in roughly the right direction. Then Ray let me have control of the rudder too. Wow! Suddenly the lightweight little plane was dancing about the heavens again and it felt like I was trying to juggle while riding a monocycle along a tightrope. I was sweating with the concentration and effort required to balance and coordinate yaw, pitch and roll concurrently. Jeepers, how do these guys manage to do all this *and* look out of the window *and* navigate *and* communicate via radio at the same time?

After about 20 minutes Ray said I could now land the plane if I liked.

'WHAT?' I said. I was having trouble keeping the plane in the sky and the right way up. *'You must be KIDDING, mate! I'd like to live to fly another day, even if you're not too fussed.'*

He laughed and said he would land it and then I could take off again. Yikes! But I figured it was less risky to aim for something big and soft like the sky, rather than something small and very hard, like the runway, so I agreed to give it a go.

I pulled out the throttle, let go of the brakes, 30, 40, 50kph then pulled back the stick and WOAH! The little plane leaped into the air and immediately banked hard left! Fortunately, Ray caught the machine before it fell back on to the tarmac and levelled the wings for me. HELL'S TEETH!

'That was just due to the crosswind,' he chuckled. *'It's kinda handy to know it's gonna do that before you leave the ground. Should have told you, ha ha ha.'*

Another 15 minutes of blatting around the sky and it was time to land. I handed over the controls as the little plane skipped, wobbled and jumped in the thermals bubbling up from the ground as we approached the runway again. I'd had 35 minutes in the air at a cost of just NZ$42.50 (£12!) and I was hooked. I wanted one. I wanted to learn to fly. I wanted to pilot my own plane. Ray told me this posh little plane would cost around NZ$60,000 (£17,000) but other microlights were half that price. Mmmm.

Having failed so far to see a kiwi bird in the wild (we were usually in bed when most of these rare creatures were about their business) we decided next morning to visit the National Kiwi Centre in Hokitika to see the birds and learn all about them.

Maybe after the duff film show in Franz Josef we should have been prepared for disappointment, but this was crap, and at NZ$10 (£3), expensive crap. For New Zealand's supposedly major display of their national identity symbol, we saw ten minutes - all we could stomach - of a poorly edited video showing lots of chewed up and decapitated kiwis (yeuch!) then went through to the 'live' displays. Here in the dark were allegedly two kiwis, but one was hiding beneath an upturned plastic bowl and the other behind a make-believe tree. The other displays consisted of a small tank of unidentified fish. And a lizard. We'd been had. In the few minutes we were there troops of people filed in, mooched around for two or three minutes then stomped out in disgust. Most of the attractions, museums and suchlike were excellent value for money, but the NZ Tourist Board really needs to clamp down on these rip-off outfits.

Nearby the One-Hour photo shop seemed to have lost the plot when they told us they would take an hour and a half to print our film, so we declined and rode out of town to do battle with the first of the West Coast's infamous Road and Rail Bridges. As unlikely as it sounds, this is where the main State Highway 6 crosses a river via a narrow, one-lane bridge which is shared by both motor vehicles *and* trains.

There are two such bridges on this stretch of highway and they can easily catch out unwary motorcyclists. Apart from checking to see there is nothing coming the other way, and no train approaching from either direction, it is essential that you keep your bike's wheels away from the tracks. An American couple crossing this bridge on a hired motorcycle a year before us came a cropper when the poor bloke got the front wheel stuck in the track, the bike was pitched sideways and his neck was fatally broken on one of the bridge arch supports. An accident like that could spoil your whole day, so we took great care to stay in the middle of the rails, and studiously ignored the rental company's advice to ride in the narrow gap between the nearside rail and bridge parapet - a recipe for disaster in our opinion.

Trains and road traffic share a single carriageway bridge north of Hokitika

After the bridge we turned off the coast highway via Stafford along the 1876 Gold Trail, a narrow tarseal road through lovely original forest to Kumara, a small town apparently named after the native potato. Here we stopped for a coffee, cookie and chat with the friendly owner who was impressed that we'd taken the time to tour these little back roads.

'Overseas visitors normally stick to the main roads and miss all this beautiful scenery,' he said. 'They don't see the real New Zealand, only the polished up and sanitised version presented to tourists.'

He also told us about a good gravel road through Greenstone to Mitchells and Lake Brunner, with a forest road to the west of the lake to cut some 60km from our roundabout route to Greymouth. Sadly this shortcut was closed with padlocked gates, so we trundled on seeing lots of wekas and startling into clumsy flight a pukeko, New Zealand's native and very colourful moorhen.

Back on tarmac heading north from Poerua the country backroad had a few crazy locals racing their cars and one nearly tangled with us on a single-lane bridge. He approached from the opposite direction around a blind bend at 110-plus kph as I was almost on the bridge. I had taken to standing up on the footrests in order to see over these tricky, narrow bridges, and to be seen, so I spotted him in time to stop as he locked up all four wheels and almost skidded into the bridge parapet. I waved him on and he tore across the bridge in a white Nissan sportster and roared away with spinning tyres. Phew!

New Zealand is the nation that invented bungy jumping and continues to dream up ever-more hair-raising risk sports, such as jumping off Auckland's Sky Tower on a wire. This is not a film stunt, oh no. Anyone can pay their money, climb to the top of the tower and throw themselves off. It was one of the city's newest attractions when we were there, with people queuing up to take the plunge.

Given this national preoccupation with thrill-seeking, risk-taking and a very evident lack of fear, it is perhaps not surprising that New Zealand motoring deaths per head of population are three times the average for the UK, although most accidents involve only one vehicle. We often saw cars wander off the road through their drivers' lack of concentration, their wheels crashing over rocks and rubble and kicking up dust from the verges. We had also noted a lack of awareness for other road users. They would pull out of side roads causing other vehicles to brake or swerve and when it came to overtaking, they frequently hadn't got a clue.

On straight and level tarmac roads our little bikes could carry us at around 95kph, a fraction below the 100kph national speed limit. Most cars would be travelling - as in the UK - at a little above the limit, usually around 110-120kph. No problem, you'd think: They'll simply overtake us and continue on their way. But often we'd see a saloon closing in our mirrors on a long, straight, clear section of road, only to brake at the last minute and drop back. Weird! Then they'd close again and drop back, close and drop back - clearly frustrated at being slowed by these two small motorcycles, but seemingly incapable of making the move to overtake.

Until, that is, we got into some bends, or until some hills obscured the road ahead. Then the driver would overtake in the most inappropriate and unsafe position possible. It wasn't at all unusual to be overtaken as we were passing a crossroads or other major intersection. On single-lane bridges we had learned to ride in the middle of the road, so they wouldn't attempt to squeeze past us, as one idiot had done. Eventually we developed our own strategy for helping them overtake us. We would show them where to overtake by moving to the left of the road and putting our lefthand indicators on when there was a clear stretch of road. And if that didn't work we'd slow right down to force them past.

Thrill-seeking, lack of concentration or poor training? Possibly all of these, but we also surmised that much of the problem stems from a lack of familiarity. Their roads are so empty, some Kiwi drivers just don't learn to deal with other traffic. Or at least, that's the way it seemed to us.

We were amused by some of the road safety posters we saw alongside the highways:

* *'No Doctor, No Hospital, One Cemetery'* (popular on the outskirts of towns and villages)

* *'Speeding ticket'* (on a photo of a label tied to a corpse's toe)

* *'Life in the Fast Lane'* (on a photo of a cross on a grave)

* *'You're a Long Time Dead - So what's the Hurry?'*

On our travels we frequently tuned in to local radio stations for the weather forecast (usually bad), the music (often good) and the local radio commercials (always hilarious). We particularly liked the police advert which had a crusty old copper saying: *'If you drink and drive, you're a BLOODY IDIOT!'* Not the most subtle approach to motoring sobriety, but it kind of got to the point.

At Stillwater we turned left alongside the appropriately-named Grey River to Greymouth, then over the bridge to follow SH6 to the north. I was feeling very dozy so, after refuelling at Runanga, we stopped at Rapahoe beach for a picnic lunch and a snooze. It was strange weather here - bright sunshine and light rain - plus the ubiquitous sandflies, so I slept on the pebbles in full riding gear and gloves but minus helmet, with Viv detailed to wave away the little varmints from my face.

On to Punakaiki and the major tourist attraction of Pancake Rocks, an unusual formation of layered limestone battered by the sea. It was a bit over-commercialised here, with gift shops and cafés and all a bit too Disneyland for our taste, but the rocks were spectacular and well worth a visit.

From Punakaiki we continued north through the most gorgeous coastal scenery, with stunning views and the best bendy roads for bikers ever. This capped a long day's first-class riding and meant we were in the best possible spirits as we rode through Westport and out to the North Beach to find our accommodation at Chrystal Lodge. The location could not have been better: Just two motel units in the garden of Ann and Bill Blythe's home, surrounded by paddocks full of horses and ponies, with a mountain range backdrop and the sounds of birdsong and waves on the beach. And if the setting was perfect, our motel was the best yet. They had just taken delivery of a new double bed that morning so we

Pancake Rocks at Punakaiki

would get the most luxurious sleep, and Ann had made muffins for us. We were in heaven and immediately extended our stay to three nights and in the morning added two more. We felt we could happily have stayed here forever.

Chapter 13

A Week In Westport

Having been as far south as the coast road would take us at Jackson Bay, with its storm-tossed fishing boats, bleak rain-lashed cottages and The Cray Pot café, we were keen to see the northern equivalent at Karamea. We rode north on the last of the West Coast Heritage Highway SH67 next morning, stopping for fuel at a quaint old garage in Waimangaroa on the way. It even had a quaint old couple running it, and both came out to chat to us about our travels, clearly delighted to have some customers to talk to.

A little further up the road we stopped at Granity for coffee. This little village was once the thriving hub for the region's coal industry, but by now had become a sleepy backwater laced with history and nostalgia. We sat at a table outside the small dairy, which wasn't as peculiar as it sounds: In New Zealand 'dearies' are café-cum-general-stores with the emphasis on dairy products, while bakeries are café-cum-general-stores with the emphasis on bread, cakes and pies. While I was inside ordering coffee Viv had attracted two young lads on bicycles, eager to chat to her about our motorbikes. They both had motorcycles they said - 80cc motocrossers - and the youngest of the two, perhaps ten years old, asked Viv if she could do doughnuts. This is where you spin the machine around in circles with the back wheel skidding wildly in a cloud of blue tyre smoke.

Viv explained that we are a bit too old for all that and gave him a ginger nut biscuit. He'd obviously never seen one before and had several unsuccessful attempts at biting it, in between more tales of his motorcycling exploits and advice on where we should ride locally to find waist-deep mud, deep water and huge rocks. They were clearly incredulous that a pair of old codgers like us could ride motorcycles at all and were testing us out. Eventually, they saw three girls approaching and quickly scarpered - ginger nut still intact - before the embarrassment of the opposite sex arrived. A few more years and all that would change.

With the lads vanished the café proprietor came out to keep us entertained. His business was up for sale, like so many on the West Coast, he told us. It was now January 8th, high summer and peak holiday season, when he might see ten customers in a day. For most of the year it was dead, he said, but he had a job at the coal mine so he and his wife didn't depend on the shop for income. Most mines had closed and much of the remaining work was automated, so there were few jobs now.

We purchased his one piece of cheese and, as we were pulling on our jackets and helmets to leave, were amused to see a delivery van arrive and more cheese supplies being carried in. We could imagine the proprietor saying: *'We've had a real run on cheese this morning, so we'd better stock up!'*

Further up the coast we crossed the Mokihinui River where the road turns inland and begins innumerable sweeps, turns and hairpin bends as it climbs past Corbyvale to the Happy Valley Saddle. There were great views from up here, out over unspoiled bush with ponga, matai, rimu, rata, kamahi and nikau palms visible in the dense growth below.

Back along the coast again we finally pulled into the appealing little town of Karamea and visited The Saracen Café, as much for the convenience of the loos opposite as for another coffee. Since every business must be multi-faceted to make a living here, the café also had an extensive display of carved wooden jewellery boxes, most crafted from sections of old fence post and cunningly constructed with magic drawers. They were made by Daniel Vos, whose Dandee Design workshops were out the back. He must have been Karamea's main manufacturing industry as he employed two men. We helped keep them solvent by buying the smallest example of their handiwork, the only size that would fit in our luggage. Or that was the reason I gave Viv. It is wise, in my opinion, to buy your wife the smallest jewellery receptacle possible. Once it is full, you have the perfect excuse to avoid extravagant gestures at Christmas and birthdays.

At Karamea Beach (turn left at the 'airport' - a grass strip and single Cessna) we sat on top of the dunes to tuck into Vogel's pumpkinseed bread and Granity's very last piece of cheese. Then the wind suddenly gusted from the sea and we were sandblasted, giving our cheese an instant crunchy coating. We retreated back over the dunes to huddle behind our motorbikes to finish our gritty lunch. Two girls arrived on foot with rucksacks and disappeared over the dunes - but soon also beat a hasty retreat from the sandblasting wind.

From here it was a metalled road for the last 15km to the northernmost point on the West Coast for vehicles and the start of the Heaphy Track, world famous among New Zealand trampers. On the last stretch of this gravel road we caught up with a girl struggling to pedal her heavily laden bicycle into the fierce headwind. Just as I started to overtake her she wobbled right across the track in front of me and I missed her by inches. She looked up startled as I flashed past - she had not heard me over the wind noise and my bike's hooter had stopped working. A bit further up the track there was a bloke with a big grin - he had seen the near-miss - and he looked vaguely familiar.

Of course! It was our old friends Ted Lewis and Shelley Trevaskis, who we'd left fishing for their supper in Lake Tennyson beside the Rainbow Road three weeks and 3,000km ago. What a small world! To have bumped into them twice - almost literally in Shelley's case - in two of the most remote and deserted places in the country was amazing.

They looked fit, brown and happy and were delighted to swap tales of our respective travel adventures since we last met. We left them setting up their tent among the trees and sandflies of the Kohaihai River mouth and promised to look out for them - and try not to run them over - on our future travels. They would be here three days, so we donated our remaining apples, bread and cheese ('scuse the sand) to their meagre rations. We had no biscuits of any kind, so no Cookie Time moral dilemmas on this occasion.

By now it was late afternoon and we still had 115km to ride to get back to Westport in time to shop for our supper, so we scooted south again, my bike running on to its fuel tank's reserve just as we entered Westport, 209km since we filled up that morning.

Next day we decided to take a break from biking and in the morning walked the four kilometres into Westport to visit

173

the Coaltown Museum. The intention was to gain a little socio-cultural insight into the region's history, but we got far more than we bargained for. There were sections telling the story of the area's aviation, marine, gold and flax developments, as well as an earthquake display and video, and all this in addition to the main coal mining exhibition. It was excellent.

We particularly enjoyed a first class film with lots of ancient footage from Denniston, the mining town in the hills above Westport. It showed the amazing Denniston 'Incline' in action - a gravity-defying cable car system that lowered half-ton coal trucks down a dizzying 1-in-1.25 gradient, each full truck's descent hauling an empty truck back up the mountain. It was a brilliant and awesome piece of engineering which ran from 1880 to 1967. At one stage 1,500 people lived up in the hills and were employed by the coal industry, including our motel proprietor Bill, who worked on the Denniston Incline cable system as a young man. Denniston was a thriving town with its own school, shops and entertainment. Now all but four of the houses had gone. By the time we dragged ourselves away from the absorbing exhibits and stumbled out into the daylight, it was 2.30pm.

Next day we decided to go see the remnants of Denniston for ourselves, as the gloomy weather forecast was 100 percent wrong and it was brilliantly sunny. How often does this happen? One analyst in the UK worked out that if Britain's weather forecasters predicted that tomorrow's weather would be the same as today's, they would be more accurate, more often, than they are currently.

The ride up to Denniston was superb, with great views back over Westport and the coast, shimmering in the sunshine. We visited the schoolhouse museum and the 'old mine' mock-up before riding off to explore Burnett Face and beyond, taking a long and increasingly steep and difficult track up Mount Rochford, a real test of extreme off-road riding skills for us, which Viv coped with extremely well, despite her still tender knee.

Back at Chrystal Lodge, Bill had lined up an afternoon of new activities for us. I was to go paddling his tiny canoe up the Orowaiti River while Viv got her first ever ride on a horse.

Nellie takes Viv for her first horse ride at Chrystal Lodge, Westport

And no ordinary horse either - this was Bill's gentle giant Nellie, a chestnut mare standing 19 hands high. Viv needed a chair to climb into the saddle but was thrilled to be taken for a trot along the silver sands of North Beach by Annie, an American horse enthusiast who had enough experience to ride Bill's lively stallion Prince.

Annie was staying in Westport on New Zealand's WOF programme. WOF stands for Workers on Organic Farms, but in practice means visitors can get accommodation and meals in exchange for a few hours work in a wide variety of businesses, many of them tourist related. We met several WOFs on our travels and all agreed it was a great way to get to see New Zealand on virtually no budget at all. Annie had heard that Bill kept horses so she cycled down to Chrystal Lodge one day to give them a carrot and a stroke of the muzzle. She got chatting to Bill, who said she could take them out for a canter whenever she liked. That's the kind of guy he is.

Viv loved her ride on the ginormous Nellie, but returned from the beach with a smile that was half grimace. Her injured leg was in agony and she needed a stepladder to get down. We would later discover that Viv's shin bone had been splintered by her big crash less than a fortnight before. It is a testament to the healing and pain-killing power of her Bioflow magnet pad that she was able to continue with our motorcycle tour at all. Had she gone to hospital, she would have been plastered from hip to toe and our travels would have been over.

After a fine home-cooked meal featuring roasted vegetables from Bill's garden, Viv decided her leg was fit for an evening stroll along the beach to show me where she had ridden. This resulted in us getting lost in dense bush and me repeating my Nelson heroics when I carried her 200 metres through a massive puddle to get us back to our motel. We slept very well.

Another brilliantly sunny day and I felt sufficiently encouraged by the more clement weather to spring-clean my face, with my first shave in seven weeks. A great bushy, and alarmingly white, beard fell in drifts into the basin and finally a chubby white chin appeared, grinning sheepishly.

Meanwhile, Ann arrived with piles of fresh towels, tea-towels and flannels again - she did the same after our second night - plus a plate of scrumptious home-made shortbread. We now felt like part of the family and couldn't face the thought of leaving the next day, so we booked to stay with Bill and Ann for a sixth night. Just as well this wasn't the first motel we stayed at, otherwise we might have got no further.

Fortified with shortbread, we dragged ourselves away from the homely comforts of Chrystal Lodge to ride back up the coast, through Granity to the tiny hamlet of Ngakawau and the Charming Creek Walk. Viv's leg had recovered from the horse riding and was now fit for a tramp in the hills.

'*And we need the exercise,*' she added, with a pointed look at my cookie-cushioned midriff.

We locked the bikes together at the start of the walk and I legged it to a nearby garage to see if they would look after our helmets, riding jackets and overtrousers for a couple of hours.

'*No problem,*' said the lady proprietor with a smile. '*You leave 'em here and we'll get a good price for 'em before you git back.*'

By the time I'd returned to Viv and the bikes, she was chatting to a German couple, Hans and Heidi from Hamburg. Okay, I admit it, I forgot to ask their names and made up the Hans and Heidi bit, but they really were from Hamburg. Truth is, I was severely distracted by the fact that Heidi was wearing sprayed-on Lycra cycle shorts, a tight white T-shirt with no bra, and was clearly very excited about the prospect of jogging up into the hills. I tried hard not to stare, but it was only after she folded her arms that I realised she had quite a pretty face too.

Aware that I was only a micro-second away from a slap round the ear from Viv, if not from Heidi, I forced my attention on to Hans and started swapping travel tales. They were taking a break from their three-year work posting in Singapore with a see-all-of-New-Zealand-in-two-weeks campervan and jogging tour. And judging by the way they sprinted off up the Charming Creek Walkway, they'd probably make it too.

Hans had confessed that he was a big fan of Bill Bryson and, as we trudged up the hill after their fast-vanishing forms, I found myself shaking my head in wonder at other nationals' ability to master a foreign language with such fluency that they can enjoy the intricate irony and gentle whimsy of Bryson's inimitable humour.

Onwards and upwards we walked over the almost-vanished sleepers of a coal mine railway, under verdant native matai, rimu and the broad fronds of pongas. In places the track skirted vertical drops into the boulder-strewn creekbed below and rock falls covered the track. Through tunnels, over bridges and finally across a gorge, via a wonderfully wobbly swingbridge, before another long tunnel and a welcome rest shelter featuring a photo-story of the timber mill which used to occupy the spot.

Rummaging in the undergrowth nearby were an elderly local couple who told us they were keen amateur botanists. They soon returned to their task of hotly disputing the Latin names of obscure and insignificant weeds.

'No, no, NO! Don't be ridiculous,' said the woman. *'Can't you SEE! The leaves should be opposing, not alternating in the Ventriculum Westwoodii. These leaves are alternating aren't they? AND they have nodulated spicules. Tut, tut, whatever were you thinking of, Ventriculum Westwoodii indeed!'*

It's nice to know that as you get older and develop new hobbies to share in your retirement years, there'll still be plenty to argue about. We left them to their botanical battles and clambered down an overgrown and broken track to perch on rocks beside a picturesque waterfall, where we munched our picnic lunch being alternately drizzled with spray and eaten by sandflies. Ah, bliss!

We set off back down the track and discovered the waterfall's drizzly mist was following us and getting heavier! Ah, maybe that's rain? The earlier clear sky had clouded over and the rain increased steadily, until we were stumbling along pressed tightly together under Viv's tiny pocket umbrella as rain hammered down in a torrent and soaked everything from our shoulders down. I knew it was a mistake shaving that beard off.

I felt briefly depressed at the return of the rain, which we so hoped had left us to torment some other poor soul, like that bloke on the Norton Commando, for instance. Then I had a mental image of Heidi jogging back down the track in a soaking T-shirt and there was a sudden spring in my step once more. Sadly, back at the car park their campervan was gone, but the sun had returned and the roads were steaming. So we treated ourselves to ice creams at the garage, partly as a way of saying thank you for not selling our gear, but probably replacing all the calories we'd burned up on our hike.

What we really needed was a coffee so, remembering there was a sign for the 'Contented Cow Café' at Gentle Annie Beach beside the Mokihinui River, 15km to the north, we rode on up there only to find a 'closed' notice now hanging on the sign.

'Why, for goodness sake?' I whined. 'It's a Friday afternoon, January 11th. It isn't going to get any busier than this - how can you be closed?'

Viv astutely pointed out that my whingeing and moaning at the wooden sign wasn't getting us any closer to a cup of coffee. Why didn't we turn around and head south again to Granity, where we sat outside a café three days ago? Good idea!

On the way we saw a distant building with TEAROOMS painted in three metre high letters on its roof, so we made a detour only to find this place had been closed for years, the only diners now being some very fat spiders which had spun webs inside the windows to trap a million flies. Pheeew!

Finally, tired and thirsty, we arrived back in Granity to find the dairy we had visited earlier in the week was closed too. What was going on? Was this some kind of conspiracy to prevent us from getting a coffee? Fortunately, there was a bright blue painted café open further up the street and we plonked ourselves wearily at a wooden table outside. The proprietor came out to serve us.

'I can't make you a coffee, sorry,' she said. 'There's no electricity to boil the kettle due to a tree falling on the line back up at Gentle Annie.'

So that explained the closed cafés conspiracy I thought, as I grumpily sucked at a carton of orange juice through a straw and tried my best to be polite to the woman at the next table. Her large and disturbingly manky dog was trying to get its nose inside my riding jacket. I wouldn't normally mind too much, but this hound was covered with scabs and weeping sores, its entire back devoid of fur but liberally sprinkled with white powder. For some reason it was attracted to me about as strongly as I was repelled by it, and despite its owner's repeated: *'No Yasmin, don't do that!'* it seemed determined to share its disease with me.

When I reached the bottom of my carton I carried on slurping so noisily and repeatedly that the woman finally came over and put a lead on her scabby mutt and dragged it away.

'Come along, Yasmin. Come and sit over here with Mummy,' she cooed and gave me a look which said: *'Your sort ought to be put down!'*

The main reason I was being testy and badly behaved was I was desperately tired and had been hoping for a shot of caffeine to keep me awake on the ride home. Instead I resorted to singing 'Good King Wenceslas' at the top of my voice in an effort to fight off the tiredness and maintain some semblance of concentration. Twice I ran off the road before we reached our motel, where I flopped on to our deluxe bed and slept soundly for an hour before waking up with a sneezing fit, convinced I'd caught canine distemper. And this is no country for chaps with a runny nose.

By now we had visited enough shops, stores and supermarkets around New Zealand to have reached a sad conclusion: This is a fully civilised, up-to-date country but in one important respect they languish in the dark ages. I am talking here about the serious matter of paper handkerchiefs.

You ladies who raise a flimsy tissue to your nose and take a feeble sniff have nothing to fear. There are plenty of tiny, dainty, flowered and scented tissues for such delicate dabs. But chaps like me who need a good snort on the old nose trumpet several times a day to keep our olfactories decongested, will be astonished at how the best New Zealand tissues disintegrate at the very first hint of moisture or air pressure.

We searched everywhere from supermarket shelves to department stores to pharmacies in our hunt for genuine 'Man Sized' tissues. The best they could do were some called 'Thicker & Larger', which Viv said should suit me down to the ground, but even these had no structural integrity in the face of a nasal blast. As Viv observed, *'S'not good enough, is it?'*

My question is this: What's the matter with you Kiwi blokes? Too timid to trumpet into your tissues? To tame to complain? Come on guys, in this battle of the nose-napkins it's time to give your tissue manufacturers both barrels - declare Nasal Warfare!

I finally resolved the problem by buying a pack of plain white 'Deluxe' paper serviettes. Huge, tough, waterproof and trumpet-proof, I found one would last me all day.

While we were searching one large department store in Christchurch for tissues we stumbled across another peculiarity of Kiwi culture. This store had a very useful central signpost to direct shoppers to the various parts of the vast, open-plan floor where they might find their purchasing requirements. There were signs pointing to: Children's Clothes, Menswear, Women's Fashions, Perfumerie, Cookware, Toys, Manchester.

MANCHESTER! We stopped and did a double-take. Yes, it really did say Manchester.

'That's ridiculous,' I spluttered. *'Manchester is on the other side of the world. Why on earth would they have a sign pointing to it from here, in the middle of a department store, in the middle of New Zealand, for goodness sake?'*

We had to have an answer. Fearing a repeat of the Taihape gumboot saga I did the only thing a chap can do in times like this: I sent Viv to ask a sales assistant.

'Aw yiss,' she said, when Viv had dragged her over to the signpost and demanded an explanation. *'Yiss, thet's Menchista. Thet's all the linens, bidsprids, sheets, all thet tarp o' thing is Menchista.'*

'But why are linens called Manchester?'

'Aw, ah dohn't know thet. They jest are. Always bin called Menchista, far as ah know.'

We'd obviously drained her entire well of knowledge. Presumably there's a connection between the cotton mills of north west England and the early colony's linen supplies which has left the city's name indelibly stamped on the Kiwi subconscious. Wouldn't it be fun, we thought, if all the country's commodities were generically labelled in the same way. The cake section would be called Dundee, solid fuels would be Newcastle, you'd search in the Sheffield department for your cookware of course and Northampton if you wanted footwear.

Another sunny day. So bright in fact that we had to keep our kitchen curtains shut to avoid the early morning glare and in the bathroom, which also faced east but had no window blind, I resorted to wearing a towel on my head while sitting on the loo to avoid a headache. Fortunately the door was locked, so no-one will ever know. By 9am it was already 25⁰C outside and Viv was bringing *in* her first washing of the day - bone dry!

It was an auspicious start for Westport's A&P day, the major event on the town's calendar when an Agricultural and Pastoral Show is held at the nearby sportsfield. All afternoon girls rode their ponies over jumps, dogs were doing circuits with their owners and marrows were judged. Viv's favourite event was the regional axeman competition which featured up to a dozen fit young men in action at once, all rippling muscles and whirling choppers as they axed their way through huge logs in seconds. While she stood mesmerised, six microlight aircraft from the Westport Aero Club flew in and landed one after another right inside the stadium. I was soon wandering around the parked planes and drooling over one with a 'For Sale' notice on it, but Viv brought me back down to earth: *'What are you going to do - fly it back to England? It won't fit in your suitcase you know.'*

By mid afternoon it was well over 30⁰C and the scorching sun was turning everybody red, so we headed 'home' to Chrystal Lodge for shade, rest and supper followed by a leisurely evening walk to the beach and river. Our final Westport sunset was stunning, with the whole sky awash with colour - blue, turquoise, gold, pink. Some areas appeared to have been airbrushed with soft salmon pink and duck-egg blue, then edged with gold, red and brilliant yellow. Skies never look like that in England. It was the most beautiful work of natural art we'd ever witnessed.

We awoke to the sound of rain. The weather gods must have known we were back on the road today. After almost a week in Westport it took a while to gather all our possessions together, double-wrap them in plastic bags, then fit them all inside the bin-liners inside the panniers, ensuring an even weight distribution. Even our washbag contents needed to be vacuum wrapped in zip-topped plastic bags to ensure that shampoo, toothpaste and aftershave didn't leak out when stuffed inside the panniers and shaken violently over the gravel roads. Many of our books, papers and souvenirs would be ruined if they got wet.

We had big hugs and kisses from Bill and Ann who'd looked after us so well for the past six days and then rode off west. You might suppose that heading west out of Westport would put us straight into the Tasman Sea, but we'd decided to visit Cape Foulwind - source of many a good flatulence joke - and its seal colony. After oohing and aahing over the seal pups and befriending the wekas which strutted cheekily about the car park looking for picnic scraps, we headed east into the lovely Buller River valley, passing Hawk's Crag and Little Hawk's Crag on the way to Inangahua.

The crags are rocky overhangs where the road has been chiselled out of a solid granite cliff. The result is a couple of narrow and twisty single-carriageway sections which wriggle between the bare rock face and a sheer drop to the rocks and the river below. They are, necessarily, one-way sections with priority arrows, but motorcyclists would be well advised to proceed only when they can see it is clear. If you meet a vehicle in these near-blind sections your choices would not be good: Head-on collision, solid rock race or a 50 metre drop to the rocks and river.

We made a brief stop to snap a photo here and, in the minute that my gloves were off and visor raised, several sandflies grabbed an early lunch. At Inangahua Junction we stayed with SH6 to the village and then turned right to follow a minor road for ten kilometres to Inangahua Landing. This was a delightful little country lane beside a stream and once we'd shaken off our escort - two lads on a Kawasaki monkey bike - we found access to the stony streambed and sat on a log for lunch.

I tried my luck with my fishing line and got lots of bites, not from fish unfortunately but from the ever-present sandflies. We were becoming hardened by now and they couldn't spoil this lovely, peaceful spot. Back on SH69 heading south we were soon in Reefton, founded when a gold-bearing quartz reef was discovered in the 1860s. The town quickly prospered and enjoyed the distinction of being the first in the southern hemisphere to get electric lighting, in 1888. You can still see the remains of the original water sluice and turbine which generated the power, rusting on the river bank opposite the town.

We checked in to the Bellbird Motel, quaint and very 1950s, but comfortable and perfectly suitable for our needs. The Reefton Visitor Centre had some good displays, but a stroll through the town itself was fascinating enough, being another with a Wild West frontier feel to it. Alfrescos restaurant provided fine pizzas and coffee for NZ$30 (£8) for the pair of us, while we provided the BYO wine. An unusual extra at this restaurant was free use of insect repellent spray and candles, which was handy, as there was no front wall to keep sandflies and mozzies at bay. We found our Hawke's Bay Merlot was at least as effective as the aerosol as far as insect annoyance was concerned. After four glasses I probably wouldn't have noticed if the owner's dog had bitten me.

Maybe it was the odd mixture of insecticide and alcohol, but for some reason I didn't sleep at all well. Consequently I was a bit sluggish next morning as we packed up and rode off towards Greymouth on SH7, past the odd-shaped landforms of old gold dredge tailings (spent gravel) and through the tiny townships of Ikamatua and Ahaura. We stopped for coffee in the latter at 'The Gallery' where oddball artist Lanie fashions Christmas Island-type heads out of ponga tree stems. Outside on the pavement was a clean, smart and original blue Morris 1000, ready to drive away at just NZ$1500 (£430). In the UK it would fetch at least four times that, but here they are still trundling around the country roads as regular transport, not as collectables.

Nine kilometres further on we turned left on a minor road signed for Nelson Creek and followed a tidy tarseal road through pretty woodland and farmland until, after 20km, it switched to a good gravel surface and shortly after Lake Haupiri appeared through the trees on our right. Its unruffled surface provided a mirror reflection of Mt Elizabeth and Mt Alexander before we arrived at the Haupiri River, where a picnic table under trees near the bridge allowed us to dine in style.

We splashed on enough DEET to keep the sandflies at bay and were serenaded by a hundred crickets, so loud we were unable to hear any birdsong, although we could see bellbirds flitting through the trees nearby.

At Kopara there was an odd collection of rusty barns and motor relics, plus cabins, a canon and a flagpole, but not a soul around. We pressed on to Haupiri, which appeared to be three homesteads scattered over a wide area, a populous village for this far into the outback, but we couldn't find our intended route around Lake Ahaura. After riding on a grass-filled track alongside the beautiful blue Ahaura River for a few kilometres, the track simply fizzled out and we were obliged to retrace our route, before turning left to pick up a gravel track to Lady Lake and Rotomanu. From here we rode through Poerua and Inchbonnie and then on to SH73 for Arthur's Pass.

Immediately the road started to climb on its way over the Southern Alps and we soon passed Jacksons, a settlement which consisted of a single building straight out of a John Wayne movie, with hitching rails for horses at the front, for real this time. I wish we had stopped there for coffee and a photo but, with a long steep climb to the saddle of Arthur's Pass ahead of us, we ground on up to Otira and a most peculiar hotel.

There's a stop here on the TranzAlpine railway but little else to tempt anyone to stay. Here's a clue to how desirable Otira is: They were offering a free house to anyone who

A moment for reflection at Lake Haupiri

would go live there and start a craft business. The poster offering this deal also listed some of the crafts you might wish to try, including jam-making, possum-trapping, hand-knitting and pottery. Just who you might sell any of these goods or services to is anybody's guess.

The only other customer was a German cyclist, disgustingly fit and skinny, with rippling buttocks in his Spandex shorts to give Viv a thrill for a change. I tried to make a joke with him that it would be a little easier going up the pass on our bikes than on his, but he argued that it was not steep, the flash git! We had the last laugh when we reached Otira Gorge a minute after overtaking him and the gradient promptly went to 1-in-3. Ha! Tell me that isn't steep, Wolfgang.

As it got steep it also got exciting, with tunnels, waterfalls, one-way bits and a concrete roof to redirect a waterfall and scree falling from the mountain above our heads. Finally we emerged on to a spindly concrete viaduct which carried the road away from the crumbling sides of the gorge and up to the top of the pass. In the carpark overlooking the viaduct we were able to observe the enormity of the engineering task undertaken to overcome the awesome obstacles of height, slope and tumbling rocks. And we got to meet some keas, the crazy mountain parrots we'd been warned about. They had a comical swaggering walk and a limping run and clearly couldn't wait for us to leave our bikes so they could attack them. The keas swaggered about like a gang of thugs looking for a chance to tear open our bike seats, so one of us stayed with the bikes while we took it in turns to ooh and aah and photograph the stunning scene below.

After another 20km we pulled up at the Bealey Hotel which provided us with a strange little room and me with ample opportunity to grumble, moan and stomp about bad-temperedly. It's funny, isn't it, how tiredness can colour your judgement. After my failed night's sleep at Reefton I arrived red-eyed and fractious and took an instant dislike to the chap at the Bealey's bar who gave me the key. Then I ranted about our tiny and peculiar room, the lack of a cooker, the awful little individual plastic cartons of UHT milk for my tea and several other insignificancies.

Cheeky kea sidles up looking for trouble at Arthur's Pass

Fearing I might go into total meltdown, Viv nipped over to the hotel restaurant to blag a bottle of milk and came back full of tidings of great joy.

'It's really very nice in the bar - I think we should go over there straight away for a drink,' she said. To which I stared at her in open-mouthed wonder and just blinked. Viv hates bars, dislikes all pubs with a passion and would not shed a tear if they all burned down tomorrow. I was speechless.

'They've got Bob Dylan playing on the bar's CD,' she explained with a smile, as she edged towards the door impatiently.

For the past 30 years or so, Viv's life has revolved around Bob Dylan's music. At home there isn't a day goes by that one of the great man's albums doesn't get an airing. But for nearly two months now Viv had gone cold turkey and she was desperate for a Dylan fix. We ran as fast as Viv's gimpy leg would carry her.

After four tracks of Bob Dylan and two glasses of Riverside Red, I was feeling altogether more mellow. I paid the barman in advance for our deficient motel room without a quibble, bought a panoramic view postcard of the mountains visible from the hotel and was even considering a game of pool with the locals when Viv reminded me I was tired. At 9pm we dodged through sheeting rain to our meagre cabin and crashed out, happy and contented.

The Bealey Hotel gained instant fame and notoriety a few years back when its previous owner, Paddy Freaney, produced a photo of what he claimed was a giant moa in the bush near his hotel. The bird had been hunted into extinction by the Maori before Europeans arrived to colonise the country, but the spark of hope that a moa might have survived somewhere was instantly fanned into flames and the press had a field day. It was good for business, of course, and the hoaxed photo perpetuated the moa myth to such an extent that there are still a few misguided souls who stalk the grounds in the hope of a sighting. As Viv wryly observed, the only moa that has been around this hotel in the last few hundred years is a lawnmoa.

We were still chuckling over this at breakfast when an item on the radio news wiped the smiles from our faces. CAA inspectors were about to visit the site near Fox Glacier where a helicopter had crashed the previous day, killing two people.

'You don't think...'

'No, no,' I shook my head, not wanting to even consider it. 'There are hundreds of helicopters operating up and down the West Coast. The chances of it being that little chopper from Lake Paringa are very remote. I guess we'll find out when we get back to Christchurch and speak to John.'

By the time our bags were packed, a watery sun had brought out every sandfly in the district looking for a quick snack. I was struggling to strap the luggage on to our bikes without being eaten alive. Viv was trying to help by slapping me and herself alternately. Our earlier 'sang-froid' had evaporated and we were both calling them 'little buggers' now. We were ready to get back to the drier east coast where sandflies are seldom a problem.

But the roads were dry and the day brightening steadily as we headed down the sweeping curves of the Waimakariri Valley road (SH73) past Lake Pearson. As ever, we were cautious on the one-way bridges, which was just as well, as

A few thousand sheep have the right of way near the Bealey Hotel

a sea of sheep poured over one as we approached. It took five minutes for several thousand woolly creatures to gallop past us as Viv smiled, waved at them and said: *'Hello, sheepies! Aaah, look at dat diddle one,'* and other such inanities that did little to enhance her tough motorcycle chick image. There are 40 million sheep in New Zealand, more than ten for every human, and long may it remain so.

It was noon when we rolled up at John and Jill's in Christchurch to find no-one home, but a note from Jill telling us to help ourselves to lunch. After raiding their fridge and pantry, we rode into town to get our faithful Serows serviced once more. The chaps at New Zealand Motorcycle Rentals found a new visor to replace Viv's damaged one and didn't bat an eyelid when we showed them their set of panniers with all the straps pulled out. It just so happened that the pannier repair man, Nigel, had just arrived with 11 pairs of panniers returned from mending, so we did a swap and rode away with freshly fettled machines plus new supplies of engine oil and chain lube. They really are exceptionally good to their customers at this bike hire shop.

After supper with John and Jill and their friend Caroline, who like us was on a holiday visit from England, we decided to play 'Chocolate Roulette' - my Christmas present sent all the way from the UK by my sister Mary Ann. This game consisted of a roulette wheel which each of us spun in turn and then ate the chocolate bullet the arrow pointed to. Eleven of the twelve bullets had a fondant centre, just one was filled with chilli powder. And guess who got the hot bullet? Thanks Mary Ann!

Next day was January 16th and cause for a double celebration. I was born on my brother John's birthday and, if he felt I made a less-than-thrilling 13th birthday present he's never shown it. John emigrated to New Zealand when I was still a youngster so it had been quite a while since we had been able to share our mutual birthday together - 46 years to be precise - and we made the most of it with an evening of partying, reminiscing, joke-telling and general silliness.

But the party spirit evaporated next morning when a newspaper report confirmed our worst fears. The helicopter crash three days previously <u>had</u> claimed the lives of Lake Paringa's Barry Guise and his hunting partner Geoffrey Rodger from Jackson Bay. Here's how the paper told the story:

Paringa in mourning yet again

Remote Lake Paringa has been struck by tragedy for the second time in six months, leaving another young widow and a fatherless baby.

The only two households at the tiny roadside clearing, 90km south of Franz Josef Glacier, are grieving again after a tragic coincidence. On Monday, pilot Barry Guise died in a helicopter crash on the slopes up the Cook River valley, leaving behind his partner and children's author Robyn Hoglund and their four-month-old baby.

In July, their neighbour and friend Brent Mahuika was killed in a freak road accident when a car skidded

191

on ice and ploughed into him as he was helping tow out another accident victim. He left behind his new bride, Nicky, and their two babies, one just a week old at the time.

Ms Hoglund grew up at the Lake Paringa Motels, where Mrs Mahuika works with her parents, before setting up house and a helicopter pad for Mr Guise at the back of the motels.

The helicopter crash also claimed the life of a well-known Jackson Bay man, Geoffrey (Gutty) Rodger, a hunter who with his wife Lisa ran the Craypot pie cart at the bay. He also left a young family.

Mr Rodger and Mr Guise died when the Robinson 22 helicopter crashed 1,370m up the Balfour Range, near Fox Glacier, while hunting thar and chamois. The accident happened in fine weather. Police said the machine struck the mountainside and then rolled about 30m, while witnesses said the wreckage was strewn through a deep gulley. Civil Aviation Authority (CAA) inspectors were flown to the accident site yesterday.

We hadn't met either of these men but felt they had touched our lives. We'd met their wives, friends and family, and we'd watched them fly their helicopter over our motel at Lake Paringa. It reminded us there were real dangers out there as we kitted up, fired up our bikes and headed for the hills.

Any hint of lethargy was soon blown away by a fine breezy ride around Banks Peninsula, taking in Godley Head, Lyttelton, Governor's Bay, Diamond Harbour, Purau and Port Levy. From here we tackled once again the lovely, twisty and narrow gravel track called Western Valley Road which we had ridden with John when we first arrived in New Zealand. It was much more fun to ride when not jet-lagged - and it was just as well I was wide awake when my bike's steering locked up as we were hurtling down from the saddle on a twisty section with near vertical drops. Having slithered to a halt in a cold sweat, I discovered a granite chipping had wedged itself between the frame's steering head and the fork yoke. A firm tug on the bars fetched it out, but it was enough of a scare to require a cup of tea and a Cookie Time cookie to soothe my nerves at Little River's Gallery Café, before we trundled back home via Motukarara and the Summit Road.

Over the next couple of days we left the bikes in the garage and borrowed Jill's old Subaru estate car to visit a Superbike race meeting at Ruapuna circuit near the airport, then the cinema to see Lord Of The Rings. We're not big film goers these days, and probably would not have chosen to go see this Tolkein 'swords and sorcery' classic but for two things: 1) It was being hailed as a great New Zealand success story, everyone was talking about it and it seemed churlish not to go, and 2) We would soon be riding through some of the set. In fact, the film was brilliant, if a tad violent, and we couldn't wait to explore some of the more outlandish scenery on our little Yamahas.

First though, John had promised to take us flying - either in a hot air balloon or fixed-wing aircraft. Like his wife, John is multi-talented and can fly just about anything that is able to take to the air. It comes in very handy in his job of aircraft accident investigator for the Government. But even he couldn't fly on Saturday due to poor weather conditions over Christchurch. While we were considering what to do next, his phone rang with a report of an accident that morning. A twin engined, six seater aircraft had crashed in the Southern Alps, killing all six occupants. This was distinctly unsettling and, coming so soon after the news of the helicopter crash, made us wonder if it was safe to take to the air at all.

John, we knew, had seen enough in his line of work to take no risks so, when the sky cleared next day and he announced it was okay to fly to Milford Sound, we grabbed our cameras and headed for the airport. At Canterbury Aero Club we pushed out of its hanger a Piper Seneca II, filled it with fuel and took off, heading west for the mountains.

If we thought New Zealand looked spectacular from the ground, nothing could have prepared us for the awesome sight from the air of snow-capped mountains, glaciers, too-blue lakes and extraordinary braided riverbeds. Over Mt Sefton and around Mt Cook we flew with cameras clicking before heading out over the West Coast, past Haast and Jackson Bay to line up for the dramatic entrance into Milford Sound. This part of Fiordland is perhaps the most popular

Looking up Milford Sound, Mitre Peak on the left

Mt Cook, Mt Tasman and Lake Pukaki viewed on our private flight to Milford

image of New Zealand's rugged scenery. We could see why as we took a heart-stopping flight between the near-vertical slopes, followed by a dizzying turn and descent to land at Milford's tiny airstrip.

The astonishing scenery and the electrifying flight down the sound were quite unreal, like something out of a flight-sim computer game, and Viv had her eyes tightly shut for the last bit. After lunch and a walk to explore the few accessible slopes, we flew back to Christchurch, identifying the lakes we'd passed and the trails we'd ridden three weeks earlier.

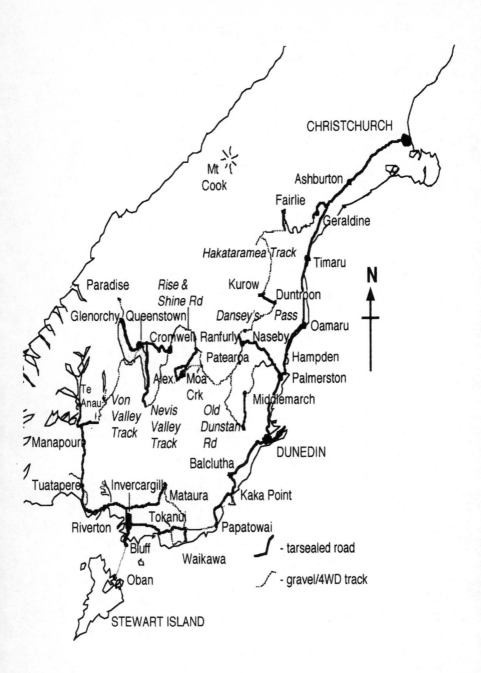

CHRISTCHURCH

Ashburton

Fairlie

Geraldine

Mt
Cook

Hakataramea Track

Timaru

N

Paradise

*Rise &
Shine Rd*

Kurow

Duntroon

Glenorchy Queenstown

Dansey's Pass

Oamaru

Cromwell Ranfurly Naseby

Patearoa

Hampden

Alex. Moa
Crk

Palmerston

Te
Anau

*Von
Valley
Track*

*Nevis
Valley
Track*

*Old
Dunstan
Rd*

Middlemarch

Manapouri

DUNEDIN

Balclutha

Tuatapere

Invercargill

Mataura

Kaka Point

Riverton

Tokanui

Papatowai

Bluff

Waikawa

∫ - tarsealed road

⌐ - gravel/4WD track

Oban

STEWART ISLAND

196

Chapter 14

There's Gold In Them Thar Hills!

We'd had a week of celebrations, feasting, fun and spectacle. We'd been shaken by tragedy. Now it was time to get back down to business, get back on our bikes and head off for the third and final leg of our New Zealand odyssey. The plan was simple: Head south west into Mackenzie country then ride the drovers' routes and old gold trails into the vast wilderness - the 'back blocks and the wop wops' - of Central Otago... and see what happened next.

It was a bright, sunny start as we roared off down SH1 to Ashburton for fuel and cash, then on to Geraldine for lunch and a mooch around the shops. The amusingly named Murch & Dice had a 1901 motorcycle on display, the first ever built in New Zealand, plus various other antiquities and novelties.

From Geraldine there is a pleasant main road (SH79) to Fairlie where we'd be staying that night, but we'd already passed that way once and were keen for adventure. So we headed off at Crotty's Corner for Hilton and Kakahu on tiny back roads, then down to Hanging Rock Bridge and a river littered with still-green trees and bushes after a recent flash flood. These were great little dirt roads which our motorcycle tyres could handle, instead of the mega-gravel that had caused disaster at the start of our last voyage. After 50km of 'true grit' back lanes we rolled into Fairlie at 5pm and renewed our acquaintance with the Aorangi Motels' Kathy and John Cassie, who were pleased to hear Viv's leg was well on the mend.

We dined at The Old Library which came highly recommended, but my meal was drowned in vinegar which soured my stomach and spoiled the dining experience. It took a 'hokey-pokey' ice cream, eaten in the street in bright sunshine at 8pm, to put me back in a good mood.

We filled up the bikes' tanks next morning and bought copious picnic goodies for a day of outback riding. It didn't start too well. We couldn't find the turn off SH8 for Limestone Valley and ended up in Albury before we saw a sign for Mackenzie Pass. Then, three kilometres down this track, there was a notice saying the road to Mackenzie Pass was closed! After a brief curse and consultation, we decided a detour through Chamberlain would do. Soon we were blasting along gravel tracks up into the wild back country and over the pass, with great views of folded hills stretching into the distance.

Nearby was a monument to James 'Jock' Mackenzie, whose name was adopted for this pass and the high pastureland around it after he became something of a Kiwi folk hero in the 1850s. Which is all the more odd since he was nothing more than a sheep rustler who, in March 1855, got caught red-handed on this spot with 1,000 stolen sheep.

Due as much perhaps to a lack of proper security as to any great skill on his part, Mackenzie escaped from prison three times over the first nine months of his five-year sentence. The fledgling authorities were clearly perplexed by this, so they decided to grant him a pardon, provided he left the country and never came back. This strikes me as a capital plan which the British Government might consider as the perfect solution to prison overcrowding in the UK.

These extraordinary events led to the Mackenzie myth flourishing around the firesides and bars of the young colony and Jock and his faithful sheepdog Friday became pioneering legends. What he did do, it seems, was to identify an area of rich pasture land around the Hakataramea River, and it was through this high valley that we now hoped to ride.

Our plan, however, was not assisted by a duff map which showed a section of the Hakataramea Pass track that simply doesn't exist. Having descended from the Mackenzie Pass on to the broad plain to the west, we found the Grays Hill Road without a problem, but there was no sign of the trail leading to the Hakataramea, which our map - from the usually excellent NZ Pathfinders series - showed heading south east from the same junction. Acting on a hunch, we headed south west on the broad gravel road which leads to Lake Benmore, and sure enough, four kilometres further on, after crossing a tributary of the Grays River, we found a track heading east between the Dalgety Range and the Grampian Mountains. Yippee!

This was a flat straight road but slippery for our bikes, due to loose gravel chippings which slowed us for a time, until the trail began to climb and wriggle between the closing hills. At the first stream crossing we caught up with two cyclists - not Ted and Shelley this time - who'd ridden down from Tekapo. We let them paddle through the ford carrying their bikes before we made more of a splash with our Serows and roared off south with a wave. Viv's confidence increased with every stream she rode through feet-up and her speed began to creep back up towards pre-crash levels. But her leg was still very tender and she was understandably reluctant to risk hurting it again.

It was a long old trail, with 80km of gravel track before we came to tarsealed road at Cattle Creek which allowed us a rapid blast down to Kurow. Despite our impressive picnic comestibles we succumbed to a hot lunch in a Kurow café, partly because we felt we'd earned it and partly because it seemed such good value for money after the expensive disappointment of the previous evening. We also had a fair bit more riding to do before we would reach our day's destination, Ranfurly, the 'capital' of the Maniototo Plain and the gateway to Central Otago.

Twenty three kilometres down SH83 we came to Duntroon where we turned right for Dansey's Pass. This was a really pretty road, winding between crumbly cliffs and green hills before becoming metalled with yellow and white gravel. It meandered up and over the hills, providing views over streambeds where gold was found in the 1860s, before dropping down between Mount Kyeburn and the Kakanui Range to the south. It was late afternoon by the time we reached Kyeburn Diggings and the historic Danseys Pass Coach Inn, built in 1862 to service a multi-racial gold prospecting community of 2,000 souls and now a haven for more leisurely travellers. But we resisted its charms and pressed on through Naseby, which proudly proclaimed itself to be '2,000 feet above worry level' and on to Ranfurly, where Robbie and Joan Dobson made us very welcome at their Ranfurly Motels.

By now we were feeling somewhat cream-crackered, having done 235km of mainly off-road riding since breakfast,

Dansey's Pass twists through folded hills

so Viv conjured up a hot meal out of our uneaten picnic while I did a neat disappearing trick with a bottle of wine from the Ranfurly Hotel's bottle store (off-licence) and we had no trouble at all sleeping.

We agreed next morning that Wednesday January 23rd would be a lazy day, for no other reason than we rather liked it here and there was plenty to see and do locally. Viv had already taken a shine to several large and very woolly sheep in the paddock behind our unit and would happily stroke and chat to them all day. So, having booked for a second night in Robbie and Joan's comfortable and quiet motel, we took a walk around the town to see Ranfurly's Art Deco architecture and soak up some local history at the railway station. This wasn't quite as strange as it sounds, as Ranfurly became the area's admin centre after the railway arrived there in 1889 on its way to linking Dunedin on the coast with Alexandra, the centre of gold mining activities in the interior of Otago province. Since the trains stopped and the rails were torn up in 1991, the station had been thoughtfully maintained as a mini-museum providing a pictorial history of Ranfurly and the Central Otago Railway.

Then we hopped back on our bikes for a ride up to Naseby and lunch at the Royal Hotel, where we were joined by motorcyclists Darren and Annette Stockman from Auckland. This couple were on a one-month trail bike tour of the South Island riding a fully-equipped Honda XR650L and said we were the only other off-road motorbike travellers they'd met. Given the wealth of glorious trails to ride, we found it quite amazing that so few chose to explore this way.

Just outside Naseby is the Glenshee Animal Park where we finally got to see alpacas, yaks, thar, deer and Wally the Wallaby, plus a herd of goats who seemed determined to eat Viv's newly-acquired, flower-patterned sunhat. By mid-afternoon the temperature was well into the 30s as we blatted back down the dusty trail to Naseby and Ranfurly in time to shop at the Maniototo Supermarket for supper. We found everything we needed here except for Cookie Time cookies, which was very distressing. When I explained to the owner that his otherwise excellent store was missing the single most important ingredient for a healthy diet and a happy life, he came up with a string of feeble excuses:

'*Those are made in* <u>*Christchurch*</u> *you know!*' as if it were the other end of the universe. I said I knew, as we'd just come from there and passed the Cookie Time factory on the way.

'*It's 80km from Palmerston - no-one will travel out here to Ranfurly,*' he said, which caused me to wonder how he managed to get any supplies at all. I pointed out that Cookie Time cookies were sold in shops and cafés in the remotest outposts of his country, in hamlets and villages all the way from Invercargill to Auckland, so there was no excuse for the factory refusing to supply him here in Ranfurly, a major town just down the road from Christchurch. I said I would call in at the Cookie Time factory when I returned to Christchurch and complain on behalf of Ranfurly that it was neglecting this town's population, and needy passing travellers such as myself.

At which point he quickly changed his tune and admitted that with Cookie Time cookies he had to order a certain number and they were date stamped, so he couldn't sell any that went out of date. Whereas the chap who supplied him with the naff, second-rate cookies he stocks (my words), would call once a fortnight to take away any unsolds, so he didn't lose any money on them.

'*Oh, I see,*' I said. '*So you choose not to stock Cookie Time cookies simply for your own convenience and blow what the customers want!*'

At which point Viv very sensibly dragged me out of the store before the discussion turned ugly and we found ourselves run out of town. I could see the headlines now: 'British Biker Banned After Biscuit Battle'. But somebody has to stand up for consumers' rights, for goodness sake, or we'd all end up breaking our teeth on ginger nuts.

I was put in a much better mood when we returned to our motel and met Steve and Marianne, a Christchurch couple who had just arrived on mountain bikes to occupy the apartment next door. Marianne was small but perfectly formed and squeezed into tight black Lycra cycle shorts. Steve, for all I know, might have been quite good looking too. It seemed only neighbourly to engage them in friendly conversation. They were having a four-day break while their two young daughters were looked after by grandparents and they'd just ridden the 'Rail-Trail', a designated cycle and tramping track on the route of the old railway line. Consequently they were hot and sticky and ready for a shower, said Marianne, wiping her hands on her hips.

For some inexplicable reason, the power of speech deserted me at this point, but fortunately Robbie, our jovial landlord, saved the day by appearing at that moment with bowls of nectarines, apricots and chocolate marshmallows - *'for pudding'* he said. What a nice bloke!

Next morning I was engrossed in books that Robbie had lent me explaining the history of the region while Viv was bustling about packing bags and tidying up. I really am a lazy git at times, but she says she loves me all the same. Just as we were nearly ready to leave, Viv spotted 'her' sheep close by the fence outside.

'Oh, my sheep have come to see me. They've come to say goodbye!' she cooed. With that she threw open the door and shouted: *'Hello sheepies!'* at the top of her voice - and, to her amazement one of them replied: *'Hello!'*

It was Steve, just outside our door, come over to tell us they were leaving. Viv recovered from her embarrassment to say goodbye and I behaved myself by staring at my feet when Marianne mounted up and cycled off after him.

While I was strapping the panniers on our bikes, Robbie and Joan turned up to say goodbye and to feed half a loaf of sliced bread to Viv's favourite sheep. Apparently this was a regular morning event and explained why the tubby animals had trotted up the fence at that moment.

'What breed of sheep are these, Robbie?' asked Viv, keen to get to know her furry friends better. *'Are they Merinos?'*

'No,' said Robbie, *'they're half-bred.'*

'In that case,' I said, *'you're obviously feeding them far too much of that stuff!'* Well, it amused me, anyway.

The 75km ride to Palmerston on the east coast is through gorgeous country on empty sweeping bends, so it's a bit of a shame the local name for it is 'Pigroot'. It earned this less than pretty title after an early surveyor was chased by a wild boar, but on our morning ride we saw nothing to discourage the poetry that started to blossom in my mind.

'Soft-folded hills, sculpted with a palette-knife and cloaked in green velvet, smudged red with the flowers of a million sedges...' I was turning into a right little Wordsworth when I suddenly remembered I was also riding a motorcycle at 100kph, and pulled back to my side of the road just in time to avoid a sheep truck thundering past the other way. Phew! That was close. If I'd crashed while concentrating on verse instead of riding, would it have been poetic justice, I wondered?

Even the onset of light rain couldn't dampen my spirits or prevent my schoolboy humour from giggling up to the surface as we passed through Shag Valley. In Palmerston we decided the now more persistent rain was a good excuse for taking time out to enjoy a leisurely lunch at the 'Derail Café & Bar' beside the station. I'm almost embarrassed to admit that we ate pizzas here, but they really were very good, and so generous that we took a doggy-bag pizza box away with us, so Viv got her second chance at pizza delivery service on our way up to Hampden, a tiny town beside SH1, where we were to spend the night.

On our ride up there we stopped off at Shag Point (well, you have to, don't you?) in order to see the seals and penguins that the promontory is home to. There were seals aplenty but no penguins so, when we arrived at Hampden Court Motels and were warmly greeted by Alice Hollows, we told her we planned to unpack then walk to see the Moeraki Boulders, for which the nearby beach is famous, then on to Moeraki Point Lighthouse to see the penguins there.

'Of course, my dears,' said Alice. *'But the lighthouse is too far to walk. You let me know when you're ready to go and I'll take you there in my car.'* We thanked her but couldn't possibly let her do that, we said. We had perfectly good motorbikes to ride.

The beach and its boulders - huge spherical concretions which have tumbled out of the cliff - were suitably impressive, even though most were covered by the high tide. Two hours later we were back at Hampden Court pulling on our helmets when Alice reappeared, holding out her car keys.

'*I have a better idea,*' she said. '*You can borrow my car to drive up to the lighthouse.*'

We were speechless. This lovely Maori woman had known us for all of five minutes. We were two scruffy motorcyclists who'd turned up from goodness knows where, and she was offering us her car to drive away. This Kiwi hospitality really is amazing! We declined again, of course, but were still talking about her generosity when we saw our first yellow-eyed penguins from the lighthouse hide, and later saw their fat fluffy chicks waiting patiently for the parents to bring home a fish supper.

Next day was overcast and cool as we rode back up the scenic 'Pigroot' before turning left at Dunback and climbing higher into ever-colder air to Macraes Flat, where serious commercial gold mining is still under way. It's cold in them thar hills! I estimated the air temperature up here to be around 5^0C and we were shivering as we turned on to a slippery gravel road, making slow and careful progress, past Moonlight and down to Middlemarch in the Taieri Valley below.

Warming up with coffee and cookies outside the Middlemarch dairy (we were back in Cookie Time country, hoorah!), who should turn up but Robbie Dobson from the Ranfurly Motels! Turned out he was an electrician and was in Middlemarch, 65km from home, to fix several people's power supplies. He was really pleased to see us and when we told him we were hoping to ride the Old Dunstan Road out to the remote Patearoa Hotel that night, he wished us luck and said he would keep an eye out for us.

We topped up our fuel tanks before leaving Middlemarch and heading down SH87 to Clarks Junction and the start of the famous Old Dunstan Road. This cart track was born out of necessity in the 1860s, when gold was discovered at Dunstan - now called Clyde - on the Clutha River deep in the interior. In order to get supplies to the thousands of miners who flocked to the river banks and streambeds of this distant wilderness, the Dunstan Road was carved by the hooves of horses and the wheels of the waggons they pulled.

From Dunedin on the coast, the Dunstan trail passed over four mountain ranges - the Lammermoors, The Rock and Pillars, Rough Ridge and the Raggedy Ranges - and through vast tracts of empty tussock grasslands for 176km. It took horse-drawn drays two or three weeks to complete the round trip and bullock waggons could take even longer. Waggoners travelled together as it was often necessary to put two or more teams on each waggon to pull them through deep mud or up steep hills.

Soon pubs and hostels sprang up along the route, at least ten licensed premises and probably just as many unlicensed grog shops, to help ease the journey for the hardy souls who used the Dunstan Road. Now they are all long gone and only the Patearoa Hotel remains, a little to the north of the original route, and it was to be our lodgings for the night... if we could get to it.

Clarks Junction turned out to be a single pub and a good landmark for the start of this historic trail. The first few kilometres were tarsealed, but after an ear-poppingly steep descent into one river valley the 4WD gravel track proper started. The first two stream crossings were very pretty, with peat-stained waters bubbling over boulders between narrow, rock-sided valleys. We perched on huge slabs of rock at Sutton Stream to munch our lunch, and took care not to impale ourselves on spaniards, large spike-tipped wilderness plants with a serious attitude problem.

Up and over the Lammermoor Range, the Old Dunstan Road wound north past a big lake at Moss Swamp and between impressive outcrops of the appropriately named Rock and Pillar Range. One such rock provided a superb vantage point for views over the Styx River and the Maniototo Plain to the north. Riding down from the 1,000-metre high pass over the mountains, we passed Paerau and the Styx Jail, where from 1861 prospectors could lodge themselves and their gold in safety. Here we picked up the level gravel road to Patearoa and our hotel for the night.

The Patearoa Hotel is itself steeped in history as photos from its early years on the walls bear witness. But, sadly, the original wooden structure complete with verandah and hitching posts were all gone, replaced with a brick facade which made it look like an overgrown modern bungalow. Still, our room was comfortable and, being a Friday night, we were served a hearty supper (meals Fri/Sat only), in the middle of which we were gobsmacked to receive a phone call. We thought there must be some mistake, since no-one knew we were here... except Robbie Dobson, who was just checking that we'd made it over the mountains okay. What a thoughtful chap!

Patearoa was a strange place. On our walkabout after supper we found it was the first town in New Zealand where the locals we met in the street didn't talk to us, but instead looked at their feet as we passed and even ignored a greeting. Back in the hotel bar all the sheep farmers down from the hills were loudly drunk by 9pm, so we retreated to our room where we discovered a few other idiosyncrasies...

There was no key for our hotel room door. The landlord said no-one had ever asked for one before and was puzzled why we should want one. Our 'en-suite' room did not include a toilet, but it did have a handbasin. Maybe in these parts handbasins are dual purpose? I didn't like to ask. Even more worrying, the loos down the corridor didn't have locks on their doors either! With drunks staggering about the place, it meant I was detailed to stand in the corridor where I could see our room and simultaneously prevent anyone barging in on Viv while she sat on the throne.

I'm sure the landlord thought I was some kind of Pommy trouble-maker when I returned to the bar to ask if they sold bottled water. He gave me a very strange sideways look. He was clearly dealing with an idiot.

'Bottled WATER! No, we don't sell _bottled_ water. We have water that comes out the tap,' he said.

Which is all well and good but, after getting upset tummies on our travels in other parts of these fair lands, we had taken to boiling all our drinking water and, touch wood, we'd since remained tummy-bug free. But, of course, this was not a motel so we didn't have a kettle.

'You want me to put some in a bottle for you?' He was probably trying to be helpful, but it sounded distinctly

Lunch stop at Sutton Stream on the Old Dunstan Road

sarcastic to me. I left the bar and heard uproarious guffaws two seconds later. At least I'd given them something to laugh about.

Next morning the sun was shining and I even got a smile from the landlord when I paid him, as if he'd just remembered a joke, so things must have been looking up. Before continuing on our exploration of the Old Dunstan Road, which would take us even further away from civilisation, we had one last requirement of modern technology: We needed to e-mail. Nowhere in Palmerston, Middlemarch or Hampden had there been a cyber-café and we were now overdue some communication to and from our children in far-off England.

I decided against asking the landlord of the Patearoa Hotel if he had a computer, in case our new-found friendship evaporated and he gave me a fat lip. We were only 18km south of Ranfurly, so I suggested to Viv that we pop back to the Ranfurly Motels to see if the Dobsons had any suggestions. Robbie and Joan greeted us like their own long-lost children.

'So, the wanderers return!' said Robbie with a huge grin, and immediately showed me into his office to use his computer. Meanwhile Viv shared a few jokes about Patearoa with Joan before heading off to the supermarket to buy grub for our lunch and supper. She was actually quite relieved to go back to the shop without me and on foot, hoping the proprietor wouldn't connect her to my Cookie Time rant of a few days ago.

While I was sending and receiving a backlog of electronic messages from up over, Robbie was busy drawing me a map to make sure we found our way over the next section of the Old Dunstan Road to Moa Creek. What a considerate person! He even explained how the blocks of schist rock from the mountain tops were attached by chains behind the gold-rush waggons to act as brakes on the downhill sections. Farmers in the treeless valleys ended up using the rocks as fence and gate posts, and we should look out for these upstanding lumps of history on our journey, he said.

Back down through Patearoa we branched off right signposted for Linnburn and then found the Old Dunstan Road part 2 behind a gate and signs warning: '4WD only - not suitable for cars. Not passable in winter.' Gulp! It was steep and rocky in places and had large patches of dried mud in others - a nightmare in wet weather for sure - but today it was infinitely easier to ride than some of the loose gravel farm tracks we'd tackled elsewhere.

There were a few gates on this section and, having propped my Yamaha on its sidestand carelessly while I opened one, the bike rolled forward and fell over. This was particularly embarrassing as I had been lecturing Viv only the day before about the correct way to leave her bike on its sidestand so that it wouldn't topple. Always ensure the bike is on level ground or facing uphill, I'd said. Make sure the stand won't sink into soft soil, I'd said. Check it's not leaning over too far, or not far enough, I'd said.

I heard the crash and turned, gate still in hand, to see my bike on its side. I was speechless. Fortunately Victor Meldrew came to my aid: '*I don't BELIEVE it!*' I fumed.

Viv, sitting astride her bike with shoulders jiggling, clearly saw the funny side of it.

'*You didn't have to demonstrate. I was paying attention yesterday you know,*' she said with crinkly corners to her eyes.

But this wasn't funny. As I struggled to get the bike upright again I saw the clutch lever had been snapped in half. Thankfully, the clutch action was light and I found I could operate the broken lever with two fingers, so we were able to continue unhindered with my ego the only casualty.

There followed some gloriously twisty, rocky, up-and-downy track that carried us over the Rough Ridge mountains and on to a high plateau where we came upon the Poolburn Reservoir, site of much of the filming for Lord of the Rings. We could see why they chose this spot. The Poolburn has weird rock formations jutting out of its waters and the surrounding smooth hills have odd rocks protruding, like bones sticking through skin. In the film you can see Auks and Hobbits swarming over this landscape and, even without them, it has a fairytale quality about it.

After a sun-kissed picnic and cooling paddle in the lake, we booted up and continued past the dam to pick up the wide gravel road to Moa Creek. At 69km from Ranfurly we spotted a tiny, hand-written sign for 'Historic Miners Village' which meant we had found Bonspiel, Keith and Sue Falconer's Moa Creek sheep station, our home for the next two nights.

For a change from the luxury and convenience of motels we'd decided to try living in a Chinese gold miner's stone cottage, built in 1866, to get a taste of the pioneers' primitive lifestyle. Keith and Sue's daughter, Sarah, told us to follow her big 4WD vehicle to find our cottage. Through a paddock, over a hill and into a hidden valley we rode and, there under two tall poplars, was a tiny stone house with a tin roof. There was no electricity, no water, no bathroom, no kitchen, no dining room and no loo other than a bucket with a seat in a stone closet with half a roof.

What we did have were bare stone walls and floor, a huge fireplace, queen-size bunk beds, two armchairs and a camping stove. Outside was a trestle table and two carboys of water - our alfresco dining room and bathroom. We loved it! To romantic and sentimental old fools like us, this was paradise. Best of all was the setting. The low doorway and two tiny square windows looked out over miles of fabulous countryside, pastures full of sheep, goats and horses, a pond rippled by paradise ducks and a backdrop of distant hills and mountains. Apart from birdsong and an occasional bleat from a lamb, we were surrounded by silence.

As the sun slipped behind the jagged tops of the Raggedy Range to the west, Viv rustled up a meal on the gas ring, I got a few logs crackling in the hearth - as much for light as for heat - and we soon slipped into blissful slumber by the flickering light of the fire.

The morning started with a refreshing outdoor flannel bath, followed by breakfast in the early sunshine serenaded by the magpies 'oodle-wardling' in the poplars. Then we busied ourselves with clothes washing and motorbike maintenance, just happy to be in this special place. But a lack of food and cash meant we had to revisit civilisation so we rode the final part of the Old Dunstan Road, a superbly scenic gravel road twisting around the contours of the hills, to Galloway and Alexandra.

Having flourished in the 19th century gold boom, Alexandra has continued to prosper from fruit growing long after the gold, and the dredges which scoured the Clutha River for it, were gone. We rode past countless orchards and fruit shops on our way into town, had a fine lunch at 'Briar & Thyme' café and found the cash and groceries we needed.

The Clutha River at Alexandra is so shockingly blue it takes your breath away. We photographed it flowing beneath the new Meccano-style road bridge which sits next to the far more elegant stone pillars of the one it replaced. Then we rode through Earnscleugh to Clyde dam and Lake Dunstan which fills the valley behind it, before heading up through

Chatto Creek to Omakau where we stopped for coffee at Rosie's café. This was memorable only for the fact that it was baking hot inside and the owner refused to open any of the windows or doors. Maybe he enjoyed sweat dripping off his nose? We took our mugs of coffee outside and drank them standing on the shady pavement. I was all for offering this chap a little friendly advice about customer care as a means of increasing his business, but Viv said I'd come close enough to blows with the shopkeeper in Ranfurly and made me stay outside while she took the mugs back and collected our helmets.

Refreshed but bemused, we rode through Ophir, over the Raggedys and back into the Ida Valley before turning south at Poolburn for the run back down to Moa Creek. We called in at Bonspiel farmhouse to give Sue some tomatoes and potatoes we'd bought for her in town and, shortly after we'd returned to our cottage, she trundled over the hill in her smokey old Land Rover. She brought us more water, another cylinder of gas, some smoked wild ham, lettuce, radishes and half a bottle of wine. How kind!

After supper we walked through sheep pastures and over the hills to find Chinaman's Orchard, where an ancient Chinese miner had once eked out a living by growing fruit after the valley's gold had all run out. After he died, a family came from the jobless North Island in 1934 to live here and scrape a living from the few flakes of gold they could find. They built three mudbrick houses and one remains, rebuilt by the Falconers as another rustic retreat. This lush and lonely, tree-filled valley could well have been the last refuge for one of New Zealand's extinct moa. The stream and settlement got the name Moa Creek because it was here that the first Europeans found bones of the giant bird with flesh and feathers still attached. They had missed seeing the last living specimen by a few weeks only.

Viv had just finished her fully-naked outdoor flannel bath next morning and was wrapping a towel around herself when a chap walked past. He was on his way with his dog and gun to keep down the rabbit population, a never-ending job in Central Otago where they are the most damaging economic pests. A sad fact of life. He strolled off with a smile and left Viv wondering how much of her fresh air bathing he had witnessed.

We thanked Sue, Keith and Sarah, paid them NZ$80 (£23) for our two-night stay and rode back to Omakau for fuel before heading north to pick up the Rise & Shine Road through the Dunstan Mountains. This 4WD track via Thompson's Gorge provided the most awesome views but also had dozens of gates to open and close along its convoluted 30km to Lindis Crossing. Before we'd even reached there we both got wet feet riding through a deep and stony stream so we decided a lunch stop was in order while our socks dried in the sun. There were no other vehicles or any sign of habitation in this gorgeous valley.

Turning left on to SH8 we rode to the old gold town of Cromwell, which proudly displays its more recent economic good fortune to the world in the form of gigantic fruit - twenty-metre-high, 3-D replicas of an apple, pear, apricot and peach. Today wine production is rapidly taking over as the major bread-winner, so I expect a humungous bunch of grapes will soon be casting its shadow over the town. We would have welcomed a little extra shade, as it was blisteringly hot and blindingly bright as we pulled in to seek rest, refreshment and a room for the night. Fortunately, the Gateway Motel had a unit free with lakeside views and a cooling breeze off the water. Owner Warren Anderson recommended we dine at the Victoria Hotel and try their blue cod, which was a good tip - it was the most succulent and delicious fish we'd ever tasted.

Chapter 15

In Search Of Paradise

Warren gave us more good advice next morning when he pointed us towards the Nevis Valley road, another 4WD track through remote gold mining country. With full fuel tanks we headed south from Cromwell across a bridge over the Kawarau arm of Lake Dunstan to Bannockburn. The tarseal road ended as we passed Carrick Station and its historic woolshed, built from the blocks of rock that Robbie Dobson told us had been dragged down the mountain to prevent the 'cart before the horse' metaphor.

The dirt and gravel road here was good but very steep. We could see why they had needed extra brakes on the way down, and why Dead Horse Pinch had been so named. Many of the draught animals didn't make the grade when hauling dredge pieces uphill for the gold workings in the valley beyond. The steep road zig-zagged up the Carrick Range and we were soon in tussock grasslands dominated by rocky schist tors with superb views back over Cromwell to Lake Dunstan.

Three quarters of the way up to the summit we met a herd of cows coming down the narrow track. With a steep hill on one side and an even steeper drop on the other, we beat a hasty retreat to a safer spot where they wouldn't nudge us over the precipice. Following his ambling cattle in his Land Rover was a farmer who stopped for a chat. He had tried the day before to get his herd through the nearby gate and down to another pasture, but they hadn't wanted to go, he said, so he was trying again today. We had never thought of cattle movement as being such a democratic process. He also told us that on a clear day it was possible to see Mount Cook from the summit of the mountain we were climbing, but we found this difficult to believe as, according to my map, the peak of peaks was almost 200km away.

As we restarted our bikes to continue our upward journey the cows were voting with their hooves to go for the fresh pasture. The farmer gave us a thumbs up as the last one

214

sashayed through the gate. Soon we were in alpine scenery, with tumbled rocks, delicate little blooms dancing in the breeze and spaniards thrusting their evil spikes skyward, eager to stab the unwary with their poisoned barbs. We had reached Duffers Saddle, at 1,300 metres the highest maintained road anywhere in New Zealand. The air was cold and thin as we took off our helmets and noticed a signpost which read, 'Mount Cook - 189km'. We followed its pointing finger and, sure enough, shining in the crystal distance was the white peak of the king of mountains. Fabulous.

The clear air and our elevated position made the views truly breathtaking. Below us to the north was Lake Dunstan, flanked by the Pisa Range to the west and the Dunstan Mountains to the east. Beyond lay the Southern Alps grinning like a row of white-tipped teeth with Mount Cook glistening triumphantly over them all. Over to the west were the snow-capped peaks of the Remarkables, a range of mountains aptly named for their majestic beauty, and all around us stood unusual chunks of rock dominated by The Two Sisters. These scarred and ragged schist tors bore witness to the ferocity of the wind which had sculpted their sides and was now making our hair dance and our eyes stream. And this was a fine day in high summer. We shivered to imagine what it must be like up here in a winter blizzard. Time to mount up and ride on.

We began the descent into the Nevis Valley and were rewarded immediately with different panoramic views of the Hector Mountains and the Garvies cradling the Nevis River, with tiny coloured specs of homesteads amid splashes of green where trees had been planted to give them shade in summer and shelter in winter. With ears popping from the steep descent, we soon passed over the bridge at Nevis Crossing and sped along the floor of the valley, past the holding pens and woolsheds, through the cloying scent of lanolin and over the cattle stops (grids) of Ben Nevis Station, an impressive homestead spread beneath the towering peak of Ben Nevis (2,240m).

A little further on we saw a tiny corrugated zinc shed sheltering beneath a few sparse trees and slowed to read its signboard, 'Nevis Valley Bowling Club - Clubhouse'. Beside it was a roughly mown patch of coarse grass. They must have strong bowling arms up here in the Nevis Valley. But how did they get a game together? As far as we could see there was just the one farmhouse...

The handful of sheep farmers and an occasional summer gold prospector who live here today contrast with the 600 gold miners, including 300 Chinese, who inhabited the Nevis Valley in the late 1860s. The settlement which sprang up at Nevis Crossing and along the valley floor included three hotels, a public house, bakery and store, school, town hall and a telephone exchange. Today it is hard to make out the crumbled remains of any of these buildings, so completely has Mother Nature wiped her slate clean. By 1902 there were no less than six dredges working the streambed, one continuing until 1939, its remains just visible, rotting beside the Schoolhouse Creek. If you didn't know what to look for, you could pass through the Nevis Valley and never know that all this life, hope and endeavour had ever toiled here through searing summers and wicked winters. A similar story was enacted, scene by scene, throughout the Otago goldfields.

It was in 1861 that Aussie Gabriel Reid discovered gold in a streambed near Lawrence, east of Dunedin, and sparked New Zealand's biggest gold rush. It is estimated that 14,000 people flocked to the Tuapeka Goldfield and Gabriel's Gulley hoping to find their fortunes, but what gold was there was soon exhausted. The following year Americans Horatio Hartley and Christopher Reilly hit paydirt beside the Molyneux (now Clutha) River at Dunstan (now called Clyde). News that they had deposited 87lb of gold at the Dunedin Treasury after just three months digging led to another mass migration to the interior region around Cromwell.

That same year Harry Redfern and Thomas Arthur found gold at the Shotover River and thousands of hopefuls poured into Skippers Canyon, then soon after into the Fox River valley to found Arrowtown, best preserved of all the 1860s gold-rush towns. But the easiest and richest pickings were soon gone and the law of diminishing returns saw the majority of prospectors switch to farming or head for the

West Coast, where gold-bearing quartz was being mined, crushed and separated from its treasure.

While it lasted, the New Zealand gold rush fuelled much of the early exploration and expansion into the country's interior and laid some infrastructure for the farming communities which followed. The gold funded most of the young colony's economy in the early years and still sets pulses racing today. There are dozens of sites around the country, especially in Otago and on the West Coast, where you can try your hand at panning for gold. For the more serious, there are half a dozen gold mining companies still operating with increasing levels of equipment and sophistication. All agree that there is more gold remaining in New Zealand's soil than has been found so far.

After a long, fast blast through the belly of the valley we crossed a steam and suddenly were climbing again, up to a winding track perched high above the gorge and the tumbling waters of the Nevis River. Below we saw a 4WD Mitsubishi and, standing in the stream, were three men in floppy hats flicking rods and lines back and forth across the water while a fourth filmed them with a video camera. This sequence would never get past the cutting room floor of Lord of the Rings II. The narrow track continued to climb higher above the rushing waters, clinging to virtiginous cliffs with stony climbs, potholes and muddy streambeds making us work at our riding.

Unladen, the Yamaha Serows were a doddle to ride in this terrain. Up on the footrests, low gear, a dab of brake, a touch of throttle and we could climb nimbly over it all. We were just beginning to feel a bit cocky and superior when we came across a diminutive Yamaha monkeybike with tiny wheels and fat tyres.

'Blimey,' said Viv. 'If he can get up here on that, I certainly ought to be able to do it on my Serow.' It was a timely confidence boost because a minute later we came to a sign which told drivers of 2WD vehicles to turn back and promised 25 fords in the next 24km.

'Oh heck! Do you think I can do it?' she asked nervously.

'Of course you can,' I said. 'You've ridden through lots of streams already, and if you can ride through one you can ride 'em all.'

After a few wobbly moments in the first couple of streams, Viv gained confidence with every crossing. Towards the end she was opting to ride through them first and gunned her little machine through the water and boulders feet up every time. Finally, we counted ford number 25 and the Nevis Valley road started to climb towards the next saddle.

Once more we were treated to wonderful views from the 1,100 metre summit of the pass as we crossed the Hector mountain range and we ate our lunch looking down on the fertile plains of Fairlight and across to the Eyre Mountains beyond. Another steep descent brought us to SH6 where we headed north alongside the southern arm of Lake Wakatipu to Queenstown.

After the morning spent in the tranquillity and isolation of the Nevis Valley the bustling 'Adventure Capital Of The World', as Queenstown likes to call itself, was a culture shock. The streets were full of noisy vehicles and road works and the pavements were teeming with people. We stayed no longer than it took to drink coffee beneath a pavement parasol and drop four rolls of film in to the Fuji shop for processing and collection next day. There was no time to dally as it was already mid-afternoon and we had an appointment with Paradise, a tiny hamlet I'd spotted on the map way up north of Glenorchy. It was like a magnet pulling us into the wilderness, so we left the hustle of Queenstown behind and zoomed along the twisty turns and sweeping bends of the lakeside road.

The views across Lake Wakatipu were like entries for a photographic competition, dark towering mountains and blue skies reflected in a mirror surface. When we rounded a bend to find the snowy eminence of Mount Earnslaw staring down the Dart Valley, where we were headed, we had to pause to take it all in. In Glenorchy we stopped briefly again to look at the map and were immediately overtaken by a large ewe and two lambs galloping down the road being chased by a panting woman on a bicycle. They obviously make their own entertainment in these parts.

Nevis Valley, our favourite off-road trail

After a right turn signposted for Paradise the tarseal road surface gave way to a reasonably good gravel road for a further 13km then abruptly turned rough, with a surface made of huge granite chunks which shook us mercilessly for the next five kilometres as we headed further from civilisation. By now I was sure we must have passed the spot marked as Paradise on our map, but we'd seen no sign of it. The further we rode the more disappointed we felt. Maybe it was some sort of Kiwi joke - you never find Paradise by looking for it? Or maybe it was more philosophical - we were already in Paradise but we just didn't realise it?

Tired and deflated, reluctantly we turned around to head back down the tortuous road. I was puzzled. Why would there be a map reference and road signs to Paradise if it didn't exist? And then I got to thinking that the low hills and trees on our righthand side looked pretty idyllic... and wasn't that the roof of a building hiding among the trees? On a hunch, I turned off down a little unmarked side track which twisted mysteriously through dense foliage, then over a rise, past a cute little wooden cottage and into a clearing with a couple of larger buildings. Out of one of them strode a young chap to meet us. I turned off my engine and pulled off my helmet.

He stuck out his hand and said: *'Hi, I'm Geoff. Can I help you guys?'*

'We've come in search of Paradise,' I replied.

'Well done - you've found it!' he said with a wide grin and proceeded to tell us the story of this remarkable place, after explaining that there were no Paradise signs out on the road because trophy-hunters stole them all.

The 300-acre property that makes up Paradise consists of pristine native beech forest and grasslands bordered to the west by Mount Alfred, to the east by Turret Head, the foothills of Mount Earnslaw and the start of the Mount Aspiring National Park. To the south lies Diamond Lake and to the north the Dart River flats. It was owned by the late David Miller, who believed he had discovered Paradise here and few would argue. When he knew he was dying in 1998 he set up The Paradise Trust to: 'Preserve and enhance the unique features of Paradise for the enjoyment and benefit of all visitors, with particular attention to the needs and expectations of people with disabilities'.

Geoff Ockwell was now the trust's manager and he lived here with his wife Grace and their three young children. I asked him what it was like being Manager of Paradise?

'Pretty good! Well, you can go see for yourself,' he said. 'We have a number of huts for rent as guest accommodation. You can go see The Garden of Eden if you like, there's no-one staying there today.' And he pointed the way through the trees, where a faint track took us for half a kilometre before we came to a clearing with a wooden cabin commanding spectacular views from its verandah, across a grassy meadow to the snow-capped mountains of the Southern Alps.

We stopped our engines, took off our helmets and heard only silence as we looked around in wonder. Then a tui sitting high in the tall eucalyptus tree beside the Garden of Eden cabin sang, bell-clear and mellifluous, across the clearing.

'I've died and gone to Heaven,' said Viv in a whisper.

We checked out the cabin. It had a water supply but no electricity. The cooker was a wood and coal-burning range, with an axe helpfully provided for splitting logs. The loo was an earth closet, or 'long drop' as they're called in New Zealand. It had all the magic of our Moa Creek gold miner's cottage with a little more luxury and scenic charm thrown in. We longed to stay, but we had an appointment with a ferry next morning, it was nearly 6pm and we were way past the back of beyond. We needed to get a move on or we wouldn't be back at our Cromwell motel before dark.

We thanked Geoff, promised to return to Paradise as soon as we could and headed off down the bumpy track for the last stage of our marathon day of riding. The 50km of swooping tarseal road from Glenorchy had our engines sniffing fumes again, so we fuelled up in Queenstown before the final 60km blast through the scenic Kawarau Gorge to Cromwell. It was 8 o'clock when we rolled in to find the New World Supermarket closed, but a nearby dairy-cum-chipshop took pity on us. It was also closed, but when the staff saw our tired and hungry faces pressed against the glass, they opened up the door and let us in while they fried us 'fush 'n' chups' for supper. We had done a monster 354km since breakfast, including the best off-road track and the bumpiest road of our journey. And we had been to Paradise and back. We were totally happy but utterly knackered and had barely wiped the grease off our fingers before we fell into bed and slept like logs.

Another bright and sunny day greeted us as I hosed down the dusty bikes and attended to their various lubrications while Viv packed the luggage for the umpteenth time. We paid Warren and thanked him for his help and hospitality. In addition to providing two comfortable nights, a bag of apricots, copious leaflets, brochures, maps and excellent advice, Warren had booked us on the TSS Earnslaw for the trip across Lake Wakatipu to Walter Peak Station. Since this ancient steamship was a foot passenger ferry with no room for cars, it hadn't occurred to us that it might be able to carry our motorbikes until Warren suggested it and then phoned them to confirm it.

This opened up a whole new route. From Walter Peak sheep station there was a gravel farm road running for perhaps 100km down the Von Valley, with a 4WD side track up to the Mavora Lakes if we felt inclined. Brill!

Back in Queenstown we picked up our photos and topped up with fuel and food before heading down to the quayside to find the ship. This was a tad tricky. Because the TSS Earnslaw doesn't carry cars there's no obvious vehicle access. However, we eventually managed to ride along a pavement and then across a wooden boardwalk over the water to get our bikes on to the dock, only to find a lorry had managed to get there via a different route and was pouring tons of coal down a chute to feed the ship's boiler furnaces.

When she was coaled up one of the crew laid a plank to the lower deck and we had several attempts at getting the bikes on board. This wasn't helped by the fact that the plank ended half a metre above the dock and the bloke supposedly helping us had never undertaken the exercise before. It seemed he'd never seen a motorcycle before either and was totally bewildered when little chunks of wood he expected us to ride over flew out from under our wheels. We resorted to lifting the bikes one at a time on to the plank, riding them across while he held each bike's rack to stop us toppling sideways into the lake, then manoeuvring them by hand in the cramped deck space. In all the mayhem Viv's injured leg took a hefty knock and she was speechless for a while.

With a toot of the Earnslaw's whistle and a hiss from her ancient twin steam engines, the ship left Queenstown behind and slid gracefully across the lake, surrounded by wonderful peaks and wooded slopes. This lovely old vessel was originally built in Dunedin, then dismantled and carried by rail to Kingston at the southern tip of the lake where she was rebuilt and put into service in 1912.

As we chuffed along in splendour a pianist played on the afterdeck, a bit like the Titanic... but no, that was unthinkable. Within 45 minutes we'd docked alongside the very grand 'Colonel's Homestead' at Walter Peak's tarted-up-for-tourists High Country Farm. By the time we had repeated the bouncing and heaving routine to get our luggage-laden Serows on to the dock, the quayside was packed with Japanese tourists all pressing forward to get on board, or simply to take a few hundred more photos, it was hard to tell. When we fired up our engines, instead of parting to make a space for us to ride through, they pressed forward even more. Perhaps they thought we were part of the Earnslaw/Walter Peak entertainment? Either way they didn't seem to grasp that they had to move to let us leave and, since my hooter still wasn't working and I have never learned Japanese, I'm sorry to say that one or two got a minor bump from my handlebars.

Soon we were clear of the madness that the good ship Earnslaw had exported from Queenstown and were riding into the sanity of the countryside on a neat gravel road between tidy fields of haybales and paddocks full of horses. As we neared the next homestead of Mount Nicholas Station, we found ourselves lost once more in a landscape of amazing views. We could see up Lake Wakatipu to snowy Mount Earnslaw 60km distant and knew that, hidden in the smudge near its base, was the little slice of Paradise we'd experienced the day before. With the midday sun burning down we moved into the shade of some willow trees for our lunch and felt sublimely happy with the world.

Von Valley Track winds through gorgeous country south of Walter Peak Station

After Mount Nicholas the road plunged southward down the Von Valley and we came upon an enormous flock of sheep ambling down the road. The shepherd urged us to ride through them but this proved more difficult than it sounds, as they all panicked as we approached and the resultant stampede kicked up so much dust we couldn't see to ride through it. Further on, we slowed for cattle grazing at the roadside - a stampede from these wee beasties could be fatal - and met the only vehicle we would see on this 60km section of farm track. The driver of the Range Rover said we should take the time to visit the Mavora Lakes as they were beautiful so, after another hour's riding and fording two streams between the Thomson and Eyre Mountains, we turned off to ride through the forest to reach the first of the lakes.

By now Viv was flagging and in need of a kip so we stopped at a picnic area where she lay down and closed her eyes. Why is it you can go all day and see not a soul, but the minute you try to get five minutes sleep the world and his wife arrives? Almost immediately we were joined by a cyclist from London who was in the sixth month of a marathon bike tour of New Zealand and wanted to tell us all about it.

Ten minutes later we were joined by the Range Rover chap with the lady friend he'd just collected from the Earnslaw, and they kindly invited us to follow them further up the lake road and join them for tea. Viv pointed wearily at her watch. It was 4pm, we still had a lot of gravel roads to negotiate, and she was struggling to stay awake. Perhaps the marathon ride of the day before had taken more out of her than I'd realised.

So we declined and headed south, rejoined the main track now running alongside the Mararoa River and almost immediately ran into trouble. The last 20km had been easy going on a wide farm road, where we had ridden side by side at up to 80kph, kicking up great clouds in our wake from the dusty surface. But now the road was layered in ankle-deep gravel, big granite chippings just like the stuff that had brought disaster near the Rakaia Gorge just after Christmas. For Viv, already drop-dead exhausted, it was the last straw. Scared of another crash on her injured leg, she struggled on slowly with skating wheels and twitching handlebars before coming to a halt, shaking with fear and frustration.

'I just can't do it any more,' she said between the tears. 'I know I'm going to fall off on this bloody awful gravel and I'm terrified of injuring my leg. If I bang it again I'll die,' she sobbed.

After a five-minute hug, her shaking had stopped. We had a mouthful of water and discussed our options. We could stop here for as long as she liked, but eventually we would have to ride on. I reckoned we were 25km from tarsealed roads but doubted whether this dreadful gravel would continue that far. If we just took it slowly we would eventually get through it. She nodded and pulled her helmet back on reluctantly.

Before we set off again, we did a little road reconnaissance. There were three clearer tracks in this wide gravel surface. On the crown of the road's rounded camber was the widest wheel track, where tyres from vehicles travelling in both directions had pushed the stone chips aside. Halfway between the crown and the road edges were narrower, fainter tyre tracks, where cars' nearside wheels had run. In between the tracks were deep and treacherous ridges of gravel, in places piled up half a metre and containing fist-sized chunks of granite just waiting to spit our wheels sideways and send us crashing to the ground. At anything more than walking pace it was dangerous.

I had found that the crown track was the least difficult to ride in, but this came at a price. When a car appeared around a bend coming hell-for-leather straight at me, I had a real panic getting my twitching, skittering wheels through the deep gravel ridge to get out of the centre of the road. If I'd fallen he would never have been able to stop on this slippery surface. Viv, understandably, didn't want to take that risk, so she battled on halfway down the slope of the road amid the grit and dust, wrestling with her handlebars at 15kph. It took us a long, long time to get to the main road, SH94, and we'd never been so relieved to see a tarsealed surface.

Half an hour later we rode into the Manapouri Glade Motel & Motor Park more than happy to be at the end of our day's riding. Proprietor Ian Wentworth was happy to see us too.

'Hello Bob,' he said with a smile, as I pulled my helmet off and walked into his office. This threw me, as I'd never met him before in my life. He laughed at my shocked expression and said: 'You told me you'd arrive on motorbikes when you phoned with your booking yesterday. See, I wrote it down - Bob and Viv Goddard on motorbikes.'

I was so impressed I booked a second night on the spot. After the day's trauma and exertion I reckoned we'd need two nights' recovery. I grumbled about the ridiculous gravel on the road to the Mavora Lakes and he said he almost wrecked a car and caravan on it, when the latter started weaving and went out of control. So it's not only motorcyclists who suffer. Why on earth do the highways department dump such great heaps of chippings on these roads? The managers should all be made to ride them regularly on motorcycles to see the error of their ways.

Our detached cabin was set among trees beside pretty Lake Manapouri, with birds singing in the bushes to help us relax over a home-cooked supper. But they were not the only wildlife, as we discovered when we got chatting to our next door neighbours and the little biting beasties (the sandflies, not the neighbours) drove us all indoors. But it didn't take long for the cares of the day to dissolve into deep and peaceful sleep.

Chapter 16

The Riviera Of The South

We were mildly amused next morning to hear a new arrival at Manapouri Glade ask the proprietor, *'What are parasites?'*

I was about to volunteer a detailed description of the nasty little sandflies that would eat him alive if he didn't watch out, when the motel owner completely threw me once again when he replied: *'They're electric hook-up points for campervans, caravans and tents.'* Then I twigged. The guest was asking about 'Power Sites', one of a range of options listed on a noticeboard by the gate.

Of course, not everyone wants a motel, which is just as well, because there were only three of these (NZ$70 - £20 per night for two people) at Manapouri Glade. In addition there were four cabins which provided a bed and not much else for NZ$30 (£9) per night for two. If you brought your own blankets, sheets and pillows these were a budget option, but that wasn't practical for motorcyclists. Hiring bed linen could raise the cost to near motel prices, but without the facilities. Cabin-dwellers shared toilets, showers and a kitchen with the campers. Cheapest of all were the 'parasites', as we would call them from now on. There were 12 of these for campervans, caravans and tents at NZ$17 (£5) per night for two. Most towns and tourist spots in New Zealand also had backpackers hostels which provided the cheapest beds for sociable types, and at the other end of the scale there were hotels, B&Bs or Homestays, where you stayed in someone's home and paid top dollar for the privilege.

After a pleasant walk through beech forest beside the Waiau River to Pearl Harbour, we returned to wash the previous day's crud off our bikes before zooming up to Te Anau, 22km north. We checked in at Fiordland Travel for the 2pm sailing to the Te Anau Glowworm Caves and left our riding gear with the friendly staff. We shared our picnic on the beach with some hungry seagulls then boarded the boat for the 35-minute voyage across Te Anau Lake to the caves entrance. Here we were shown into a reception building for a video film showing the geology of the caves and the biology of the glowworms, then we were taken in groups through water-sculpted tunnels to a lake where small boats floated us in awed silence into the glowworm grotto. A thousand tiny blue lights lit up the cave roof like a starry night sky. It was delightful.

New Zealand glowworms are actually the larvae of small flies called fungus gnats. These tiny maggots produce a brilliant glow to attract other flying insects that become caught on their sticky silk fishing lines and are hauled up to be eaten.

Friday February 1st dawned dry but cold, with the local radio station predicting a high of 15^{0}C compared with 25^{0}C the day before. The good news was the chill air discouraged the sandflies while I crouched in the gravel to adjust both bikes' chains. This was the first time the chains had needed adjusting - other than at service intervals - on our epic New Zealand journey, now approaching 10,000km. I guessed this was due to the dusty conditions of the farm trail from Walter Peak Station. I had been diligent with chain lubrication, but dust can cause the chain to overheat and stretch.

We headed south on SH99 - the Southern Scenic Route - with the soft rolling hills of the Takitimu Mountains on our left and the rugged Hunter Mountains on our right. After 70km we rolled into the tiny hamlet of Clifden and turned right on to a minor road in order to visit Lake Hauroko, the deepest lake in New Zealand. The first 12km were fine until the tarseal ended, then suddenly we were back on a deep and rough gravel surface again, making both bikes skate around alarmingly. After five more kilometres of fighting to keep the Serows upright and pointing roughly the right way, we stopped and agreed that another 20km or so of this was too much like torture to be worth the effort.

We were just turning round when a big old Mercedes pulled up, its driver's window dropped and a sweet old lady asked us if we were okay. I explained that we were fine, but the gravel was far too deep and difficult to ride on safely with motorbikes.

'Yes, it really is dreadful,' she said. 'I don't know why they do this - it just makes our roads really dangerous for everyone.'

We'd done thousands of kilometres on unsealed roads by now so we were no novices. If we could not ride them safely, they must be a nightmare for cyclists, to whom the New Zealand tourism industry appeals repeatedly to, *'Take to the backroads and have an awesome adventure!'* These unnecessary Southland graveltraps are not awesome, they're awful.

It was time for a consolation coffee stop in a strange little town called Tuatapere. We followed signs for 'Town Centre & Information' and ended up in a backpackers hostel, where the owner directed us to ride a further two kilometres and over two bridges to find the shops and café right on the edge of town. Still, the café was warm and friendly and the staff maintained a cheery, jovial mood while serving an unexpected coachload of British pensioners, all demanding odd and difficult drinks and snacks which were not on the menu.

An elderly couple from Gloucestershire sat at our table and the wife quizzed us about our motorcycling, the trip and the weather, while her husband quietly ate his hamburger together with his paper serviette. When he had finished picking the remnants of paper from his teeth he asked how we managed to do all this bicycling. BICYCLING!? We were sitting in our motorcycle jackets and our helmets were perched on the table. He'd nudged one with his elbow several times while tucking in to his serviette-burger. Our Yamahas were parked only inches away on the other side of the window. We hoped the extra roughage helped his digestive system run a little more freely than his brain.

A little further south at Te Tua we turned off the main road on to a pleasant little gravel track leading into the Longwood Forest and found a quiet spot for lunch, sitting on a huge horizontal tree trunk in a valley full of trees, deer and birdsong, with bellbirds and their fledglings fluttering in the branches above our heads. Then we rode on past wind-sculpted macrocarpa trees and glistening white surf fringing a deep blue sea before arriving at Riverton 'The Riviera of the South'. Here the Aparima and Pourakino rivers meet in a broad estuary before pouring out into the great Southern

Ocean that circles the globe. No surprise then that it became a settlement for Maori fishermen and later - in 1835, 1836 or 1837 depending which history you read - became a whaling station and reputedly the first European settlement in the South Island. It is still a fishing town today with colourful boats clustered around its pretty harbour.

Our accommodation for the next two nights was Riverton Beach Motel where we turned up, unfashionably early as usual, and woke up landlord Carl. He was trying to get some kip, he told us slightly groggily, because he works nights while his wife Cecilia works days. No shortage of work ethic here. He gave us the keys for a pleasant first floor motel with balcony and great views over the bay.

Saturday dawned with an auspicious date - 2/2/2 - and a glorious sunrise, its golden beams pouring into our bedroom. With the sun came a fresh breeze so there was no stopping Viv, who had spotted an impressive-looking line in the garden, from getting most of our clothes out of our bags and into a bowl. She liked nothing better than doing the laundry by hand, bless her, pummelling our shirts and trousers in foaming water. If we lived in Africa, she would be the first in the river every morning, beating our clothes on a rock.

While she was industriously pegging the dripping and flapping items on the washing line, I was indulging in a nostalgic enterprise of my own, trying to track down a mystery electrical fault on my bike. Despite all the horrendous weather we'd been through earlier in our travels, the little Yamahas had been remarkably reliable. After the rental shop's repair of the short circuit that had prompted me to rediscover my bump-starting talents back in Akaroa in November, we'd had only one blown headlamp bulb. The bikes had been almost faultless. But now my machine's indicators had packed up and I was keen to get the blinking things working again. As I spread the Serow's tiny toolkit on the seat and worked out what sort of surgery I was equipped to perform, I was reminded of a similar problem in the dim and distant past.

230

My first little motorbike, a 1965 Honda 90, was in many ways a miniature marvel as it came equipped with flashing indicators which were virtually unheard of on motorcycles of any size at that time. My sister Jane still drove a car with trafficators, for goodness sake, those ridiculous illuminated wands that were supposed to pop out from either side of a car's roof to show which way you intended to turn. Of course, they either didn't pop out or didn't light up and never, ever popped back in again after the manoeuvre was over. This left her little Austin trundling down the road with one or two orange tongues sticking out, blowing raspberries at passers by.

My Honda 90 was nowhere near so cranky. My winkers blinked, but so dimly and so slowly that they were useless for warning other road users of my intentions. No problem, I thought. Hand signals were reliable and unmistakable. Who needs indicators, anyway?

I did, it seemed. As my first motorcycling summer slipped through autumn into the cold, dark days of winter, it became clear - even to a 16-year-old wearing ginormous jackboots and vast rubber jacket - that nobody could see my hand signals in the dark. The black sleeves of my Black Prince jacket ended in black leather mitten gauntlets and no matter how earnestly I thrust them out, no-one could see I was about to make a turn once the sun had set. After a couple of near misses I had a bright idea. I would equip myself with flashing gauntlets.

At about this time Motor Cycle News was my sole source of serious study in the school library. In it I'd spotted an advert for a 'DIY Flashing Gloves Kit' which seemed like the perfect solution to my problem. The manufacturers of this wondrous equipment - I don't recall their name and suspect they went out of business the day after they cashed my ten shillings and sixpence postal order - promised a fabulous transformation that would dazzle my friends. I couldn't wait for the package to arrive.

When it did I found it contained two large orange plastic hemispheres, each containing a tiny bulb and with two lengths of wire attached, plus four brass paper filing clips. The instructions came straight to the point, 'Take a bradawl or other sharp implement and makes holes in the thumb of the glove, the index finger (or, in my case, where my finger sat within the mitten) and in the back of the gauntlet. Now push the wires from the orange indicator lamp through the hole in the gauntlet, bending tabs inside to hold it in place. Push brass button A's tabs through hole in thumb and brass button B's tabs through hole in finger, and attach wires before bending tabs back to secure. Now clip battery (not supplied) to the battery connector and your flashing gauntlets are ready for use. Simply bring thumb button A into contact with finger button B and the lamp will illuminate. Make and break the circuit repeatedly to achieve flashing indicator'.

I was ecstatic. No-one at school had anything like this. I could not only indicate my intentions on my bike, I could now flash to my heart's content while walking up the High Street and I could show off in the school library. In short, I could win friends and influence people simply by winking my gauntlets at them. I could flash in stereo and at any rate of my choosing. I was a blinking marvel!

Imagine my dismay then, when my flashing gauntlets produced nothing like the admiration I had fondly imagined, nor the respect promised by the manufacturer's advert. In fact, instead of gasps of wonder from my school pals, my proud demonstration of my flashing gauntlets drew howls of laughter and snorts of derision. By the end of that school day I had taken to hiding my flashing gauntlets in my school bag and everywhere I went voices rang out down corridors:

'Oi! You winker! Give us a quick flash!'

With red cheeks and burning ears I rode out of the school gate to jeers and laughter. Philistines! What did they know anyway? Most didn't even have a motorbike. They were obviously just jealous.

After supper that evening I set out into the winter darkness for a marathon ride through the Fens to make full use of my new flashing gauntlets and erase the taunts from my memory. I rode for miles, flashing here, flashing there, until a light rain started to fall and grew steadily heavier. I was halfway home when I noticed to my horror that both gauntlets had taken on a dim orange glow as the rain shorted out my gloves' electrics. By the time I got home, both batteries were dead.

I rode to school for the rest of that winter with rain pouring steadily through six empty holes in my gauntlets, a constant reminder of the folly of believing advertisement promises. Within a week or so my schoolfriends had tired of calling me names and the demands to: *'Show us your blinkin' gloves then, Goddard!'* had fizzled out.

As soon as I could afford it, I took my little Honda along to Watson and Garwood's motorbike shop in Holbeach, where Wally Garwood took less than a minute to diagnose my machine's winker problem: For nighttime riding I needed to turn the ignition key round another notch to step up the alternator's charging output to power the lights, he said. I'd been riding around with a constantly flat battery, hence the winkers wouldn't wink. I was so pleased I could have kissed him, but he was an ugly old geezer, so I showed my gratitude by buying a new pair of gloves and slipping my holey old gauntlets into his wastebin.

Back in Riverton my Serow's indicator problem didn't take much longer to fix. Grit from the dusty trails had got into the switch and once this was removed the blinking winkers flashed happily again. With indicators fixed and washing flapping in the breeze we set out for nearby Invercargill, the capital of the south coast, to find a Fuji shop to process our films and a bank to cash a cheque. It was a total waste of time as Invercargill didn't have a Fuji shop and all the banks were closed.

Undeterred and with only the faintest of cursing, since this was a wonderfully sunny day for a motorbike ride, we headed north on back roads stopping in tiny Otautau for coffee before heading up gravel tracks to explore the eastern side of the Longwood Forest. My map showed a maze of tiny dirt roads crisscrossing this area of woodland and within half an hour we were gloriously lost. The mixture of pine trees and native forest was so dense we only got a clue as to our whereabouts when the tracks brought us to the brow of a hill. But it didn't help much as all we could see from up here was more forest, so I resorted to my upside-down solar navigation technique and we forged onwards, up and down hilly tracks that were so overgrown the gorse bushes swept both handlebars simultaneously.

Eventually, we emerged on to a tarseal road at Fairfax, stopped to photograph a tiny shed which claimed to be 'Gropers Bush Library, est. 1880' (what went on in the romance section there, we could only speculate) then passed the cute Gummies Bush Church on our way to the coast. Back in Riverton the tide was up, the sun still shining and everyone was enjoying themselves, the youngsters by throwing themselves off the town bridge into the swirling waters of the harbour, which looked to us like a sure recipe for drowning, while the older ones were pottering along the beach, helping grandchildren dip nets into rock pools.

On days like this Riverton does indeed look like 'The Riviera of the South' and, when we saw in an estate agent's window details of a detached, three-bedroomed family house on a half-acre section (plot), with garage etc for just NZ$20,000 (£5,700), we were seriously tempted. Back in England a tiny beach hut only just big enough for changing into a swimming costume had sold recently for an astonishing £60,000, so this seemed an unbelievable bargain.

Back at our motel Carl was consulted on the dining out possibilities of Riverton. He recommended the Beach House Café which turned out to be a fair old stroll along the coast road, so by the time we got there we were moderately ravenous. Which was a shame because, despite the meal being the most expensive we'd encountered anywhere in New Zealand, there was almost nothing to it. My small piece of grilled fish was stylishly sliced, fanned out and accompanied by an artistically presented salad garnish. But two thirds of my plate was empty. I waited patiently for the waitress to bring a dish of steaming vegetables and a tray of French fries to go with it, but when she didn't I made discreet enquiries as to the whereabouts of the rest of my meal.

'*Aw no, sorry. Thet's it! Thet's all thet comes with it.*'

'*But there's nothing here except a tiny piece of fish and a few bits of shredded lettuce. Could I have some potatoes please?*' I asked politely, through clenched teeth.

'*Aw no, sorry. Chif doesn't do potatoes at all. Doesn't believe in 'em,*' she said.

'*Doesn't BELIEVE in them!?*' I spluttered and would have gone into orbit at this point had Viv not been holding my clenched fist down firmly on the table top. She had that '*Please don't make a big scene*' look in her eyes.

So instead I asked in my sweetest voice: '*Would Chef mind awfully if I had another bread roll then?*'

After I'd paid the exorbitant bill I smiled at the waitress and said, '*I'd like to give you a tip.*'

She looked surprised, but delighted. '*Aw, thenk you sir!*'

'*Sack the chef!*' I said and walked out. Always wanted to do that. Call me old fashioned, but when I pay twice the norm for a meal it seems reasonable to expect it to be pretty well perfect. So why is it that fancy-smancy, hoity-toity restaurants charging prices close to the total of Third World debt, frequently leave me seething?

As I paid Carl for our two-night stay at his excellent motel next morning he asked: '*Howdja get on at the Beach House Café last night?*'

'*Horrendously expensive, tiny, arty-farty portions and no bloody potatoes!*' I replied.

'*Yeah, that's just what everybody else says. You'd be better off in the chip shop next door, I reckon,*' he said. Yeah, right. Thanks Carl.

We rode east on SH99 past Invercargill through the flat southern farmlands, productive but uninspiring, looking for some bush tracks to make our journey to the Catlins more memorable. But first we needed fuel or it might be remembered for us having to push our bikes to the next town. All the road signs pointed to Dacre and every milestone gave its distance, so we decided it must be a pretty big place and we could fill up and have coffee there. But when we arrived Dacre consisted of a crossroads and one distant farmhouse.

Next place on the map was Edendale, which had a fuel station but, being a Sunday it was shut. The plan had been to ride from here into the wilds of the Catlins Conservation Park, but with 180km on our trip counters we couldn't be far from running out of petrol. There was nothing for it but to head north to Mataura, which turned out to be a major industrial town with factories, shops, people and an open fuel station. Right next door was a bakery serving coffee and sticky cakes. Perfect.

Fully refreshed and refuelled in all departments, we crossed over the railway line and the river bridge to the east and then turned south again on little backroads to Wyndham, past the Tuturau Maori reserve and a monument marking a major inter-tribal battle of 1836. These were all tarsealed minor country roads through gently rolling sheep and cattle country, the lush green hills drawing us deeper into the Catlins through Redan and Mokoreta, although you would never know it as these tiny hamlets had no village signs to identify them.

Finally we came to a stretch of dusty gravel road and turned off to find a peaceful picnic spot beside the Waikawa River. This was a promising landmark as we were heading for Waikawa Harbour, about as far distant as it was possible to get from the Waikawa Bay near Picton where we stayed before Christmas. However, before we could go to our lodgings we first had to find the owners, June and Murray Stratford, who live in Progress Valley. Thanks to poor signage and a confusing map we ended up riding round in circles and became lost and disorientated. As we turned down the same gravel road for the third time I spotted a car coming the other way and flagged it down to ask for directions. As it pulled alongside we read 'Catlins Farmstay' on the door. It was the Stratfords, hoorah!

June and Murray run a 1,000 acre sheep, deer and cattle farm where they provide accommodation for up to eight guests plus hearty farm-style meals. Six kilometres away in Waikawa was Harbourside Cottage where we had booked to stay the next three nights. Armed with the key and fresh directions we found our way first to the 'Niagara Falls of New Zealand' that we'd seen on the map. We were quite excited by the prospect of viewing a colossal cataract pouring millions of gallons a minute down an enormous cliff and producing vast clouds of spray and rainbows. So when we discovered it was really a modest ripple in the tiny Waikawa stream we burst out laughing. And that's the idea, it's a Kiwi joke. After a twisty stretch of gravel road, we arrived at Waikawa Harbour and located Harbourside Cottage overlooking a wide expanse of mud. This wasn't a joke. The tide was out.

We were surprised to find we had rented a full-sized, three bedroomed house with large kitchen, shower and bathroom and a spacious lounge. Our delight was short-lived as further inspection revealed the house was shabby, poorly equipped and clearly hadn't been cleaned in quite a while. We'd been assured that Merril, who lived nearby, would be along to clean the place and provide fresh linen shortly, so we went for a stroll.

The old Waikawa church is now a general store and café where we chatted to its owner, Cecilia, while we sat on pews to drink coffee and munch her homemade flapjack. We had quite enjoyed the unsealed road which brought us down from the Southern Scenic Route to Waikawa, but to Cecilia it was a curse.

'These old gravel roads are dreadful for business,' she said. *'The Japanese tend to crash a lot, they've never seen gravel roads before. And the car and campervan hire companies ban tourists from driving on gravel roads, as they're not insured. We need tarseal roads to bring the tourists here.'*

We bought a few items to help keep her in business while she waited for the road building programme to roll past her door, then walked down to the harbour mouth where we stood on a rickety pier to watch the waters swirl as the tide rushed in. We didn't stay long though, as we were bitten to death by the accursed sandflies, and beat a retreat to Harbourside Cottage to see if Merril had finished the extensive spring-cleaning the place so desperately needed. But there was still no sign of her having been near the place. So we used the can of fly spray we'd bought at Cecilia's shop, left the air full of insecticide to deal with the swarms of fat bluebottles that infested the house, and went for a ride.

Porpoise Bay nearby is reputedly the place to see Hector's dolphins, some of the rarest and smallest dolphins in the world, but they proved to be either too rare or too small for us to spot in the gathering gloom. We did see a single yellow-eyed penguin waddling his lonely way up the beach before the darkening dusk made further nature watching impossible. We returned to grimy Harbourside Cottage where I cleaned up the fat-encrusted grill and washed the days-old dirty dishes before making cheese on toast for supper, while Viv searched the cupboards to find clean sheets to make our bed.

After a night of rain and seagulls clattering about on the tin roof we got up to an overcast sky and a damp and blustery morning. Never mind. We had a lot to see and do and, by the time we returned, the mysterious Merril would <u>surely</u> have turned our drab house into a sparkly-clean holiday cottage.

Still no dolphins (had they stayed away on porpoise?) so we pressed on to Slope Point, the most southerly tip on the South Island, via a gravel road which caused more problems for Viv. She was still wary of hurting her injured leg again and found the moderately slippery surface distinctly unsettling. On the way back up the track to Haldane we stopped outside a backpackers hostel for a breather and a look at the map and the helpful proprietress came out to offer advice. We had two choices of route to Tokanui, she said, a 50km trek on tarsealed roads via Fortrose, or a direct 13km unsealed track through farmland and bush to the north. Despite feeling less than keen on this particular day, Viv agreed on the gravel road and we made slow and wobbly progress to the Tokanui Dairy and Takeaway for coffee, shopping and to check out the possibility of a fish supper.

Like a fool, I forgot to fill up our tanks at the garage next door before we set off to see Cathedral Caves, 45km to the east. I realised the oversight when the tarseal surface gave way to gravel and I stopped to check that Viv was willing to continue. This stretch of the main coast road, the Southern Scenic Highway, is not only short of tarmac, it's thin on fuel stations too. We wouldn't make it to the caves and back to Tokanui's fuel pumps on our remaining petrol. The only option was to continue to Papatowai, a further 25km of gravel road further on, and Viv agreed reluctantly.

The road was full of sweeping bends, but was wide and could be ridden fairly fast provided we stuck to the tyre-polished grooves and avoided the wide and deep lanes of chippings in between. But it was busy too, with cars overtaking and spraying us with gravel, which didn't boost

Viv's confidence much. At least she rode feet up, unlike the Moto Guzzi rider we saw wobbling nervously in the opposite direction with both feet trailing on the road. Did he really suppose his leg could save his hefty 1,000cc touring bike from crashing to the ground if his front wheel skidded out from under him?

We were relieved to pull in to Papatowai's do-everything store. Here you could fill up with petrol, enjoy a coffee and snack meal, buy groceries, get your booze from the bottlestore, buy fishing gear and a licence and stay in their motels. It was an oasis on an otherwise deserted coastal route and was doing the roaring trade it deserved.

Back along the metalled main road for ten kilometres we turned down a rough and rocky, muddy and slippery, narrow track to the Cathedral Caves car park where we paid NZ$2 (60p) each, left our helmets and rucksack at the office, and hiked for a couple of kilometres down to the beach through steep and lovely native bush. People heading the other way told us the tide was coming in fast and was already at the cave mouth, but we'd staggered this far down the zig-zag track, with Viv's injured leg making itself painfully known and we weren't going to turn back now.

After another ten minutes tramping across the soggy sand we could just make it between the waves into the first cave entrance. It was very dark inside the huge cavern and with such a big swell pushing the surf right into the caves I was worried we might be trapped by the rising tide. After a couple of hurried photos we came out of the other entrance and skipped through the foam and water to keep the sea from going over the top of our boots. By now it was raining steadily and we got thoroughly soaked on the long, slow and - for Viv - painful climb back to the cliff top car park.

Despite the conditions we made faster progress on the gravel road and arrived back at Harbourside Cottage late on a dull, wet afternoon to find the cleaner still hadn't been. So, damp, cold and grumpy, we set about sprucing the place up ourselves. Viv found a vacuum cleaner in a cupboard and set to in the lounge, which was filthy with spilled food on the carpet, crisps ground into the settee and the sticky remains of sweet fizzy drinks congealed on the table and most of the surfaces.

I decided to light the 'Yunka' multi-fuel burner, but it obviously hadn't been cleared out in months. It took me almost an hour to dig out three bucket loads of ashes, chicken bones, beer bottle tops, nails and goodness knows what else before the fire was fit to use. Finally I had some logs producing welcome heat and a rosy glow and Viv had cleaned, dusted, mopped and polished to make the lounge a habitable room and was now setting about the kitchen, which was in a most unsanitary state. The 'mini-kitchen' cooker was almost useless and with no café, restaurant or takeaway within 25km, one might suppose the self-catering aspect of the property would be of paramount importance. We had a second evening meal of cheese on toast.

After another night of rain and high winds which blew open the front door in the wee hours (aptly named, as I'm usually tottering to the loo at this time), we awoke to a blustery, rainswept morning. It was not ideal for motorcycling, so we donned cagoules and walked up to the Waikawa & Districts Museum based in the old village school. For such a tiny hamlet, this turned out to be an impressive collection and display of the area's history, from the time of the early sealers and whalers who used Waikawa Harbour as a base, to the loggers, sawmillers and gold miners who all added to the region's colourful past during the 1800s.

By the 1920s the railway had arrived, the entrance to the harbour had silted up and the boom time was over. Finally, it was the fishermen and farmers who developed more sustainable resources. As Waikawa's fortunes waxed and waned in the early years the settlers established a school, a jail and even a coach route over the sands when the tide was out. Otherwise, communication with the outside world before the railway came, was by ship alone.

As always, it was the human stories which brought the past to life. Captain Wybrow came for the whales in the 1830s and set up a whaling station at Waikawa. He married a Maori woman called Manuca and she bore him two daughters and a son before she died in 1846. Then in 1853 the salty old seadog was married again, this time to a 14-year-old white girl from Codfish Island to the west of Stewart Island, and she gave birth to several more children. Which helps to explain the spread of the Wybrow family name throughout the region, with some of his descendants dusky and some pale.

After an absorbing couple of hours we crossed the road to the Old Church Café where Cecilia made us coffee and we fell into earnest conversation with two motorcyclists from Nelson. They had stopped for tea and pies to warm them after a cold, wet journey along the south coast on a BMW 650 Funduro and Kawasaki 1100. The temperature by now had crawled up to 13^0C but, with the rain and windchill, it felt much cooler. We'd promised ourselves a hot meal so, despite the uninspiring conditions, we togged up and rode off for a fish and chip lunch at the Tokanui Dairy.

Back at Waikawa we stoked up the Yunka, Viv had a hot bath and I settled down to read an article in a Kiwi magazine all about water - not as boring and irrelevant as you might suppose. When we had first arrived in civilised Christchurch we were assured that New Zealand water was not only safe to drink, it was in fact some of the best in the world. Despite the looks of pity from most people we admit this to, Viv and I often drink water and on our motorcycle excursions we have found it essential to carry a couple of bottles of water to avoid dehydration.

As our journey unfolded across the picture postcard landscape of this wonderful country we both developed intermittent gippy tummy... until we decided to boil all our water supplies. Just as well it seemed. This article entitled 'Turn Off The Tap!' reported that nationwide research had shown mains supplies were sometimes contaminated and even when they were not, the chemicals used by the water companies to kill off the bugs could also cause upset tums. Boiling the water killed most of the germs and helped to drive off some of the chemicals, it said.

That was mains supplies, but in the rural areas where we had been staying most of the time we'd been travelling, rainwater is collected from roofs, piped into tanks and delivered to taps by gravity or by pumps. For Kiwi country-folk, the idea of filtering or sterilising their water supplies is as unthinkable as we might find it undrinkable. These rainwater tanks, according to the article, '*...also have problems due to the build up of slime, dead snakes and breeding frogs*'. A bit of journalistic licence here, since New Zealand doesn't have any snakes, but it is inevitable that anything that the rainwater can carry off roofs and gutters is going to end up in the tank, including dust, dirt, bird-droppings, snails and insects. It was confirmation, if we needed any, that our policy of boiling the tap water was entirely justified.

Chapter 17

Stewart Island

Next morning we would have been glad to get water of any kind. It was Wednesday February 6th, Waitangi Day, a national holiday to celebrate the founding of modern New Zealand. We might have felt festive, but we woke to no electricity and soon realised there was a district-wide power failure.

This meant: 1) no tea or coffee (poo!); 2) no toast (double poo!); 3) no water for washing, as an electric pump feeds water from the rainwater tank (poo-er!); and 4) no water to flush the toilet (poo-ee!). We decided to pack up and leave as soon as possible. The Tokanui Dairy should be able to provide coffee and breakfast and we could use their toilets and washroom.

We left NZ$140 (£40) instead of the $200 (£57) we'd agreed, with a curt note for June and Murray Stratford explaining the lack of cleaning and the various shortcomings of their cottage. I didn't feel too happy about leaving this way, but resolved to phone them at the first opportunity to set the record straight.

Leaning into the biting wind and horizontal rain, we rode for half an hour to reach Tokanui where the grumpy owner of the dairy said he couldn't make us a coffee as he'd got no electricity - although he was standing there drinking a steaming mug of tea! I felt in no mood to argue with him. I was unwashed, unshaven, unbreakfasted, my teeth were unbrushed and his lack of compassion was unwelcome. As we squelched back outside to mount up and ride west, I noticed a lad waiting in his car by the petrol pumps of the fuel station next door, so I went to have a word. This young Australian chap was almost out of fuel, couldn't understand why the garage wasn't open at 9.30am and was bewildered by the dairy owner's unfriendly and belligerent attitude.

I told him about the power cut, explained that the garage might not open at all due to the national holiday and suggested he drove slowly and frugally to Fortrose. We would follow in a few minutes, after I'd made a phone call, and would keep an eye out for him. As he puttered out of Tokanui trying not to press the accelerator pedal, I plucked up my courage, dialled June Stratford, told her why we'd departed Harbourside Cottage in a hurry and explained why we'd left her only $140. I expected anger and indignation, but instead she apologised about the mix up over the cleaning - she'd only just discovered that Merril had gone away - and insisted that we owed her nothing! She would send the money I'd left back to my brother's house in Christchurch, she said.

We passed the fuel station in Fortrose with no sign of the Aussie chap's car along the way, so we guessed he'd made it okay. At least he was warmer and drier than we were. The bitterly cold, wet and fiercely windy weather felt more like December in Scotland than summer in the southern hemisphere. I guessed that being nearer to the South Pole than the equator meant a cold snap was possible at any time.

After warming up over a coffee and breakfast bun in Invercargill we continued south to Bluff where we had arranged to meet John and Jill. The plan was that they would drive down from Christchurch, we'd garage our vehicles at the ferry depot then hop on the Foveaux Express, a high speed catamaran, to take us across to Stewart Island, the third and smallest of New Zealand's main islands. John's work colleague had a bach - or crib as they call them in the south - where we could leave the cares of the road behind for a few days.

But we were early. The power failure that had encouraged our prompt start, plus the wintry weather that had discouraged any sightseeing, meant we now had six hours to kill, so we made friends with Geoff at The Lighthouse café near the ferry quay. Geoff supplied us with coffee, advice on what to see and do and tales of his wayward youth racing motorbikes up Bluff Hill. He also had a computer, which allowed us to catch up with news from home, and space behind his counter for our luggage while we set out to see what the town had to offer.

There's not a lot of excitement in Bluff on a wet and windy day, despite the blandishments of the town's glossy tourist brochure. It's a major commercial port handling 1.7 million tonnes of cargo each year, including exports from the nearby aluminium smelting works which, for the terminally bored, offered Tiwai Smelter Tours. We decided to give it a miss, along with 'viewing by arrangement' at Johnson's Oyster Factory and Big Glory Seafoods, which we imagined would be just as smelly and fun-packed.

We could, perhaps, have whiled away an hour or two in Bluff Maritime Museum, especially as the town claims to be the oldest European settlement in New Zealand, its 1824 date eclipsing nearby Riverton's 1935/6/7 'oldest town in the South Island' bid for fame. But we were all historied up on whaling captains and shipwrecks after Waikawa. We decided that a ride to the Lookout Point at the end of State Highway 1 would give us views over the 35km Foveaux Strait to Stewart Island and whet our appetite for the trip to come.

Whet wasn't the word for it. We got soaked as we stood peering through sheets of rain, with streaming eyes and trousers flapping to a blur in the southerly gale. But we did work up an appetite and retired to the warmth and comfort of The Lighthouse again for an excellent meal. Afterwards we walked in watery sunshine to the only remaining tourist attraction, the Paua Shell House. This is a bungalow filled from floor to ceiling with thousands of paua shells, even overflowing out the door, one man's collection-obsession. It was mildly entertaining in its own quirky way, but the paua or abalone shell, which is so startlingly colourful and beautiful in ones or twos, loses much of its charm when presented by the truckload. By the time we had mooched around the place and walked back again it was time to thank Geoff, collect our luggage and proceed to the ferry terminal to meet up with John and Jill.

They turned up in good time but almost hadn't made it at all. Jill had been wracked with violent stomach cramps for the previous 48 hours, feared she had appendicitis and had travelled the 690km from Christchurch clutching a bucket between her knees. The poor girl looked like death warmed up and in no fit state to tackle the bumpy sea crossing to Stewart Island.

But Jill is a tough cookie and, as the catamaran lurched and slammed through the waves, she stood chatting to the skipper and brightening by the minute, while I felt queasy and Viv clung to her seat for grim death, with white knuckles, green gills and wide, terrified eyes. Gradually the smudge on the horizon materialised through the waterfall of sea spray cascading down the windows into a beautiful green island. An hour after leaving Bluff we slipped into the calm of Half Moon Bay to dock at Oban, Stewart Island's capital and home to a resident population of just 390 people.

Jayne from Oban Tours & Taxis picked us up in her minibus and deposited us five minutes later at the 'Treehouse' crib of Ken McAnergney, known locally as Three Persons. The crib's name was easier to fathom as the charming wood cabin was built on stilts on a steep hillside, with a balcony overlooking the treetops to the gorgeous Golden Bay and Paterson Inlet beyond. You couldn't wish for a better location or views.

With the solid fuel stove crackling and glowing to ward off the evening chill, we tucked in to a huge lasagne which Jill, despite being desperately ill, had made the day before and I spotted a large parrot-like bird flying overhead calling 'kaa-kaa!' It was a kaka, the forest parrot, and soon we saw a dozen more with one cheeky chap landing on our balcony and peering in through the window to see if we'd left him any supper. Cedric, as we christened him, was soon standing on one leg and nibbling at chunks of bread clutched in the other while posing happily for close-up photographs.

After the rigours and excitements of the previous day we all felt we needed a leisurely start to our Stewart Island sabbatical, exploring the cute little town of Oban, nosing round the shops and tramping through several short bushwalks before a takeaway supper of 'fush 'n' chups'. Cedric paid us another evening visit, but turned his beak up at leftover chips. He preferred bread, he said, as he kicked our potato offerings through the trees and flew off with an ear-splitting 'Squaarkk!' We decided Cedric must be pure-bred, unlike the Ranfurly sheep.

Stewart Island is an extraordinary and wonderful place. It is the most natural of New Zealand's three main islands -

the least farmed, least logged, least burnt and least built upon - and is the newest of the nation's national parks. Only a tiny fraction of the island's 172,000 hectares is inhabited, the land outside the Oban area being covered in original native rainforest, bush and scrub. There are just 25km of roads and 245km of walking tracks, but the majority of the island is not accessible at all. Consequently many species of plants and animals thrive here exclusively.

Besides the kaka, Stewart Island is inhabited by the flightless weka, kakapo, yellow-eyed penguin and kiwi. The Stewart Island Brown Kiwi is easier to see than its cousins on the mainland due to its habit of searching the shoreline for food by day as well as by night, often ignoring any human presence. On smaller outlying islands the New Zealand Department of Conservation (DOC) is helping to preserve surviving populations of endangered species, such as the New Zealand dotterel, Stewart Island Saddleback and red-crowned parakeet. Of the five species of lizard found on Stewart Island, three are found nowhere else, including the small-eared skink which was new to science when discovered here in the early 1990s. The DOC's work necessarily includes controlling the populations of cats, rats, deer and our old friend, the possum, which we still hadn't seen in the wild, despite a low-key possum hunt of our own last time we'd holidayed with John and Jill.

It was during our Christmas holiday break at Wainui that we told them we'd never seen a live possum and had some niggling doubts that they were the prevalent menace that most people claimed. So, having consumed another of Jill's fabulous meals, together with a bottle and a half of fine New Zealand wine, we stumbled out into the darkness to find one.

We'd be sure to spot one in the roadside trees, its eyes illuminated by our torch, they said. Jill even gave us a rendition of a possum call - a rasping, back-of-the-throat sound - so we'd know what to listen out for. Feeling a little frisky and keen to encourage the possums to show themselves, at the first rustle in the bushes I mimicked the possum call - 'Ccrrrck!' - and quite convincingly too it seemed.

'There's one!' said Jill. *'Quick, shine the torch.'*

After a minute of fruitless searching, she said, *'That's strange. I distinctly heard it calling. Can't understand why we can't see it.'*

By now I was much too embarrassed to admit that the invisible possum was me. Sorry Jill. Despite our best efforts on subsequent nighttime forays, armed with a torch and my best possum call, we never did get to see one. We have yet to be convinced they are the common pest they're made out to be, but of sandflies we had no doubts. Even without imitating their mating call we could summon up a cloud of the little beggars and were permanently covered with itchy lumps from their bites. Perhaps the Government scientists could genetically engineer a possum that eats sandflies instead of trees? Now there's a thought.

In Maori mythology, Stewart Island was 'Te Puka a Te Waka a Maui' or The Anchorstone of Maui's Canoe. The island's land mass held the canoe (the South Island) secure while Maui and his crew caught and raised the great fish, the North Island. The modern Maori name for the island is Rakiura or Land of the Glowing Skies due to the Aurora Australis and the spectacular sunsets and sunrises that frequently light up the heavens in these southern latitudes.

It got its English name from William Stewart, first officer of the Pegasus, a seal hunter ship which put in to the island's southern harbour in 1809. Stewart charted this part of the southern coast in a little more detail than the much-acclaimed Captain Cook, who thought this lump of land was merely an extension of the South Island. He must have been having a nap the day HMS Endeavour sailed this way, since the 35km wide Foveaux Strait would take his ship something like five hours to cross in anything other than a strong following wind. He could hardly blink and miss it!

Ignoring the lack of roads, we hired a car next day to drive out to Lee Bay and spend the afternoon tramping through fabulous primitive rainforest on the Garden Mound Track. John and Jill helped us to identify the magnificent rimu, kahikatea and totara, the tallest of New Zealand's southern trees clothed in creepers, mosses and lichens, together with dozens of different ferns, from the tiniest frill-leafed species to the mighty ponga.

That evening at the Treehouse crib, I produced an evening meal which, to everyone's amazement, did not consist of a takeaway pizza. Inspired by a fine Kiwi cab-sav/merlot, in the best Keith Floyd tradition, my Wiener Schnitzel, potatoes, carrots and broccoli were all quite edible. The crystal clear night sky, unsullied by industrial pollution or sodium street lamps, sparkled with a billion stars and the broad brilliance of the Milky Way splashed a glowing river of light across the dark ocean of the night.

While John and Jill explored the rare bird sanctuary of Ulva Island on a guided tour next morning, Viv and I walked to the Ackers Point Lighthouse at the eastern tip of Half Moon Bay. This eight kilometre trek featured 574 steps as our path clambered along the clifftops and was a good measure of the recovery of Viv's leg. Spurred on by the fairytale charms of Lonnekers Beach and the gin-clear waters sparkling between giant gum trees, we made it to the tip of the peninsula. Our reward was a soul-renewing view of the Muttonbird Islands and schools of porpoise and pilot whales cleaving the shimmering seas in rhythmic formation.

On our way back to the Treehouse we stumbled upon the smallest flea market in the history of the world. Oban's school had two tiny tables displaying an odd assortment of hand-knitted bags, jars of honey and worn-out shoes. We seemed to be the only two visitors to this touching but pitiful attempt at commercial enterprise, so felt obliged to buy something and paid an outrageously inflated price for a small spiced apple cake. Whoever had conjured up this rare confection had even less idea of cookery than I had. It was inedible and even Cedric, after chewing a couple of rubbery crumbs for a minute or two, flew off in disgust.

We had better luck that evening when we dined at The Lighthouse Café (yes, another one!) and Wine Bar, which specialised in delicious wood-fired pizzas. Our 'last supper' on Stewart Island was eaten with fingers, washed down with two bottles of Hawke's Bay's finest and left us light-hearted but lead-tummied on our final evening stroll up the hill to the Observation Rock for a view over Golden Bay to Iona

Island and the broad Paterson Inlet in the dying light of another fabulous day. As the final flight from the mainland - a ten-seater Islander - flew overhead to make its touchdown at the Stewart Island airstrip, I suddenly remembered that I had nearly learned to fly at a much younger age.

I was twelve years old when my eldest brother, Bill, came up with a great plan. He had this theory that if you had enough old parachute material and some long bamboo poles, it ought to be possible to make a contraption that could lift a person off the ground.

'*How would you like to learn to fly?*' he asked me, in that big brotherly way that promised excitement and adventure. Twelve year old boys don't need asking twice.

If I had any sneaking doubts when we hopped into his Ford Zephyr and headed for a deserted Fenland lane instead of the local flying field, I don't remember them. If I was worried when I saw the enormously long, three-inch diameter bamboo poles and flimsy material I didn't show it. I do remember it was blowing a gale, which was an essential ingredient in the plan.

The poles and material were assembled into a gigantic kite, a strong climbing rope took the place of kite string, and a hefty car tow rope with a brick tied to the end formed the tail. Heath Robinson, eat your heart out. With the long line at full stretch and attached to the car towbar I was instructed to lift the kite and, as the first gust caught Bill's flying machine, I took off.

I had often daydreamed of flying. I would be Baron von Richtofen, Biggles or Douglas Bader, depending which book or comic I'd been reading last. These flights of fancy had a wonderfully smooth, magic-carpet quality to them. Reality was somewhat different. My arms were suddenly jerked out of their sockets, my feet left the ground and my short life rushed before my eyes. Fortunately, the levitation was temporary. After a heart-stopping second I crashed back to the ground with a knee-buckling thud and had the surprising good sense to let go.

The danger, however, was not over. Lurching around above my head the monster kite was flicking its tail to and fro, as kites do. But this was no ordinary kite. This kite had a full-sized house brick attached to its tail. I was oblivious to its murderous intent at this stage yet above the howl of the wind and the buzz of the material crackling in the gale I clearly heard Bill's urgent shout: *'GET DOWN!'*

From a crouched position I dared to look up and saw the heavy missile whipping past my head. It's surprising how fast you can move on all fours in situations like this. I joined Bill at the back of his car which was gyrating to the strain of the humming kite line.

'I don't think this is such a good idea,' said Bill. My thoughts exactly. *'A bit too windy to maintain proper control. If we walk along the rope and apply our combined weight to it, we should be able to bring the kite back down to the ground.'*

We didn't get far before the kite grew impatient with this restriction on its line. It flicked its tail and threw the brick half way across the neighbouring field, then turned and dived into the road with a sickening crunch which snapped the main bamboo pole like a matchstick.

'Now you don't need to tell mother about our little kite flying expedition,' said Bill thoughtfully as we drove back home. *'It'll be our little secret, all right? And I'll make you a tent out of the parachute material and pole, how does that sound?'*

It sounded just fine to me. Strangely, this experience did not put me off the idea of flying, but it did make me very wary of kites and gave me recurring nightmares featuring tethered house bricks.

After an early morning ferry crossing over a glassy sea, we split up on Bluff's dockside with John and Jill heading back for Christchurch and our faithful Yamahas carrying us east once more. On our way out of town we called in at the Bluff BP Garage to top up our petrol tanks before tackling the fuel-station-starved route ahead and to buy chain lubricant. The last of the chain lube from the bike rental company had expired back in Manapouri and I'd been transferring engine oil to the rear drive chains with a stick. This was, even for one of *my* bodges, faintly absurd, so I was delighted when the garage proprietor came up with a much better solution. He supplied me with an old transmission oil bottle topped with a transparent pouring tube so I could apply oil to the chains instead of the wheels and my clothes.

The kindly garage man had moved here from Warrington 35 years previously and still retained a rich Cheshire accent. He was awed by our three-month odyssey through the backroads and byways of New Zealand and wished he could leave his business and do exactly the same thing. He watched longingly as we pulled on our helmets and headed off for the last leg of our journey.

The Southern Scenic Highway, which had been a trial of endurance four days earlier when we'd battled through a storm-force headwind and freezing rain, was now bathed in sunshine. Feeling in a sunny, happy sort of mood we decided to call in for coffee at the Tokanui Dairy for old times' sake. Would the owner be in a better mood now that his electricity was restored?

As I approached the counter with what I hoped was a friendly smile he turned promptly on his heel and walked into a back room. I was so amazed at his rudeness that I followed him into his office to see what kind of urgently pressing business was causing him to snub a customer, a regular no less! He was sitting staring into space, twirling a pencil. I was tempted to give him one of my famous pieces of business wisdom, along the lines of: '*Do you know what time it is when you no longer have a smile for your customers? Time to become a lumberjack!*' - but fortunately I spotted a plump and pleasant little lady in the kitchen who responded politely and brought us our coffee with smiling efficiency, so I let the matter drop.

The gravel section of the Catlins highway seemed less bothersome, perhaps because we knew what to expect and how best to ride it, and we were delighted to be met with a cheery welcome at the Papatowai multi-purpose store. We refuelled our bikes and ourselves before heading on up the coast and around the south east corner of the country to arrive at Owaka where the domain (village green) looked so inviting I laid down and instantly fell asleep.

It was only a short ride from Owaka to Kaka Point on the coast where Rata Cottage awaited us, a small and tidy example of accommodation perfection. Owner Jean Schreuder was a wiry little white-haired lady with an amazing amount of energy. As well as our immaculate and fully-equipped cottage, she also provided bed and breakfast, kept a well-tended garden, and in her spare time held down a job. For a person of advanced years Jean was a real dynamo. She brought us breakfast cereals, juices, bread and jam shortly after we arrived because she had to take her car for repair to Balclutha next morning.

'I have to leave very early so I can catch the bus back here,' she said. 'Otherwise I'll have to walk home. I don't mind walking, but it would take too long and I've rather a lot to do.'

I checked on the map. Balclutha was 30km away!

After a reviving cup of tea we left our bags and headed for Nugget Point which boasted a lighthouse built in 1869 and promised fur seals, elephant seals, Hooker sealions, gannets, sooty shearwaters, shags and yellow-eyed penguins. The walkway to the lighthouse was an excellent elevated path along the spine of a narrow ridge of land, with wildlife sunning itself on rock ledges below.

Back at Rata Cottage, Baxter, one of Jean's two ancient cats, helped us out with our 'fush 'n' chups', which was a familiar habit, judging by his colossal size and friendly nature. Concerned that we might soon resemble Baxter, we went for an evening stroll along the one-hour bushwalk that starts right next to the cottage. Well, it would have been one hour, had we not got lost several times, but we enjoyed every misguided minute of it. The silence of the forest contrasted with the frantic birdlife of the glades, with acrobatic fantails fluttering around our heads to catch the insects we'd disturbed.

A misty morning following overnight rain provided a good excuse for us to make a leisurely start and gave me time to read up on the history of the region, thanks to the books thoughtfully provided in the cottage.

Amazingly, most of the southern towns were planned and named half a world away in Scotland in a pompous and paternalistic display of colonial autocracy. Even the rivers couldn't escape the 'enlightening and edifying hand' of the region's new Caledonian landlords. The mighty Clutha had formerly been named Matau by the Maori, then Captain Cook had called it Molyneux in honour of Robert Mollineux, sailing master of the Endeavour. But back in Scotland in 1846 it was considered: '*Molyneux and Matau are meaningless and unpronounceable. As the mouth of this river must soon become the site of an important town, it is thought to provide for this town having some reference to the city of Glasgow as Dunedin has to Edinburgh.*'

Therefore Clutha, being the ancient name for Glasgow's River Clyde, was adopted and Balclutha (the town on the Clyde) eventually replaced The Ferry, which was the original name for the settlement which sprang up after James McNeil built his bark hut on the bank of the river in 1852 amid 12-foot-high flax, and, in 1853, established the first ferry service across the river.

Where the Clutha emptied into the Pacific Ocean stood Port Molyneux which was destined to be the new 'Edinburgh of the South'. By the mid-1800s up to ten schooners could be seen unloading at the port's wharf at any one time, and Port Molyneux had two hotels, customs offices, many shops, a church and a school. But in 1878 the Clutha showed why it is unwise to take any New Zealand river for granted. A huge flood spread from the mountains to the sea, devastating all in its path. Stock and property were washed away from the lower Clutha basin, including Balclutha, Stirling, Inch Clutha, Kaitangata and Port Molyneux. On October 14th the Beaumont Bridge came floating down to Balclutha and that afternoon the Balclutha bridge was swept away too.

On the coast, the debris of dead animals, wrecked houses, bridges and trees was piled so high that pressure against the spit became too great. It gave way and a new exit to the sea was formed, closing Port Molyneux harbour for all time.

If some place names were chosen by Scottish elders for aesthetic reasons, others like Iwikatea and Kaitangata had less savoury origins. In 1750 the Maori Kati-Mamoe fought and beat the Ngai-tahu, whose bodies were left on the riverbank, bones whitening in the sun. 'Iwi' means bone and 'katea' white or bleached, so the town's name celebrated the demise of their enemy in a most graphic way. Fifteen years later the Ngai-tahu took their revenge by killing the Kati-Mamoe's chief Mokomoko and eating him, immortalising their cannibal feast with a town named 'Kai-' (food), 'tangata' (man).

By 10am the mist had lifted, we said goodbye to Baxter, who was delighted to receive the remains of our milk, and to Jean, who'd returned from Balclutha and was now busy pegging out her washing, and set off north through flat farmland.

We rode past the forgotten remains of Port Molyneux, whose epitaph ought to read: 'The best laid plans of mice and men oft go awry', and over the mighty concrete multi-span bridge at Balclutha, designed to foil any more tantrums from New Zealand's largest river. We rode past Lovells Flat and The Old Sod Cottage (we didn't stop to see if he was in) and on to Dunedin.

After coffee at a pavement café in the city centre, we headed south again to enter the Otago Peninsula and to ride a bendy harbourside road for 33km to Taiaroa Head and the Royal Albatross Colony. This turned out to be a beautiful but long-winded trek and we were disappointed to be told on arrival at the visitor centre that the only way to see these magnificent birds was to join an organised tour. Besides our dislike of being herded around with others, the next available tour would not be until 6pm and by then we needed to be 120km further north. So we ate our lunch sitting on the clifftop grass and fed the seagulls.

After riding back down the long and winding road beside the pretty Otago Harbour we rejoined SH1 and made such rapid progress to the north that we decided to reward ourselves with a coffee break at the unpronounceable town of Waikouaiti. Here it was good to see the elderly male residents keeping alive a Kiwi fashion statement which had all but died out elsewhere. These old boys all wore shorts with thick white woollen socks pulled right up to their knees, leaving knobbly white kneecaps and a mere hint of pale wrinkled leg on display. Only a few years ago this was what all trendy New Zealand men wore to work in offices and shops, with the addition of white gumboots for factory workers. Marvellous!

We pulled in to Hampden Court Motels to a fine welcome from Bruce and Alice Hollows. This couple represent the two great cultures of the country living in harmony. Bruce's family came to New Zealand from the UK in the late 1800s for the kauri gum and the coal mining. Alice's great-grandfather was the head of a Maori tribe from the Bay of Islands and was one of the chiefs who signed the Treaty of Waitangi.

Early morning sunshine greeted us for our final day on the road, but by the time Viv had packed our panniers for the last time and I'd topped up the oils and lubed the chains, a fresh southerly breeze had pulled a blanket of cloud across the sky.

We sped north with a following wind and light drizzle, stopping only for fuel in Oamaru and coffee in Timaru, before arriving back in Christchurch early in the afternoon for big end-of-trip hugs from John and Jill.

Our last couple of days in New Zealand were spent catching up with chores, emails and packing parcels to send home as we had collected far more than we could carry on the plane. It was hard to believe our great adventure was almost over. It had been an amazing journey and a life-changing experience. New Zealand's awesome beauty, space and peace had brought about fundamental changes to our perceptions of planet earth. New Zealand's wonderful, cheerful and hospitable people had warmed our hearts and shown us the best side of human nature. We had mixed emotions. We couldn't wait to get home to see our children and our granddaughter, but we didn't want to leave this lovely country. We hadn't missed our home or possessions at all.

Finally, and sadly, we returned our trusty steeds to New Zealand Motorcycle Rentals. The little Yamaha XT225 Serows had performed almost faultlessly for 11,000km over tarsealed roads, gravel tracks, 4WD trails, over rocks and through streams and mud. They had carried us and a hefty burden of luggage up mountains and down valleys to explore volcanoes, rain forests and the vast, untamed wilderness. They had survived days of torrential rain that had conquered our clothing and all but beaten us. And they'd coped with blazing sunshine and clouds of choking dust.

Apart from that initial short-circuit, an oil leak and a blown headlamp bulb we'd suffered only one silent hooter and an indicator briefly on the blink. We'd checked their oils and chains daily but otherwise they'd needed surprisingly little maintenance. Of course, the ever-helpful bike rental company had serviced them every time we passed their Christchurch or Auckland depots and our trouble-free trip is a testament to their care and attention to detail as much as their bikes' inherent reliability.

We handed the Serows over, paid for the minor scrapes and breakages we'd caused, and walked out of the rental shop feeling strangely bereft. Those little bikes had been our friends throughout our voyage of discovery and it seemed we were deserting them at the end of our travels.

Half way to the door, Viv had a sudden thought and turned around. She gave Gordon and the other guys a big smile and in her best Arnold Schwarzenegger voice said: *'We'll be back!'*

Appendix - Useful Information

New Zealand Motorcycle Rentals: Motorcycle hire and tours. Recommended

Auckland office: 31 Beach Road, Downtown Auckland, PO Box 106156, Auckland, New Zealand Tel: (09) 377 2005. Fax: (09) 377 2006.

Email: info@nzbike.com. Website:http://www.nzbike.com

Christchurch office: 166 Gloucester Street, Central Christchurch, PO Box 13200, Christchurch, NZ. Tel: (03) 377 0663. Fax: (03) 377 0623.

Email: chch@nzbike.com.Website:http://www.nzbike.com

NZ Tourism Board:

PO Box 95, Wellington. Tel. (04) 917 5400. Website: www.purenz.com. (In the UK) New Zealand House, Haymarket, London, SW1Y 4TQ. Tel. 020 7930 1662

Cookie Time Cookies:

PO Box 16141, Christchurch, NZ. Factory: 789 Main South Rd, Chch, NZ. Tel. (03) 349 6161. Fax. (03) 349 6141. Website: www.cookietime.co.nz. (In the UK) Kiwifruits - The New Zealand Shop, 6 - 7 Royal Arcade (just behind NZ House), Pall Mall, London SW1Y 4UY. Website: www.kiwifruitsnzshop.com

Bioflow Magnotherapy products:

Obtainable in the UK and via mail order from: Clearstream, Stables Bungalow, Mill Reach, Buxton, Norwich, NR10 5EJ. Tel/fax 01603 279053.

Obtainable in NZ from: Magnoheal NZ, 102 Pharazyn St, RD7, Feilding, NZ. Tel. (06) 323 2250

Independent Distributors of Ecoflow Plc.

Bob Goddard was for 20 years a journalist and editor with EMAP, IPC, Southern Newspapers and other publishing companies.

Working mainly in magazine publishing, Bob wrote for, edited and published titles such as: Motor Cycle News, Amateur Winemaker, Motorcycle Mechanics, Tennis, Southern Life etc.

Since 1992 he has run his own marketing and distribution business, but keeps his hand in with regular freelance articles published in Practical Boat Owner, Trail Bike and Enduro Magazine.

In recent years he and wife Viv have travelled widely, usually exploring far from the tourist trail on motorbikes to experience the colour, culture and humour that are often overlooked.

These off-beat travels have included: Cuba, Turkey, Cyprus, Egypt, Montenegro and New Zealand, the latter being the subject of 'Land Of The Long Wild Road'. Further travels and other books will follow.

Born in 1953, Bob has three grown up children and one granddaughter. He lives in rural Norfolk, England with his lifelong sweetheart and long-suffering wife, Viv.